Praise for the Edition

'This book reminds us of the perils of chasing poorly defined notions of success – a revised edition could not be more timely or essential.'
Matthew Syed, Olympian, Broadcaster, Journalist, Author

'The Long Win will prompt you to unlearn and relearn what it means to be a success, individually and collectively, in a way that reflects the world of work around us. Every team is better when they spend some time learning from *The Long Win*.'
Sarah Ellis & Helen Tupper, Co-Founders of Amazing If,
Co-Hosts of The Squiggly Careers Podcast,
Authors of The Squiggly Career and You Coach You

'This book approaches the idea of success from a whole new angle, equipping us to think about what it would look like for all of us to win together in the long term, not just for me to beat you. It is a vital handbook for us as we face the challenges of our time, which will demand we work together as citizens, not simply to take what we can get as consumers.'
Jon Alexander, Co-Founder of the
New Citizenship Project and Author of 'Citizens'

'I could relate to everything in this book which applies to any leader wanting to take a long-term view of business success. In business, there is no final destination or finite measure of what winning means, so it's essential for our teams to enjoy the journey.'
John Morgan, Group CEO of Morgan Sindall Group plc

'The Long Win offers a powerful blueprint for shifting paradigms and achieving enduring impact - a must-read for those seeking to reshape the meaning of winning.'
Dr Ruth Gotian, Thinkers50 ranked #1
emerging management thinker in the world, author of
'The Success Factor' and the 'Financial Times Guide to Mentoring'

Praise for the First Edition

'This is a deep and rewarding exploration of human motivation in sport, politics, business and our personal lives', *Financial Times*, 10 October 2020

'Collaboration, not challenging, is a better way to live our lives. A self-help book that should be read by all', *Daily Mail, 17 December 2020*

'A stimulating book that takes the concept of succeeding and gives it a makeover. Powerful and profound.'
Matthew Syed, Olympian, Broadcaster, Journalist, Author

'Winning and losing are the simplistic ways that modern Western societies consider success. But Cath Bishop shows how much more complex the lived experience of competition really is. What a joy to read someone talking about this crucial subject from lived experience, showing how much more there is to understand about the way that we judge ourselves and everyone else. Anyone interested in motivation should read this book and think deeply.'
Margaret Heffernan, Professor of Practice at Bath School of Management, CEO, Author

'Looking at life from a different point of view is a rare skill. Built on in-depth research and broad experience as well as original thought, this book will change your outlook on everything.'
Clare Balding OBE, Broadcaster, Author

'This is an absorbing, candid, nicely crafted book that, using helpful illustrations, forces us to reconsider what we mean by "winning". It persuasively argues the merits of taking a longer-term view. This "long win" is grounded in a considered take on what it is we genuinely want from life and, working backwards, how this might shape our choices today.'
Professor Mark de Rond, Professor of Organizational Ethnography, Judge Business School, University of Cambridge

'A gold medal is a simple goal, near impossible to win. Beyond the brutal simplicity of sport, can the concept of winning help us? What exactly do we want to win, and why? By posing and examining this question, this book helps us learn more, know ourselves better, and connect with renewed purpose with the world of business, family, life.'

Matt Brittin, President of Google EMEA, Olympian

'I wholeheartedly support the thoughts in this book. I firmly believe the only way to change a culture is through educating society as to why it should be changed. And then offer a better way. This book proposes many thought-provoking questions that will serve to inspire the change our world needs and our youth deserve.'

Valorie Kondos Field, UCLA Gymnastics Coach, PAC-12
'Coach of the Century'

'This book is powerful and brilliant. Cath clearly has a deep understanding of what athletes go through and goes further to give a way forward in pursuit of improved performance and personal growth, with concepts I have experienced and observed to work and produce results in elite sport. A must for any manager in elite sport, any teacher, any leader.'

Dr Eva Carneiro, Consultant in Sports and
Exercise Medicine, Former Premier League Doctor

'In sport and life your sense of value depends on the measures of success you choose to judge yourself against. Cath's book will help you open up a whole new freedom to succeed on your own terms and to render outcome hijack and results obsessions things of the past. Don't change the game, change what it means to win, for you.'

Dr Chris Shambrook, Director of Planet K2, Psychologist to British
Olympic Rowing Team 1997–2019

'This book is so relevant, timely and exciting for any person or organization wanting to investigate what success means to them. It couldn't be a more relevant book right now and Cath's exceptional ability in so many areas of life makes it a gripping read with a lot of key takeaways whatever your area of interest. I wish every leader could immediately read this book as the world would be a better place if they did!'

Goldie Sayers, Olympic Medallist in the Javelin, Business Coach

'In a world where sustainability and inter-connection have gained wide recognition as core drivers for business success and purposeful work, Cath Bishop's book *The Long Win* is a timely and important contribution to re-define what success and winning mean. She re-emphasizes the importance of people at the core of the "Long Win". The three Cs – Clarity, Constant Learning and Connection – are based on her rich personal experience as Olympic rower and champion, diplomat and leadership speaker, writer and consultant and they build the foundation for sustained winning. An inspiring and personal book on one of our greatest leadership challenges today!'

Smaranda Gosa-Mensing, Fellow of
Judge Business School, University of Cambridge

'Intelligent. Articulate. Timely. Cath Bishop has written a crucial read for anyone whose life is linked to performance. This GB Olympic rower floats a simple question, "Why does winning matter so much?" And, perhaps more importantly, how does our obsession with being the best ultimately serve us, our goals and the greater good? Told with gripping and, sometimes, poignant story-telling, *The Long Win* presents a compelling case for reflecting, re-thinking and re-strategizing the way we strive for and achieve success.'

Jason Dorland, Author, Coach and Olympian

'*The Long Win* is a thrilling book for anyone who believes that there must be better ways of achieving our potential, both as individuals and societally. It's not a simple fix but this book highlights precisely where we must shift our focus, across multiple disciplines. Cath's captivating experiences at the pinnacle of three such disciplines provide the book's hypothesis with both authenticity and authority. I am convinced that within sport the Long-Win approach will lead to more positive, engaging experiences and better performance. I want every athlete I work with to be exposed to the insights held within this book.'

Laurence Halsted, Performance Coach, Director of Mentoring at
The True Athlete Project, Olympian

'Long Win Thinking shifts our mindset from a focus on "winning is the only thing" to a process-based orientation that fosters a more inclusive and reflective attitude to success. A great reflective work that shows how shifting our approach to success can lead to happier and healthier outcomes.'

Professor Alex Gerbasi, Deputy Pro-Vice Chancellor and Professor of
Leadership, University of Exeter Business School

'*The Long Win* fills a gaping and growing chasm in our understanding of what defines success. It is indispensable for anyone interested in not only achievement but in finding a way to shape our pursuits for the better. While reading *The Long Win* I was informed, emboldened and energized by the way Cath has meticulously and comprehensively laid out the case for strategic thinking that stretches beyond the now, the immediate, the results, to a stronger way of being!'

Dr Steve Ingham, Director and Performance
Scientist at Supporting Champions

'*The Long Win* is a genuinely thought-provoking and fascinating insight into the potential benefits of redefining our mindsets both on an individual and a collective basis. Cath's refreshingly honest account of her own experiences provides a unique backdrop to the concepts of her philosophy. I would thoroughly recommend *The Long Win* and I challenge anyone not to take something from it.'

Sophie Hosking MBE, Legal Counsel at the FA and
Olympic Champion in Rowing

'I love this book and all it stands for. Whether you think you have won it all, or you think you've never won in life, Cath skillfully blows apart our taken-for-granted notion of winning and all that we take it to mean. Using her own poignant story and drawing on many other walks of life, she gives us an inclusive view of what winning means, so we can create a healthy and sustainable 21st century world.'

Dr Alison Maitland, Sport Psychologist,
HR Director and Consultant

'A book which challenges the reader to re-examine their fundamental beliefs about the nature of success and reward. Cath has experienced the top level of elite sport as well as the cut and thrust of diplomacy in conflict zones, giving her a unique personal perspective on the question of how we can redefine winning and losing.'

Annie Vernon, Journalist, Author and
Olympic Medallist in Rowing

'*The Long Win* brings a new narrative to the language of success, challenging the traditional expectations, including those around grades, targets and rankings, prevalent in educational settings today. I would recommend this book to all as a vital read for those who are interested in going beyond the pure gain of A* grades and instead are interested in developing within their schools a culture of collaboration and risk taking, with the mindset and skills to enable the next generation to flourish and live fulfilling and happy lives.'

Suzie Longstaff, Former Headteacher and Olympian

'A thorough and fascinating journey through sport, education, diplomacy and business piecing together the elements that build genuine and sustained success and, as importantly, pinpointing what gets in the way. It will make you think hard about your own team's approach and priorities.'

Roger Bayly, Managing Director, Alvarez & Marsal

'Increasing performance is the most important conversation within teams and organizations searching for success. Cath Bishop's thought-provoking and illuminating book is a compelling guide to how to do it. This visionary book draws on the latest research and Cath's own experiences as an elite athlete and a high-level diplomat. Everyone who is interested in performance should read it.'

Dr Philip Stiles, Senior Lecturer in Corporate Governance,
Judge Business School, University of Cambridge

'The win-at-all-costs culture generates enormous amounts of human unhappiness and is counterproductive to the wellbeing of society as a whole, the "winners" as well as the "losers". Cath has done a thorough job of marshalling evidence from a wide variety of sources, including her own experiences as an Olympian, and weaving it into an articulate and very readable narrative. Her vision for a more compassionate and collaborative world is a world I would want to live in.'

Roz Savage, Ocean-rower, Environmental Advocate,
Author and Speaker

'In this time of change, *The Long Win* provides an excellent, much-needed perspective of how we should be viewing success in the future. I'd rank Cath's writing and insight alongside that of Matthew Syed and Malcolm Gladwell. It's a must-read book for anyone interested in developing themselves and others.'

Ben Hunt-Davis, Olympic Champion in Rowing, Founder of Will It
Make the Boat Go Faster? Ltd

'It is easy to overlook and underestimate how deeply the cultural obsession with "winners" and "winning at all costs" runs, but Cath shines a much-needed light on the topic. She makes a powerful and convincing argument as to why it is high time we updated and evolved our way of playing, educating and living. *The Long Win* presents a compelling vision of a healthier, happier and more creative way of being, and I believe it has arrived at exactly the right moment in human history.'

Simon Mundie, BBC Broadcaster

'I love this book. It is a must-read for educators, business executives, policy makers, politicians and indeed anyone who wants to understand why we need a new narrative around winning and success. We need a lot more Long-Win Thinking in our homes, businesses and institutions and Cath's book is the place to go to find out why – and how we get there.'

Dame Helena Morrissey

The
Long
Win

*There's more
to success
than you
think*

Fully
revised, with
new chapter

Cath Bishop

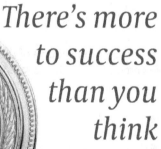

First published in Great Britain by Practical Inspiration Publishing, 2020

This edition published 2024.

© Cath Bishop, 2024

The moral rights of the author have been asserted

ISBN   9781788605878   (hardback)
           9781788605250   (paperback)
           9781788605274   (epub)
           9781788605267   (mobi)

Every effort has been made to trace copyright holders and to obtain their permission for the use of copyright material. The publisher apologizes for any errors or omissions and would be grateful if notified of any corrections that should be incorporated in future reprints or editions of this book.

Want to bulk-buy copies of this book for your team and colleagues? We can customize the content and co-brand *The Long Win* to suit your business's needs.

Please email info@practicalinspiration.com for more details.

Practical Inspiration
Publishing

For my Dad, Brian,
whose infinite curiosity has always inspired me
to explore things a little further

Contents

non teneas aurum totum quod splendet ut aurum.
(Do not take as gold all that shines as gold.)

Alain de Lille (*Parabolae,* c1175)[1]

Why a Second Edition?

Change is happening.

When I first started writing *The Long Win* back in 2016, I felt an outlier. I worried that its approach would feel too radical, that its thinking could alienate me and that its uncomfortable examination of engrained parts of our attitudes and behaviours would be dismissed.

Yet by the time *The Long Win* was published in October 2020, shifts were already starting to take place across society: the COVID-19 pandemic was disrupting all our lives and forcing us to reconsider what matters most; that same year an Olympics was postponed and the Netflix documentary *Athlete A* opened up athlete abuse on a scale never admitted before, with its ripples changing attitudes and continuing to affect the world of sport; and cultural crises in business were accruing, connecting to a growing emphasis in certain organizations on purpose, wellbeing, environmental responsibility and social impact.

The imperative to redefine success and our pursuit of success in business, sport, education, politics and our personal lives grows daily. This revised second edition aims to advance our capabilities and ambitions further so that we can better reimagine and redesign success for ourselves and the world around us. As *The Long Win* continues to resonate with the new audiences and leaders I've been working with, I wanted to update it, encompassing what I've learnt over the last few years to help more leaders work out a better way for themselves and their organizations to succeed.

One consistent line of feedback has been a request for more help and practical steps to implement 'Long Win Thinking'. A new final chapter in this edition shares a collection of short stories of Long Winners, providing snapshots and insights into how leaders are putting Long Win Thinking into practice. Also new is the section on tips and tools at the end of the book. I hope this book supports and inspires you on your own Long Win journey.

Original Preface

This book covers experiences from the frontlines of the Olympics, warzones, boardrooms and classrooms. I have combined stories, commentary and research to make sense of these high-performance professional environments across business, sport, education and politics. I have spoken to athletes, academics, psychologists, teachers and business leaders. And a breadth of insights from history, biology, psychology, philosophy and anthropology have helped me investigate how winning touches our lives.

Winning is a huge part of our culture but it's hard to pin down. It can look quite different on the surface from how it looks underneath. As it is part of our conscious and subconscious thoughts, I have broadened my perspective to include a range of opinions, attitudes, biases and beliefs alongside more conventional evidence.

Writing this book has been a fascinating professional project. It has also been an intensely personal process, enabling me to make sense of the different worlds I have been privileged to experience first-hand – sporting, diplomatic, educational, business and family.

This book attempts to balance breadth and depth in a wide topic area. The chapters seek to inform, entertain and provoke. I want to challenge our assumptions, the way we think and act, the language we use and hear around us, and the deeper motivations that drive us, our families and friends, teammates and colleagues.

Finally, I want to encourage and enable you to explore what success and winning mean to you, as I have considered what they mean to me. I believe this offers a way to open up more opportunities, possibilities and ambitions for ourselves, for the world we live in and for future generations.

Prologue

9.10 am, 21 August 2004, Lake Schinias

I sat on the start line, straight and ready in lane two, and took several deep breaths. Our main opposition – Romania, Belarus, Canada, Germany – was to the left of us, and there was one crew – New Zealand – to our right. I could feel my heart rate rising even though I was sitting perfectly still. The gentle undulation of the surrounding Greek hills outside Athens offered a stunning backdrop. They had seen some history in their time. More deep breaths. I took a fleeting look round at my crewmate, Katherine: our eyes met, a slight smile and a thousand unspoken words exchanged. I looked beyond her to the 2,000 metres of calm water that awaited us. I turned back and exhaled loudly amidst the nervous silence of the starting area. I could see the giant-sized, coloured five rings in front of me, fixed to the front of the box where the start judge waited. Even deeper breaths. I focused in on the first stroke, visualizing it, as I had practised over and over again. Somewhere deep in the recesses of my mind, I was also processing the importance of the next seven minutes, as I had over the weeks, months and years leading to this point. I knew the rules of the game. Only one result counted.

9.15 am, 21 August 2004, Lake Schinias

By this point, the pain was growing with every stroke. I was struggling to breathe and my focus was beginning to blur. I was only partially aware of what was going on around me yet felt incredibly alert. Deep inside I knew I was approaching the last critical part of the race: 90 seconds of my life that would have a profound impact on whatever followed.

All of my conscious brain was concentrated on what I was doing with an oar, in a boat, on that lake, at that moment. But somewhere in my subconscious mind, different moments in my life flashed past – trying hard in school tests, hopeless sports days, discouraging PE (physical education) teachers, encounters of sibling rivalry with my brother, bringing home exam results, my first encounter with an oar – so many highs and lows along the way, the chances and choices that had culminated here.

As we approached the final 50 strokes, instinct told me that significant extra effort would be required, regardless of our levels of exhaustion. I could tell from my blurry peripheral vision that we weren't out in the lead but hadn't been dropped either. We needed to bore down into our reserves and drill deeper than ever before to generate more speed.

I knew before the race that two storylines were waiting to be written. Years of conversations with coaches and teachers, reading articles on the sports pages and watching awards ceremonies had taught me how they would sound. The first: a tale of glory, of history being made, of dreams coming true and of a sports career finally to be celebrated. The second: a tale of repeated failure, of falling short again and of not delivering when it mattered. Both were possible. Each would have a significant impact on me and my life to follow.

9.16 am, 21 August 2004, Lake Schinias

In those final, vital strokes, I drew on all my remaining resources to drop my oar into the water as quickly as possible, accelerate it through as powerfully as I could and extract it again with as much surgical precision as I could manage, despite devastating levels of depletion. I was tuned in to my rowing partner's monosyllabic race calls, honed over thousands of hours of training. At times, I could hear them telepathically.

More distinct thoughts flashed across my subconscious mind: all the people who loved and supported me; a realization that it was now or never; a total lack of comprehension as to how I had ended up here; the clear knowledge that I was never going to do this again; the need to find something extra within me.

We were alongside the packed grandstands now. The noise of the crowds vibrated through our boat and bodies. Their hollering and stamping resounded in my ears, even though my hearing was fading as my body focused its resources purely on what it needed for the task in hand. I was now operating on instinct.

9.17 am, 21 August 2004, Lake Schinias

As we crossed the line, the crowds stopped chanting. My body, one moment straining to be stronger and more powerful than it had ever been before, now flopped over my oar. The urgency of the preceding minutes vanished. As my hearing brightened, I was deafened by my lungs gasping to inhale fresh oxygen. My mind and body automatically jumped to post-race processes. My body set about dispersing the vast quantities of lactic acid from its muscles and tackling the ravaging effects of oxygen debt. My mind began processing what had just happened and what it might mean. One question quickly came to the fore: 'Had we won?'

A number of supporters from the three countries that had won medals continued to cheer and brandish their flags. As I looked up, I could just make out a few Union Jacks still being shaken.

A mundane electronic bleep signifies you have crossed the line. The end of years of striving. Hopes and dreams are over for the majority. When crews are close, the bleeps come in quick succession. Despite overwhelming fatigue, your mind instantly unravels which bleep applies to you. I knew which bleep was ours but couldn't immediately take on that knowledge.

Because rowers face backwards, we could see those who finish behind but not those ahead. As we slouched over our oars and drifted, I could see most of the other boats we'd been racing up until a few seconds ago. Except one. There was one boat I couldn't see. I knew what that meant.

9.20 am, 21 August 2004, Lake Schinias

Not long after finishing, officials directed us to turn our boat round and start rowing up past the crowds to the pontoon with the podium. This was a new route for me. Only twice had I been pointed to row in that direction at the World Championships, and never before at the Olympics. At the two previous Games I had competed in, having failed to finish in the top three, we had just skulked away back to the boating area, devastated, defeated and destroyed.

I stared up in bewilderment at the strangers madly waggling flags at us, straining to see if I could recognize any faces. My memories are patchy; my body was still not fully recovered from the seven-minute all-out effort that had ended just moments ago. At the pontoon, I was in a haze getting out of the boat, instinctively hugging Katherine, then sitting down for a moment as my legs suddenly gave way. One of our fantastic support team brought us some water as the sun beat down on our weakened bodies, severely dehydrated and depleted from the recent physical effort. The water tasted so good.

We were quickly ushered over to the waiting BBC sports presenters, including legendary five-time Olympic champion Steve Redgrave, for our 'on the spot' interview. Microphone under my nose, I was asked how I felt about the result. I had no idea; I had only just begun to try and work that out. I can't remember exactly what I said. My mind was still whirring away, untangling what had happened and what it meant. I think I said something about it being a privilege to be out there racing and that we had given everything. I didn't really answer the question.

After the interview, we were lined up ready for the medal ceremony further along the pontoon. Gold in the centre, silver to the right, bronze to the left. We stood on the right. The medals were put round our necks, laurel wreaths imitating the ancient Olympic ceremonies placed on our heads, flags raised and the anthem of another country sung.

My mind was still frantically processing feelings, thoughts, hopes and doubts. I felt deeply drained, relieved that the pre-race nerves and years of waiting had ended, and unsure. A circular thought process was whirling round my mind: we had done everything we could, we had made the podium, we had come second. How should I make sense of that?

Winning and losing

As my internal post-race analysis continued that day, I moved on to wondering: 'What would others think of our result?' I thought first of my rowing partner, who had spent hours sitting just two feet behind me. For me, it was my first Olympic medal; for Katherine, it was her second Olympic silver medal. No one wants two. This is an elite world where only winning counts. We had shared clear aspirations to upgrade from her previous Olympic experience and had spoken openly about our belief and ambition that we could be the first British women to win an Olympic rowing gold medal. That dream was over. But we had had a far from smooth run-up to the Games. Beyond that lake and the podium, we had been through situations that only the two of us would know and share for the rest of our lives.

Next, I wondered: 'What would our coach say?' His crew had won in Atlanta in 1996 and then painfully finished second in his home Olympics in Sydney 2000. I knew second place wasn't what he wanted in his first Olympics leading the British team. I didn't know where he was at this point, but I knew he would be going through his own reckoning process before he saw us.

Then my thoughts moved on to: 'What would others say?' The journalists sitting up in their commentary positions would already have given their verdict, as they wrote up tomorrow's reports and waited for the next race to come past. Other judgements would be flowing too. Voices on the riverbanks back home would soon be determining who were the heroes and who were the chokers, who had fought valiantly and who had bottled it.

Finally: 'What would my parents think?' That changed the frame of reference considerably. My forehead unwrinkled and I felt my body relax and let go. If I'd had enough energy to laugh, I would have. Bless them, for, wonderfully, they didn't really care about the result, beyond knowing it mattered to me. They had never spent any time in the sporting world until I dragged them into it. Their reaction would depend largely on mine and they knew to gauge my response first. They had got that wrong in the past, congratulating me on a great race when I hadn't won. My reaction had been distinctly uncelebratory. Since then, they had quickly learnt to adjust their expectations in line with mine. They'd be anxiously waiting to gauge my response.

Thoughts and questions about what winning means, what success looks and feels like and where my experiences fitted into that flowed like rapids through my mind after crossing the finish line. I've continued to reflect on them ever since.

They reverberate around us all. The question I get asked most when giving talks is still: 'How did you feel when you crossed the line?' For a long time, I got wrapped up in introspection, trying to find the answer. Until I realized that it was as much about the questioner as it was about me. It was about our shared need to work out what constitutes winning and that pull to relate to someone else's experience to make sense of our own criteria for success.

For a while, I thought it was my own personal dilemma.

Now I realize it's in all our minds.

Introduction

When I retired from sport, I thought I was leaving a world obsessed with winning behind me. But across the worlds of diplomacy, business, parenting and education, I found a continual recurrence of the theme of winning everywhere I looked. Realizing that this wasn't unique to sport or to me, I became hooked on understanding how and why the idea of winning pervades our lives and society so deeply and how it is playing out in practice.

As a diplomat, I discovered a world of winners and losers in political negotiations with much higher stakes than my sporting races had ever had. After I changed careers again and started working in leadership development and organizational performance, I met a stream of leaders and companies vying to 'be No. 1' in their respective marketplaces and to smash their competitors, searching relentlessly for the 'winning formula' and the 'secrets of success'.

When I became a parent, I was thrust back into a world of school winners and losers through the preoccupation with examinations, grades and rankings, and the labelling of children as 'talented' and 'gifted' or, at the other end, 'demotivated' and 'disengaged'. University friends who had gone into careers in law, financial services or management consultancy were all toiling and competing like Olympic athletes to become the best in their cut-throat professional worlds.

We are surrounded by the language and culture of winning. Literally millions of books and products promise to turn us into 'winners'. Some of the most famous songs of the 20th century focus on winning, such as 'The winner takes it all' by Abba, 'Winning ugly' by the Rolling Stones and Queen's anthem 'We are the champions'. TV screens, billboards and social media posts feature countless images of society's anointed 'winners', our role models for success in the form of heroes from the sports pitches, fashion models with 'winning looks', politicians or business idols. How do these everyday images of winning influence our view of the world? Who do we aspire to emulate, and how do they teach us to behave? Are we competitors or colleagues, friends or foes, primarily out to support those around us or get one over on them?

The language of winning has seeped into our everyday conversations, reaffirming consciously and subconsciously the belief that we are all trying to win. It can feel hard to challenge it (that's what a 'loser' would do) but that's what I am daring to do. Simple, narrow definitions of what winning means can lead to serious unforeseen consequences. The dichotomous 'winning is good, losing is bad' view doesn't hold up to the scrutiny of real life. In fact, that mentality is damaging us. This book aims to look at the dark underbelly of what winning can mean, beyond those glorious trophy moments, so we might better reshape success in the future.

Defining success

What assumptions do we bring to this topic? When I asked friends or audiences 'What does winning mean to you?', common themes and images leapt out: medals and podiums, trophies and cheering crowds, being the best and beating everyone else. Physical gestures were mentioned too: big grins, fists pumping and arms held high. A few phrases were spontaneously quoted, most commonly 'everyone loves a winner' and 'it's not the winning; it's the taking part' (usually said in a sarcastic tone). They also mentioned personal moments of achievement, iconic Olympic victories, sporting idols past and present, adventurers through the ages over sea and land, leading entrepreneurs and global business giants, as well as historic figures from Napoleon to Mandela.

These images and idols are universally heroic, at times superhuman. They recall moments that seem magical and otherworldly. Such deeply instinctive responses to what winning means echo all around us in our personal and professional lives and in social norms. Winning equals success, success must mean winning and, mostly, that involves beating the opposition.

The saying 'competition brings out the best in us' was quoted many times in conversations on this topic. We often attribute certain remarkable human achievements to the presence of competition – from radical scientific discoveries to the race to the South Pole and the historic moon landing in 1969. But I don't think it's that simple, and we miss a lot by assuming that competition is always a positive driving force.

We hold up iconic figures as our heroes and role models for success, but I am curious about their wider stories and experiences. Take those early heroic, pioneering astronauts – what were their lives like beyond the moment they stepped out of their space capsule in the first moon landing? How did they feel when they returned to earth? I discovered stories of widespread depression. Buzz Aldrin, one of the first two humans to land on the moon, applied a haunting description of the view from the moon – 'magnificent desolation' – to his own life on return to earth.[1]

The race to the moon was part of international politics, a world drowning in the rhetoric of winning and losing. Yet winning in politics seems increasingly disconnected from success in tackling the major issues of our time, whether it be climate change, terrorism, global health or social inequality. In the ultimate win–lose arena, a glance at the military annals over recent decades shows that where victory was promised, none came, from Vietnam to Iraq to Afghanistan. Debates rage as to who won the Cold War, the ultimate unwinnable war, perhaps best portrayed by the incessant, futile competition between George Smiley and Karla in John Le Carré's fiction.

We cling to the alluring simplicity of what winning means: coming first and beating all the competition. 'Winning isn't everything; it's the only thing' is just one of the clichéd phrases that echo around boardrooms, sports pitches and homes. Mostly we take it for granted that this is 'the way life is'. Everyday language and habits reaffirm our belief that winning is a universally powerful force for good in our lives to which we should all aspire. We can accept it and carry on as we are. Except we shouldn't accept it. Heretical though it may seem, it's time to face up to the fact that it's not working well for us.

Like those times when winning doesn't equal success, such as when Lance Armstrong was stripped of his seven Tour de France titles due to doping. Or when England's top-scoring rugby player Jonny Wilkinson expected to fight depression and find joy winning more caps, more titles, more points even though, in his own words, 'It's never enough.'[2] Or when I heard the story of an Olympic champion who walked into the changing rooms and threw their medal in the bin, because the experience leading to the result had been so miserable.

What is this different picture of success we start to see? What are the costs that winners have paid? What about the others in those races and matches, who we dismiss and ignore? What talent, brilliance and future success might we have discarded due to the narrow success metric that doesn't go beyond simply coming first?

In education, where school systems revolve around grades, targets and rankings, vast numbers of teachers are leaving the profession. Multiple studies have shown that A-grade students, the clear 'winners' at school, do not go on to have the most successful careers. To take a few high-profile examples, Bill Gates dropped out of Harvard and neither Steve Jobs nor Richard Branson excelled at school. In business, how many of the battles to be the best have turned sour? How do we view 'serial winner' Fred Goodwin, who led the Royal Bank of Scotland (RBS) to the largest annual loss in British corporate history and an unprecedented bailout by the British government in 2008? Or leading investment manager Bernie Madoff, who ran the biggest investment fraud the world has ever known? Or business giants such as Enron and Volkswagen, who fell short over the long term? Looking across the organizational world, flatlining levels of productivity and declining engagement across sectors alongside record levels of burnout show us that commonplace company narratives urging 'be the best', 'destroy the competition' and 'be No. 1' in the marketplace are not working.

I have heard sales managers admit they would *turn down* business with colleagues and clients in another region if it prevented them from hitting their targets. All in the quest to 'win'. I met a Harvard Business School alum who is now working in investment and earning $1.2 million a year. He told me he had achieved most of what he had defined as success back in business school, yet admitted he hated going into the office, saying 'I feel like I'm wasting my life.'

The desire to win plays out with problematic consequences across every part of society. It has been proven to impact negatively on the quality of journalism, academic research and our adversarial legal systems. Some of the biggest legal cases play out in the news and live on in Hollywood because of the drama that comes from the polarity of the courtroom – a place where diversion, distortion and even deceit can play a role in the need to win the case and beat the other side.

When we re-examine the 'winners' from a longer-term and broader perspective, our common definition of success starts to buckle. Common images of what winning means focus largely on a single moment in time: the winner on the podium, the announcement of a company's annual profits, a legal battle won or the declaration of a landslide electoral victory. Chris Evert is famous for saying that the high of winning Wimbledon lasted about a week. What happens after that?

What does winning (or not winning) mean for a sportsperson over the course of their life? What might business success look like over the longer term if the perspective focused on employees, the local community and wider society? How do top school grades prepare students for their later lives? And when society's political leaders win the right to govern, how does electoral success translate into progress in tackling the key issues of our time? If success is temporary, what follows?

Legendary US gymnastics coach Valorie Kondos Field told me that our obsession with winning is producing 'broken human beings' in education, sport and business. As she explains in her TED Talk, *Why Winning Doesn't Always Equal Success*:

> we have a crisis in the win-at-all-cost cultures that we have created... As a society, we honour the people at the top of the pyramid. We effusively applaud those people who win championships and elections and awards. But sadly, quite often, those same people are leaving their institutions as damaged human beings. Sadly, with straight As, kids are leaving school damaged. With awards and medals, athletes often leave their teams damaged – emotionally, mentally, not just physically. And with huge profits, employees often leave their companies [having been] damaged.[3]

If winning isn't working in so many cases, then it's time to explore what's happening at a deeper level, work out how we got to this point and see if there is a way to change.

This book is far from a blanket rejection of all winning, competition or the desire to do our best. It is certainly not about lowering standards. Quite the opposite. It is about challenging the framework we put around winning, competition and success in order to consider how we might do it better. It is about looking at what we normally turn away from or brush under the carpet in order to understand more about those occasions when winning doesn't actually bring meaningful success into our lives. It is only by seeing both sides of the coin, the light and the shade of what winning can mean, that we can redefine success and start to pursue ambitions that could last longer and go far beyond simply coming first for a moment. There is more to success than we may realize.

Examining such a deeply engrained cultural phenomenon means exploring both what we can see and what we can't immediately see. It always surprises me how accidental and un-thought-through our lives can be. We schedule all our visible tasks each day – the meetings, the briefing calls, the project planning – but seem to leave out consideration of the most important part of us – our minds and the way we think, believe and feel. Yet these invisible elements govern most of what happens in all those visible tasks and drive the way we behave and interact with others. In the chapters that follow,

I aim to look at both the visible and the less visible components of success in our lives.

In the chapters in Part I, I look at how we arrived at our current obsessive relationship with winning, through the lenses of language, science and history. I consider a range of influences across linguistics and culture, religion and philosophy, psychology and biology – by no means exhaustive but enough to help us become more conscious of how we have formed our views about what winning means.

Part II tells the broader story of how our fervour for winning plays out across education, sport, business and politics. I analyze, through different perspectives, examples I have seen, experiences others have shared with me and situations within the public domain. This deeper examination of the dark side of winning also serves as a stimulus to start considering how we might rethink and redefine success.

In Part III, I explore the 'Long Win', an alternative approach to defining success. I probe how we might actively create a different picture of what success means for ourselves and our communities, rather than accepting entrenched views from the past. And I consider questions and strategies to put Long Win Thinking into practice. Tools and guidance are provided in the appendices of this second edition to help further.

This book is unapologetically full of questions which offer a way to deepen our understanding, develop our thinking and spur us into acting differently. If we are to challenge some of the beliefs, assumptions and 'universal truths' that we take for granted, then we need to rediscover the world through a different lens and reflect on what we notice as a result. I am reminded of the anecdote about the fish that asks another fish 'How's the water?', to which the other fish replies, 'What the hell is water?' I want us to see afresh what winning has come to mean in our lives.

Let's start by delving into the hinterland of this topic. In the next three chapters, we take a tour through the language, science and history of winning to trace how it has come to dominate our lives.

Part I

What Does Winning Mean?

Who wins is the factor that shapes our lives more completely than anything else.

Professor Ian Robertson, neuroscientist (*The Winner Effect: The Science of Success and How to Use It*)

Chapter 1

'Loser!'

The Language of Winning

University tutors warned me against following the route of the 'losers', trying to steer me away from spending too much time playing sport or propping up the bar. I had an Olympic rowing coach who for years taunted me and fellow athletes with the question: 'Are you a champion or a loser?' He had a particular knack for asking this at the times we felt particularly vulnerable, weak, struggling with self-doubt or simply exhausted. One of my first line managers at work advised me not to complain if I didn't get a fair go at something, 'because nobody likes people who whinge; they tend to get seen as losers and don't advance far'.

'Do you want to be one of the winners or one of the losers?' I have heard this question throughout my life and seen it used in films, books and speeches. Sometimes explicitly, sometimes implicitly, urging me that if I didn't do whatever they were advocating, I would fail, I would lose. These messages often came from figures in authority, those with power. They reinforced that I had clear choices in the essential dilemma of life: whether I was a winner or a loser. Leaders, teachers, coaches and managers constructed a binary world that seemed so self-evident as they perpetually reaffirmed that life was essentially about that central battle between opposing forces.

This language, way of thinking and understanding of the world around us is part of a deep, long-standing story of victors and heroes in our society. It still dominates our workplaces and businesses, schools and homes, and it prevails in the media. Hundreds, thousands, millions of book titles, speeches and products promise to reveal the 'secrets of winning' and turn you into a 'winner'. They span almost every category and genre, from hair products to marketing campaigns to online sites that promise to teach you 'how to win a gold medal in blogging' or any activity you choose. Books range from

Jack Welch's classic management guide, *Winning: The Ultimate Business How-To Book*, to Olympic champion and International Association of Athletics Federations President Sebastian Coe's *The Winning Mind*, UK political advisor Alastair Campbell's attempt to 'set out a blueprint for winning' in *Winners and How They Succeed* and England rugby coach and businessman Clive Woodward's *Winning!*, imaginatively followed up by his book on leadership, *How to Win*. *New York Times* correspondent Neil Irwin wrote a book about how to navigate a successful career with a title that sums up the conundrum facing us all: *How to Win in a Winner-Take-All World*. I could list many more.

Whether you look in the business, sports, politics, history or self-help section of a bookshop, it doesn't take long to find a book with 'win' in the title, full of rock-solid tips, tools and formulae for how to be a winner. Much like the dieting industry, readers avidly return, eager to find the latest book: the one that really will turn them into winners this time.

In businesses, the vocabulary of winning and losing underpins board-level conversations about profits and market share, aspirations to be market leaders and ambitions to destroy competitors. The daily news from the stock exchanges around the world perpetuates an ongoing list of winners and losers.

Sports fans and journalists alike love watching and describing gladiatorial Wimbledon finals, fierce warring derbies in England between Premier League football clubs and epic Ryder Cup battles between US and European golf teams. High-level sport is a joy to watch, something special to savour, and I'm a huge fan of it. But our interpretation of what we see, and the perspective we see it from, forms an important part of what sport represents. Is it just about who wins? Isn't there more to admire and consider in what we watch?

Sporting heroes are invested with a god-like status and superhuman powers, then unceremoniously deposed as soon as their form slumps and they lose. You are up or you are down; there is little in between. But there is another picture: soaring numbers of mental health issues across elite sport, startling and rising numbers of suicides in the US National Football League, waning audiences for the Olympics, widespread corruption and major doping crises. All of this suggests that all that is gold does not glitter in the sports world.

In schools, the language of winning resounds in the playground and the examination hall. Children learn from the world around them that they must compete to know all the answers, to get picked and come out on top. In many countries, schools have to compete in league tables to secure their future, in much the same way as football clubs.

Politicians overuse the language of winning, perhaps hoping that if they say it enough, they'll become associated with it and come out on top the next time they face the electorate. President Trump played this card time and time again:

> we're gonna start winning again, we're gonna win so much, we're gonna win at every level, we're gonna win with the economy, we're gonna win with the military, we're gonna win with healthcare and for our veterans, we're gonna win with every single facet... we have to keep winning, we're gonna win more, we're gonna win more.[1]

The rhetoric of winning has been the politicians' 'go-to', whether in response to a pandemic or a terrorist attack. But although politicians have (over)used this language for centuries, there is an increasingly uncomfortable incongruence between the language of winning and the complex world we inhabit. It increasingly hinders our collective response to the unpredictable, uncertain challenges we face across society. Politicians, like the rest of us, need to adapt and expand their approach to fit the times.

A whole 'industry of winning' runs all year round, way beyond the world of sport. There are competitions to win scholarships, write the best book, be the best pianist in the world, be the best business to work for, run the best marketing campaign or design the best invention. And an endless cycle of award ceremonies and events celebrate the latest winners.

But what is the meaning of these events? For a start, large numbers of people have to spend a lot of time filling in the forms to nominate or be nominated, and then these have to be read and ranked. The winning criteria are usually pretty arbitrary and narrow, sometimes defined by those who have won before (despite assertions of independent verification). When you look a little closer, you can often 'buy' yourself a better chance of winning a business award by being an event sponsor or joining the panel of judges. There is often little or any real meaning conveyed or any sense of deeper human impact in the world beyond being ahead of competitors on some arbitrary criteria.

Take one of the most visible competitions of all – the competition for who can build the highest building. This has gone on for centuries. Historically, the tallest man-made structure was the Great Pyramid of Giza in Egypt, which held the position for over 3,800 years until the construction of Lincoln Cathedral in England in 1311. From then until the completion of the Washington Monument in 1884, the world's tallest buildings were Christian churches and cathedrals in Europe. Skyscrapers were pioneered in the US in the 20th century, and then the boom in construction in Western Asia, China and Southeast Asia kicked in, with the Petronas Twin Towers in Kuala Lumpur and then Burj Khalifa in Dubai reaching new heights. An international body, the Council on Tall Buildings and Urban Habitat, fulfils the role of certifying which building is the 'world's tallest'.

As new buildings spring up across the world, there is a constant desire to show power, dominance and strength by building the next tallest tower. I saw how a similar goal played a hugely symbolic role in the ongoing bitter battle for dominance between the Bosnian Muslims and the Bosnian (Catholic) Croats in the ethnically divided city of Mostar. The prominent positioning of their respective places of worship on opposing sides of the river provides the citizens who live there with a stark daily reminder of the divisions. The determination of the Catholic community after the fighting in the 1990s to rebuild its bell tower higher than any minaret in Mostar, adding an enormous Christian cross on top, spoke volumes about the bitter mentalities still at play.

Everyone jumps on the bandwagon, not just war-torn cities and wealthy billionaires. Leaders are seduced by the language of winning, keen to associate themselves and their companies with winning, seeing it as a way of increasing their worth. Yet how do these accolades and awards, and the effort to win them, actually strengthen our world in any meaningful or sustainable way? What will these wins mean in a few years' time, after others have won subsequent awards, built higher buildings, received the next round of plaques and rosettes?

Phrases about winning have become an integral part of our everyday language. We've become so used to this that we barely notice it. But it's worth noticing and reflecting on whether this is helping or hindering us to achieve what we want to achieve.

Here are a few examples of how winning pervades our everyday language:

How did we get here?

Let's consider the origins of the word 'win'. The word has Germanic roots dating back to the Middle Ages and is based on two concepts: *gewinn* and *wunnia*. The *Oxford English Dictionary* gave the meaning of *gewinn* as 'to work, labour, strive, contend' – emphasizing effort and hard work – while the meaning of the closely related *wunnia* was 'joy, pleasure, delight, bliss'. In the early stage of language, then, winning was about effort and pleasure, not defeat, loss or beating others. It was about the human experience rather than any material outcome, and it was not about a moment in time, but an ongoing activity or state of being.

From there, winning quickly became subsumed into the dominant view of history and the world of battlefields, fighting and war. It didn't take long for its meaning in the *Oxford English Dictionary* to develop into an 'act to conquer, subdue, overcome (an adversary), defeat, vanquish, beat (an opponent)'. The meaning of the related word 'competition' was similarly warped from the original meaning of 'to strive together' (from *competere* in Latin), based on a common synergy, to the present-day depiction as beating and destroying others. 'Competitors' have gone from being those you cooperate and collaborate with to being your fiercest opponents, who you must overcome and defeat.

Winning continued to be used in the military context for centuries, until war moved to the marketplace, to political parliaments and onto sports pitches. The language of the battlefield transferred neatly into the world of commerce. As a business, the enemy is your market competitor; victory requires you to destroy them economically.

As the Industrial Revolution accelerated the pace of change in society, so too did the language of machines quickly infiltrate the vocabulary of business success. Workers became numbers; today we still talk about human 'resources' and 'assets'. Processes and targets became central to success. Human emotions and feelings exited the stage in almost every workplace. Winning was about profit and material wealth. Only towards the end of the 20th century did the impact and importance of culture in the workplace start to be taken seriously. A much-needed rehumanization of the workplace is still very much in its infancy.

A binary win–loss mentality pervades much of our current understanding of what winning means. Companies still focus on beating competitors and driving them out of the marketplace. Politicians compete to crush the opposition; the weaker your political opponents the better off you are, even in societies which claim to uphold the principles of democracy and accountability in government. School pupils compete to be top of the class, seeing their fellow pupils as competitors to prove superiority over, rather than as friends or collaborators to support each other's learning.

How far winning depends on defeating an opponent is an important question to consider in our own lives. Do we need to beat someone else to feel successful? Are our achievements less if they have not involved diminishing another? When we did well at school, did we judge our success on our own positive performance or on our performance relative to others around us? If you get 8 out of 10 and everyone else gets 7 out of 10, do you feel better than if you get 8 out of 10 but others get 9 out of 10?

At work, if you get a promotion and no one else does, do you feel more successful than if all your peers are promoted too? If your business grows, but a competitor grows by a greater amount, do you consider your own growth in a less positive light? If one athlete breaks a world record, it is a truly remarkable achievement. But if the person they are racing with breaks it by a greater amount, then is the achievement of the now second-placed athlete irrelevant?

How far we prioritize this 'relativization' component of winning in our definition of success has a huge influence on how we think and behave towards others. It affects whether we trust or mistrust, share our best ideas or keep them secret, support or deceive, collaborate or work alone, encourage or put others down, unleash potential or rein it in. In my view, it's a dangerous element of winning that can mislead, distract and damage our chances of achieving what we're capable of in the long term.

There is a crucial 'time', or 'perspective', component to the language of winning too. The original definition from the Middle Ages, which focused on effort and pleasure, was not clearly time-bound. Winning described effort put in along the way, rather than any single outcome, and focused on experience rather than a particular end moment. Yet winning has shifted to become associated with brief moments in time – a split second when an athlete crosses the line first, or the moment when the daily stock exchange share values are recorded, or those brief points in time when victory is announced or awards presented.

Much of sport still operates around an annual time frame; this is the case for the football leagues, the Tour de France, Six Nations Rugby and the world championships in many sports. Business strategies focus on quarterly results, driven by maybe a one-year business plan; strategies rarely stretch beyond three to five years. Governments barely think beyond the next election date, a maximum of four or five years away, often less. 'Long-term' thinking in sport stretches out to a four-year cycle between World Cups or Olympics, with some more recent radical planning looking eight years ahead, over two cycles. Yet all these could and should be considered outside of these cycles. Sportsmen and women have lives either side of the moments they cross the line; businesses impact the welfare and experience of employees for the time they are at a company (and after), and they affect communities and society too; politicians make decisions that can change lives, sometimes for generations.

Beyond time, what is the scope of our definition of success? Is it an individual achievement or a wider shared aim? Do we see societal success within our national frontiers or on a global scale? The answers to these questions drive different ways of thinking and behaving. As we face unique and complex challenges in our lives, not least how to protect the planet, it's important to consider both the timescale and scope of success that we choose to work towards. To do that, we need to question our own assumptions of what winning means so that we can start to reshape our definition to serve us better.

Our winning delusions

There are so many prevailing (mis)assumptions about what winning means. Let's have a look at a few of them; you'll soon start to spot more around you. The first involves the question of strength. We tend to think of winners as strong and losers as weak. Strength is seen as a stereotypically male trait, and it's no coincidence that winners through history have typically been male. This is how winning has become associated with masculine qualities of heroism, competition and dominance. The superheroes who follow the simple format of beating the baddie, saving the day and coming out the winner are predominantly male. Despite advances in gender equality over the last century, there remains a huge imbalance in the stories and pictures we see of male and female sporting winners, political leaders and business leaders. Studies of 'gender-coding' in the workplace identify language used in meetings, recruitment and promotion processes which support and protect the dominant, usually white, male leaders.[2] 'Winning', 'competition' and 'confidence' are all examples of words which appeal to men more than women. Of course, many women and men learn to play this winning game, against their initial instincts. They learn to use this language and develop the expected winning way of operating, as it's the only way to succeed in many situations. This is a world where the winners are those with hierarchical power, the dominant ones, the 'in' crowd, the ones you don't want to get on the wrong side of and, at times, the bullies.

Alfie Kohn, author and expert in human behaviour and education, explains how a belief that everyone should be competitive becomes a self-fulfilling prophecy:

> competitive people (falsely) assume that all others share their orientation – and indeed those who declare most vociferously that 'it's a dog-eat-dog world out there' usually are responsible for more than their share of canine consumption – which impels them to redouble their own competitive orientation.[3]

I have come across organizational leaders who believe they have to talk about 'winning' in their town hall speeches and communications, claiming that it's what people want to hear and feel part of. The connotations of strength and success associated with winning make it a powerful aphrodisiac. But winning can become closely defined by power, a means of dismissing challenge and questioning, and used to justify behaviours that are extremely damaging yet hard to stand up to, especially lower down the hierarchy.

Associating winners with superheroes and all-powerful leaders brings huge psychological pressure. Alongside associations with superhuman strength, well-worn phrases such as 'winners never quit and quitters never win' link winning with persistence and endurance. People who give up on things are considered weak and quickly tagged as 'losers'. When winning means persisting at all costs, it also strengthens 'sunk cost' bias. We continue with failing projects despite knowing they will not work, simply because of that deep belief that keeping going is a winning behaviour. Such beliefs also create immense personal pressure, meaning that if we fall short in some way, we can quickly feel worthless or suffer in other ways with our mental health.

We become reticent to experiment and risk failure, even though it is a crucial part of learning and innovation. The rise of entrepreneurism is challenging this conventional thinking, unafraid to prove that sometimes the faster you quit, the better off you are.

The ubiquitous talk of war and winning battles when referring to patients fighting diseases, especially cancer, has long made me uneasy and has now been proven to do more harm than good. While the language may be intended to motivate people to be vigilant and proactive, one study found no evidence that this was the case and, in fact, found that battle metaphors could undermine people's intentions to engage in healthy behaviours.[4] Most damaging of all, the underlying implication of these metaphors is that the people who die from cancer, COVID-19 or whatever the disease, didn't try hard enough, didn't fight bravely enough and ultimately 'lost'.

The metrics trap

Part of the allure of winning has always been its measurability. The finish line of the sporting world gives us that certainty we all crave. The industrial measurement of output and productivity in the Industrial Revolution seduced leaders into thinking they could measure success properly. But metrics have played a key role in the distortion and narrowing of what winning has come to mean, as we see in later chapters. Sitting comfortably at the top of what measurement is usually aimed at, winning is often its own justification for measurement.

Metrics have proliferated across society. Governments use metrics to prove accountability or transparency, irrespective of what actually gets measured. Statistics gain additional value simply from having been through 'a measuring process'! If something is quantifiable, then it feels 'scientific'; it seems serious. Gathering data and measurement information becomes a sign of progress, creating a myth of success when in fact no progress has been made at all. (Scientific) data is widely assumed to be more reliable than an individual's judgement, and no one seems to challenge that assumption any more.

Metrics drive behaviour – if we are going to be measured on something, we pay more attention to it. I have seen students arriving on business school programmes ask as their first question: 'What am I going to be assessed on?' Not 'What am I going to learn?' 'How can I get the most out of this course?' 'What are the opportunities for me to grow?' In *The Tyranny of Metrics*, Jerry Muller details the way in which metrics distort every aspect of society – from the police to healthcare, academia and business.[5]

Goodhart's law reminds us that 'When a measure becomes a target, it ceases to be a good measure.' While the intentions behind measuring may be positive – a desire to improve effectiveness and results – we must notice the adverse impact of metrics on behaviours, mindsets and the way we define success. As Nobel Prize-winning economist Joseph Stiglitz warns: 'If we measure the wrong thing, we will do the wrong thing.'[6]

Media narratives

BBC commentator at the end of my Athens Olympic final race (commentator's voice rising throughout, **bold** for commentator's emphasis):

There's no doubt Romania are tiring out front... 150 metres remain. Romania are holding on. Great Britain easing up, every stroke, they're just level now with Belarus. We've got 75 metres remaining... It's just into the silver medal position. Now **let's go for Romania,** the last 10 strokes for the Olympic gold medal. **Let's go Great Britain!** Up and give it everything, push it on for gold. **Let's attack, let's attack...** Up to the line, they're through but they're **only** in silver medal position...

The media help create and sustain an unquestionable view of winning as so wonderfully clear-cut. You're a winner or a loser. Nothing else matters and there's nothing else going on. The images we see of winning sports stars, politicians and business leaders become simplified, exaggerated stereotypes that mostly ignore the breadth, contradictions and complexity of each of these individuals.

They are slotted into a few simple formats: hero against the odds, born leader, people's champion. The stories become repetitive, and as readers we know in advance what we're going to read. There's a formula to how each 'face of the Olympics' gets portrayed or how each landslide-winning all-conquering politician is seen. We are robbed of the ability to contemplate paradoxes within them, nuances in their approach, complexities in their thinking, or to see others 'behind' them. This constrains both those individuals and those of us who are watching them.

In this binary world, a politician can only be a winner or a loser, right or wrong. There is no space to show a more versatile approach, one that involves admitting and learning from mistakes or understanding different, even opposing, viewpoints. The rules of winning are clear: compromise is weak, dogged views are strong. We see two sides pitted against each other, and we wait to see who will win and who will lose: the climate change sceptics versus the environmental activists, left versus right, rich versus poor. Soon we become divorced from the reality of the issues that are actually playing out and their long-term consequences. The gap between the complex decisions that our politicians need to make and the understanding of most of the electorate widens. It becomes harder to make compromises, collaborate with others traditionally portrayed as opponents or rivals, or take decisions with difficult short-term consequences (those that could be construed as a 'loss' in the short term) to achieve a better outcome in the long term (what we will come to call the 'Long Win'). We are just shown the winners and the losers – all neatly summed up in a 500-word article or a set number of characters on social media.

A perennial short-termism drives print journalism, broadcasting, filmmaking, blogging and social media. Today's newspapers grow old quickly; online news is constantly updated and replaced; social media posts are forgotten within seconds. Studies have shown that the competitive nature of journalism lowers its quality in the long run – it's not difficult to work out why. A 1980s study of science reporting found that reporters felt a strong motivation to distort their coverage to win the competition for prominent display of their stories.[7] Studies since have continued to prove this.[8] Shortcuts, assumptions and oversimplifications only increase. Media coverage becomes increasingly out of kilter with the lives we experience – which are typically getting longer, not shorter, and more complex, not simpler.

Why language matters

Reading this, you'll begin to notice more consciously the language, images and metaphors of winning everywhere – on the political, business and sports sections of newspapers, around the dinner table, and in parliaments, classrooms, stock exchanges and boardrooms around the world.

The language of winning and losing battles is so well established that we typically accept it without question. We barely notice it any more. But is it really helpful for the modern world? Is it an appropriate frame for the lives of the majority of people in the world who are not at war? Is it fit for the mobile, diverse, fast-paced business world in which companies need to adapt, innovate and collaborate to thrive? Does winning actually help us to reach our potential and explore what's possible together? Is winning 'the only thing that counts'?

Through the following chapters, I continue to investigate the impact of language on the way we think and behave. We see how it can trap us into a false, binary world and prevent us from exploring any other outcomes that are more sophisticated than winning and losing.

But first, we need to resume our examination of how we have come to be obsessed by winning and address the assumption that it's simply the way we are made. Can we absolve ourselves of responsibility for the way our human minds and bodies respond to winning and simply blame science and nature?

Chapter 2

'It's How We're Wired'

The Science of Winning

On leadership programmes, I have always used activities to unlock insights into human thinking and behaviour. The aim is to support leaders to think about what's happening at a deeper human level in their work environments. One exercise uses a pseudo real-life business setting of a stock exchange, where teams have to decide whether to buy or sell stocks. Their choice to buy or sell mirrors the prisoners' choices about whether to support or betray each other in the prisoner's dilemma, a well-known game from behavioural psychology that demonstrates the tensions between self-interest and cooperation.[1]

In the stock exchange exercise, if teams all 'buy' stocks in each round, then each team gains. If one buys and the other 'sells', then the one that sells does extra well at the cost of the one that buys, which gets a negative return. If both sell, then both achieve negative outcomes. The objective is clearly set out as finishing in profit, *not* as having more than the other teams, *nor* as working to ensure another team goes bankrupt.

Each time I introduce this exercise, I feel nervous that the groups will quickly spot that the obvious solution is to cooperate, all teams simply buying the stocks each round. I worry that if each team states they want to buy in each round, the exercise might end up rather dull, finish quickly and demonstrate the blindingly obvious (and leave me with a gap in the schedule). But I have yet to see a group where all the teams opt simply to buy, choosing to cooperate to reach the required outcome.[2]

Some voices usually realize early on that all teams need to buy to reach the objective, but strong voices always challenge them, urging their teams to sell, to 'shaft the other team' (their language, not mine!) in a determined bid to 'win'. This is despite the fact that their definition of winning – having more than the other teams and/or the other teams losing badly – does not align with the clearly stated objective of the activity: simply to finish in the black.

For some, the importance of winning, defined (by them) as 'beating the other teams', outweighs any option to win through achieving the stated objective. Assumptions are made about what winning must look like: it must involve 'competitor' teams doing badly, working for the common good cannot be a 'winning strategy' and there can only be one winner.

Within each team, challengers to this thinking see the greater benefits of a cooperative approach. They question what the bigger prize might be and, to try to work out the meaning behind the activity, start asking: 'What are we actually trying to achieve?' Initially, this can often feel like the 'weaker' position in the team discussions, with the former position advocated as one of strength and superiority.

Part way through the exercise, each team sees how the other has voted and team representatives can talk to each other. This is an opportunity to build trust and potentially begin anew with fresh cooperation. The approach and communication style in the negotiations play a significant role in whether cooperation follows. Do the team representatives issue threats and accuse each other of betrayal or treachery? Or are they thinking about what they need to do to influence others to cooperate? Sometimes teams realize that cooperation is the clear way to success. But when teams haven't understood or accepted that, it gets frustrating. Most commonly, assumptions about what winning means leads the teams to avoid cooperation. Some even go so far as to create a fictional winning strategy for themselves, which completely fails to achieve the objective set for all the teams to finish in the black and act in the collective best interest.

The debrief with the participants always takes some time. It can be challenging to support the teams to recognize their own (conscious and unconscious) instincts and behaviours, to understand their impact on the rest of the team and wider group of teams, to consider how this sort of behaviour shows up and affects their real workplace and, finally, to discuss how to create a workplace that does not engrain limiting, self-defeating behaviours but creates space for cooperation and acting for the good of a longer-term shared purpose, rather than for narrow, individualistic, short-term outcomes.

This is often the start of a new thought process, an incredibly valuable one that can release us from the winning trap. Our underlying calculations, assumptions and beliefs are critical to how we think, act and make decisions in the workplace. They determine whether a desire to win overrides working collaboratively with colleagues to achieve the best overall outcome.

The same fundamental psychological dilemma is at play in our own lives, with self-interest and short-term gain balanced against longer-term, collective interests. It's echoed in international issues too, from doping in sport to the international nuclear arms race and climate change negotiations.

Often people respond to my questions with: 'That's just how we're wired'; 'We can't help it'; 'Winning is part of who we are'; 'Competition brings out the best in us'; 'It's human nature.' But that's always the argument used to defend the status quo. Alfie Kohn points out in *No Contest: The Case Against Competition* that 'the characteristics that we explain away in this fashion are almost always unsavoury; an act of generosity is rarely dismissed on the grounds that it is "just human nature."'[3]

In this chapter, I want to explore what is and isn't 'natural' about winning and consider different perspectives across anthropology, ethology, biology and psychology.

Perspectives from anthropology and ethology

What assumptions are we making about how we behave and think based on what we (think we) know about our ancestors or the animal world? Instinctive views seem to dominate. These assert how human it is to need to win and prove we're the best or strongest, the explanation being that that's how we survived as cave dwellers. Or that's how animals show us survival works in the animal kingdom.

We have certainly all seen pictures of lions eating their prey and large fish gobbling up smaller ones. But on closer look, this is really a small part of nature. There are also many examples of mutualism, which we seem to quote much less often. For example, oxpecker birds land on rhinos or zebras and eat parasites that live on their skin, thereby feeding themselves and providing pest control for the larger animal. Baboons and gazelles work together to sense danger, and chimpanzees hunt cooperatively and share the spoils. We seem to learn about the cycle of life as a bloodthirsty dog-eat-dog (or dog-eat-cat) world, but tend to overlook examples of behaviours in the animal kingdom which value relationships, show empathy, offer consolation and display a sense of fairness. From chimpanzees to dolphins, there are animals which know how to repair conflict and reconcile differences through behaviours that would be 'superfluous if social life were ruled entirely by domination and competition'.[4]

American palaeontologists Stephen Jay Gould and George Gaylord Simpson point out in their work that there is no necessary relationship between natural selection and competitive struggle. In fact, as Kohn says, natural advantage comes less from struggle and more from

> better integration into the ecological situation, maintenance of a balance of nature, more efficient utilization of available food, better care of the young, elimination of intragroup discords... exploitation of environmental possibilities that are not the objects of competition or are less effectively exploited by others.[5]

If success in the natural world is defined by leaving offspring that survive, then there are as many 'cooperative' strategies, such as symbiosis and mutualism, as there are 'competitive' strategies, such as 'survival of the fittest', the one we usually hear most about and which fits neatly into our cultural 'win at all costs' obsession.[6] Interestingly, we even seem to have twisted what Darwin meant when he used the term 'struggle for existence', interpreting it as a win–lose battle. In fact, he explained that he was using the term in a 'large and metaphorical sense, including dependence of one being upon another'.[7]

I have encountered surprise and confusion that as an Olympian I might not fully sign up to the 'fact' that 'all life is a competition'. One Olympic champion, now retired, said to me that she felt 'competitively burnt out' after years of living as an athlete vying to be the best every day, as required by the training environment, and living an inherently selfish lifestyle. She was relieved that she didn't have to be like that any more. Yet, while she considered herself to have moved into a different phase of her life, others expected her still to be immensely (and pointlessly) competitive about everything and exhibit a win at all costs approach at all times.

Why has this thinking become so entrenched? It's clear that we learn about competition from an early age, partly because we see it all around us. We have often only encountered a single route to success and been taught that winning requires an outcome, reaching a predefined standard and involving other people as comparators, and that winning is inherently good and losing is inherently bad. As social learning theory tells us, learning takes place in a social context;[8] if a particular behaviour is rewarded regularly, it will persist; if it is punished regularly, it's likely to desist. Much of our society encourages and rewards competitive ways of thinking and behaving when it is really only one way to be.

We shouldn't overlook the findings of multiple anthropologists that it was cooperation – rather than brain size, the use of tools or aggression – that defined the first humans. What sets us apart from the animal kingdom is our ability to cooperate in large numbers, communicate through sophisticated language and connect through expressing ideas and stories. As our means of communicating and thinking continually develop, we have the potential to develop our means of connecting and collaborating further. That's good news, as none of our complex social, economic or environmental challenges can be solved by individuals working alone. Our brief trip back into ethology and anthropology is a reminder not to leap to assumptions about what's 'natural'.

Insights from biology and psychology

In a scientific experiment, matched pairs of male mice were put together to see who would come out on top in 'the mouse equivalent of the boxing ring'. A small amount of sedative was slipped into the pre-match food of one mouse in each pair. As expected, the non-sedated mice won. Nothing unexpected there, but further consequences emerged in further bouts. When both new mice and the winning mice from the rigged matches were pitted against tough un-sedated opponents, those with the previous experience of victory against a sedated mouse won more often than the new mice, which had not had this experience.

Behavioural scientists talk of this experiment as evidence of the 'winner effect',[9] referring to the idea that an animal that has won a few fights against weak opponents is much more likely to win later bouts against stronger contenders. It's easy to see how this applies to humans too. The winning experience triggers hormones which influence behaviour, decision-making, self-esteem and confidence. We start to see the 'biology of power' at play. But it is double-edged: short-term gains can turn into long-term losses. The confidence gained can become dangerous when the animal goes up against too many or much stronger opponents still thinking that it can win. It's not difficult to find examples of this sort of thinking and behaviour in business, sport, education and politics.

The mouse experiment just illustrates one way that a winning experience might play out. There is no single scientific description of winning. Rather, there's a complex patchwork of knowledge, with new discoveries emerging all the time as the fields of neuroscience, biology and psychology continue to uncover more about how we think, feel and act.

We still do not fully understand how the different hormone systems in men and women affect their ability and desire to win. We've all heard of testosterone, which is frequently linked to dominating, aggressive and antisocial behaviour. Men have higher quantities than women and so are assumed to be more competitive, natural heroes and winners, more ambitious, more driven to win. But results at recent Olympic Games where women have been represented at levels never seen before should provide enough evidence to dispel these myths.

Traditionally, testosterone has been linked to dominance, power and success. But it has also been proven to impede judgement and emotional intelligence, increasingly viewed as important qualities for building successful teams, effective leaders and organizational performance in the modern world. Again, our definition of what success looks like is critical when it comes to which behaviours we choose to develop and reward.

Although testosterone affects behaviours, it works the other way round too. Harvard psychologist Amy Cuddy's famous recommendation of 'power poses' was proven to raise levels of testosterone in women and men, thus increasing feelings of power and confidence for individuals themselves, and perceptions of their power and confidence in the eyes of those around them.[10] This brings into play the age-old debate of nature versus nurture and challenges the view that some dominant behaviours are natural and innately human. We may have much more choice on how we actively develop our behaviours than we sometimes think. To make better choices, we need to understand how winning impacts our brains. As well as increasing confidence, as we saw in the mouse experiment, winning a race or receiving an award leads to an increase in dopamine, the 'feel-good' hormone. This leads us to want to experience winning again. Winning becomes seductive and addictive – not attributes which are usually seen as positive. It's no surprise that athletes are particularly vulnerable to gambling because of their heavy socialization around competition and extrinsic rewards – two common traits of gamblers.[11]

In business, competition and rewards (such as bonuses and promotions) are often prominent indicators of success and addiction to these quickly starts to drive leaders' behaviour. Success is seen as the next promotion rather than as part of the bigger picture of collective progress towards a shared purpose. Short-term, this approach can work; long-term, it can be less successful and cause a lot of damage to others along the way. The darker, destructive sides of 'winning behaviour' can be found in stories like that of the rogue trader Nick Leeson or the investment fraudster Bernie Madoff, both of which ended in a vicious circle of diminishing performance and self-destruction.

The enjoyment we get from addictive activity decreases each time we do it. Few of us associate addicts with success in life; more usually we see them as sick and weak, in contrast to the 'strength' we associate with winners. This is one of many paradoxes behind what winning can mean in reality when we examine it more closely.

Sportsmen and women who feel emptiness the moment after winning and immediately turn their energies to winning the next competition start to resemble gambling addicts. In *Bounce*, Olympic table tennis player Matthew Syed describes 'the metaphysical hollowness that often accompanies a long-desired triumph'.[12] He argues that it is part of a natural process of disengaging from one successful outcome in order to move on to the next challenge. Certainly, on one level, an athlete needs to shift focus on to the next goal in order to keep improving. However, the extremes of 'hollowness' manifest in many elite athletes and coaches are close to the edge of diminishing rather than increasing performance.

Sir Alex Ferguson is always held up as the epitome of this approach, with his ruthless refocusing on the next season, even immediately after winning the historic 'treble' (Premier League, UEFA [Union of European Football Associations] Champions League and FA [Football Association] Cup) with Manchester United Football Club. Although it undoubtedly drives a team towards the next performance, it brings risks and can easily tip into a self-destructive approach that leads to diminishing performance and wellbeing over time. World Cup winner and legendary England rugby player Jonny Wilkinson provides a clear example of someone who drove himself throughout his career to win more and more – caps, titles, points – but admits, looking back, that it didn't help him at all. He spent years trying to fight his depression with "'another Six Nations Championship, or some more caps, or titles, or points". "Surely," I told myself, "that will keep you off my back?" It doesn't.

It's never enough.'[13] In the 1990s, Dr Robert Goldman asked athletes whether they would take a drug that would guarantee them overwhelming success in sport but cause them to die after five years, a famous study known as the Goldman dilemma. Approximately half said they would.[14] (More recent research suggests this figure is slightly lower[15] but the phenomenon remains.) It is one of those tantalizing hypothetical questions that intrigues and haunts us all, the tantalizing Faustian bargain – what would we do if we were in that situation?

But for athletes, the risks of doping are massive. Long-term health and reputation are risked for the sake of a potential increased status and a 'winning experience' in the short term. So great are the distortions and glorifications of what winning seems to mean that it can seem a worthwhile risk to take. Yet any gains are often short-lived (and destroyed if the cheating athlete is caught) and bring feelings of anti-climax and emptiness in most cases. All the more so when the risks taken have been high.

Former elite squash player and psychologist Tal Ben-Shahar coined the term 'arrival fallacy' to explain the widespread misconception that achieving a goal – in his case, winning a squash game – would lead to feeling happy afterwards. Psychologists Timothy Wilson and Daniel Gilbert also found that impact bias leads us to overestimate the duration and intensity of the positive emotions we may experience as the result of an event. Basically, our ability to predict future emotions – that is, our 'affective forecasting' – is poor. All of these findings lead us back to the importance of carefully reframing what success looks like and not giving in to seductive assumptions and flawed thinking. Getting to know our brains better is key to developing Long Win Thinking.

Certain aspects of our biology and psychology give us the ability to undertake urgent, short-term action, based on our survival needs centuries ago. If a tiger is approaching, the 'limbic' part of our brain will kick in and ensure we act quickly and instinctively. The challenge is to avoid over-relying on and overstimulating this part of our brain. Instead, we could choose to consciously develop the other parts of our brains that determine how we behave and think. By engaging the rational, thinking part of our brain, we could focus on working towards something with greater meaning and purpose over the longer term. The powerful role of meaning and purpose in our thinking is a critical part of redefining success, as discussed in later chapters.

The 'winning mindset'

Is there such a thing as a 'winner's mindset'? We hear motivational quotes at school, on the sports field and in the workplace about winning as an attitude. Take basketball legend Michael Jordan's famous quote: 'I play to win, whether during practice or a real game. And I will not let anything get in the way of me and my competitive enthusiasm to win.' Or the words of Tiger Woods: 'Winning takes care of everything.' I think of this as an old-fashioned winning mindset that doesn't hold up to scrutiny, real-life experience or insights from psychological research – but it's still prevalent on the sports pitch, in the classroom and in the workplace.

The challenge of understanding and knowing how to develop our mindsets reminds me of when I was starting out as an Olympic athlete. I tried really hard to work out how to optimize my state of mind and understand the different thoughts swirling around in my head. I was constantly confused about what was myth and what was fact. Talk of who had winning mindsets and who didn't in the Olympic environment, particularly by coaches and managers, led to a sense that it was innate rather than something that could be developed. This naturally worried me a lot, and I wondered if I had a winning mindset or not and how I might be 'found out' as not having one.

Of course, I didn't like losing; it didn't feel good. And all the authority figures around – the coaches and performance directors – didn't react well when we lost and expected us to exhibit behaviours to show demonstratively that we disliked it and didn't want it to happen again. To be happy or relaxed about losing was seen as a poor indicator of your potential to be a future champion, so you didn't want to be seen doing anything other than tearing your hair out and experiencing extreme grief when you lost. I, too, hounded others who weren't sufficiently miserable when we lost races. In hindsight, I realize these emotions did nothing to help us think clearly about how to go faster next time and kept our mindsets in a fear-based 'survival' mode. Over time, the rational part of my brain learnt that losing was inevitable and could actually be helpful to making the improvements needed to win next time. But it was hard to challenge the dominant outcome-focused narratives held up as the 'right way' by those in charge and those who had won previously; we were afraid of being tainted as unlikely future winners.

Despite the constant reinforcement in that environment to value 'the will to win' above all, revered as the ultimate winning character trait, I was realizing that *wanting* to win did not in itself seem to be connected with going faster. Rather, it was focusing on the 'performance process' – what was required to make the boat go fast – that was effective. Devoting my energy to finding ways to get faster, exploring the possibilities, rather than *wanting* to get faster and *willing* myself to go faster, was a subtle but crucial shift that took place over time in my mind as I started to reframe what success meant. It moved me away from an obsessive approach to winning and towards a mental space where, ironically, I would have a better chance of winning.

This also introduced me to different aspects of the psychology of motivation, goal orientation and competence. Do we have an 'ego orientation' whereby we compare ourselves to others to work out if we are doing well or not? This is at the heart of a world defined by rankings and medals. Or do we have a 'mastery orientation' whereby we are trying to improve one day to the next, comparing ourselves against our own achievements, less reliant on external markers of success?

Athletes have to operate and survive in a world defined by extrinsic measures (medals, rankings). But to thrive and perform consistently at the highest levels, their approach needs to be connected to a more intrinsic mastery mindset, which is so much more energizing and helps sustain performance. Both psychology and philosophy combine within the concept of a mastery mindset. It is a way of focusing on the present and letting go of the need for outcomes when pursuing a task or when defining our approach to life. We see central tenets of this in Long Win Thinking, discussed later.

Loss aversion

To understand the psychology of winning, we need to understand the psychology of losing. Psychologists have shown that if you lose £20, that will register much more strongly as an experience than if you gain £20. Rationally it feels like the impact should be the same, but our basic survival instincts mean we have a stronger reaction to threats and negative events. This is described as 'loss aversion'.

Some argue that this is why we are driven to win – if we enter a win–lose situation, our terror of losing drives us to win. Sports coaches and business leaders driven by the fear of losing assume this is the only way to motivate people. But as with addictive behaviour, this is a limiting strategy, with possible short-term benefits but significant long-term costs.

The more importance placed on winning, the more debilitating losing becomes. Fear-based motivation shuts down our ability to be creative, build collaborative relationships, and grow, learn and adapt, all of which are often central to success. In the long term, it's a recipe for high levels of anxiety. Stress prevents us from accessing the rational part of our brain and regulating our emotions. We effectively make ourselves 'less clever', less able to analyze what has happened and how we might do things differently the next time. Why would we choose to make ourselves less clever by trapping ourselves in win–lose thinking and reducing our ability to learn and improve? For any job or occupation requiring creativity, collaboration, decision-making or problem-solving, relying on motivations stemming from a fear of losing is a recipe for decreasing performance and minimizing learning.

If losing is a powerful negative experience that affects us deeply, then it is interesting that we choose to reinforce this by persisting with win–lose narratives and situations that require many losers. When we define winning and success solely as coming first, then there are multiple occasions where most people will lose most of the time. As was pointed out to me by another Olympian, that's the basic set-up of the Olympics, if you take a step back and look at it. Ten thousand of the best athletes from across the world gather at the opening ceremony, each full of dreams, hopes and excitement. Two weeks later, they all return for the closing ceremony. This time, just over 300 are celebrating, and if we have a binary mindset, the rest have become failures, most never mentioned again, many flooded with shame, self-doubt and a deep sense of inadequacy.

Psychologist Frank Ryan points out that it is often the more successful competitors who struggle most with losing. Bitterness and bad feeling about losing are indicators of a successful competitor (which we are all encouraged to become), and a winning record can increase these unsavoury behaviours.[16]

Sports psychologists nowadays explain that you don't win by wanting to win and advise choosing and developing a completely different response to losing – to focus our minds on the objective of learning rather than on the outcomes of success or failure. Part of being able to learn entails accepting the full range of thoughts, emotions and feelings within us so we can rebalance our mental approach and avoid leaping to judgements about what losing must say about our self-worth. Later in the book, we see that this forms part of Long Win Thinking.

The psychology of negotiations

It's not difficult to see how the choice between self-interest and collective interest plays out across business and beyond, in the international world of global trade, climate change and security.

For example, international climate change negotiations closely mirror the prisoner's dilemma discussed earlier in the chapter, where both parties have a choice whether to defect (that is, choose not to cooperate) because the (economic) risk of choosing to cooperate while the opponent exploits them is too great. Although cooperating is by far the best option for the collective good, nation states have been reluctant to commit to significantly greater cooperation that incurs individual costs. Climate change summits have ended up as a gathering of countries fighting to ensure that their own individual targets are not greater than each other's – at this point, the real aim of working out what will best protect our planet is lost. There are some regional examples of cooperation, such as the Nordic Council of Ministers working on a 2030 vision for Nordic cooperation, including issues relating to healthcare and the environment, but these remain exceptions rather than the rule.

How we define success collectively in international politics is crucial when so much is at stake. During the 12 years I worked for the Foreign and Commonwealth Office as a diplomat, I was involved in a range of political negotiations, including negotiations on European Union (EU) directives on asylum, trilateral negotiations on increased cooperation with Spain and Gibraltar, and negotiations on advancing much-needed political reforms in Bosnia and Herzegovina (hereafter Bosnia) after the violent break-up of the former Yugoslavia in the 1990s. Where disputes become entrenched – the Spanish–Gibraltar sovereignty dispute dated back to the Treaty of Utrecht in 1713, and the ethnic hostility after Bosnia's bitter civil war in the 1990s followed centuries of battles – you typically find yourself stuck in a rigid zero-sum game mentality. It is then phenomenally difficult to move forward. For one side to feel they have made progress, it must be at the other's expense.

Our job as diplomats and negotiators was always to seek out opportunities, however small, to craft a new narrative, step by step, to allow both sides to feel they could make gains; the hardest thing was accepting that your opponent should gain going forward. It's hard work and takes years, and as events in the Middle East demonstrate, it can seem almost impossible. But this approach is working in many parts of the world to prevent unstable situations from falling into conflict.

In one diplomatic role, I worked as the Head of the Political Section of the British Consulate in Basra, Iraq, in 2008–2009. Our main objective was to persuade the local political leaders and the heads of the militias and paramilitary organizations that were fighting each other on the streets of Basra on a nightly basis not to achieve their gains through violence, but to work together to create a peaceful and more prosperous city in which everyone could play a part. For years, we got nowhere, as all the local groups fought constantly to see who would be the winner, the dominant and strongest party, the future 'kings of Basra'. Our beseeching about democracy and holding peaceful, democratic elections fell on deaf ears.

But by 2008, a new dynamic was emerging. With growing fatigue locally due to the fighting on all sides, an increasing death toll and other consequences, there was a realization that no one was getting what they wanted. All that was being achieved was the destruction of the beloved city that the various parties longed to preside over, with no end in sight. The increasing shared appetite for change gave us a tiny opening to start developing a new narrative and a new way of thinking about finding a more cooperative way forward and some common ground. With all the many different stakeholders, we needed to start to redefine a shared vision of what 'winning' might mean. It was a messy process, full of ups and downs in a complex and volatile situation. But some new momentum was emerging.

When we started asking the local leaders, politicians and heads of militias what they wanted and why, we heard some overlapping themes. They all talked about making Basra great again, harking back to the prosperous days when Basra had been known as the 'Venice of the Middle East'. We wanted that too. The contrast between this ambition and the reality of a town more and more battered and blasted to pieces each day gradually helped us to start to change the way people were thinking.

While the parties were consistently rejecting the international community's urging to establish democracy and hold peaceful political elections, another more attractive shared objective was emerging. All sides wanted greater prosperity, which became the basis of developing a powerful longer-term vision in which everyone needed to play a role. Several leaders spoke of creating a 'Dubai' in southern Iraq and started to develop a shared language which provided an opportunity to create some 'win–win' thinking rather than 'zero-sum game' thinking. Of course, things didn't change overnight; it was not a smooth process and there was still further bloodshed. In such a messy, conflict-affected situation, there were many actors with different motives. But a noticeable shift brought a small but significant increase in stability once there was wider buy-in to working towards a shared vision of prosperity, rather than Western-imposed democracy or a world where only one 'gang' could win by destroying all the others.

Diplomacy shows the importance and challenge of shifting mindsets and the behavioural psychology at play underneath the political and technical issues being negotiated. You have to identify the 'game' being played through the language used, and then make a decision about whether to play within the constraints of that game or change your language, thoughts and responses and move away from a zero-sum game. We all have more choices than we may realize about the game we see ourselves in, whether it's sport, business or life, and how we can choose to play it.

Why understanding the science of winning matters

While some biological, psychological and social aspects of our make-up respond to competition and zero-sum game thinking, we can respond in other ways too. The opportunity and challenge is to create environments where those other ways of thinking, behaviour and motivation are valued and rewarded. Are our work and home environments full of confrontation and threat, sparking short-term stress responses? Or do these environments foster a deep culture of support, acceptance and safety? Not completely without conflict, but with conflict that can be resolved constructively and compassionately.

It would be wrong to conclude that competition and self-interest are simply how we function, and it's certainly false to think that's how we create the best outcomes. But we need significant re-education and rebalancing across our lives to understand the 'winning trap' and avoid this self-limiting thinking. Science isn't telling us not to bother to try and create longer-term cooperation or build diverse collaborative teams; it's telling us we need to create different approaches to create the necessary conditions where we can all thrive and develop successful relationships and effective teams. To understand our cultural assumptions about winning further, let's take a look back over time to see how winning has played out in the history books.

Chapter 3

'To the Victor, the Spoils'

The History of Winning

As the gladiators entered the Colosseum, swaggering and brandishing their swords, the crowds cheered and bayed loudly. The combatants drew swords and as they clashed and jousted in their fierce contest, the atmosphere became intensely febrile, the spectators growing increasingly agitated. They all knew that this was a live competition of nerve and skill that would go all the way. All eyes were on these two men, who were fighting according to one clear, universally understood rule: there can be only one winner. The vanquished gladiator would pay the ultimate penalty for defeat.

Crew selection for the Olympics operated on not entirely dissimilar rules. You win and you are selected; you lose and you don't make it, you don't get the kit, you don't go to the Olympics, you don't get a medal, you have failed, you are forever a 'loser'.

Seat racing in rowing is the key method of selection, and a pretty brutal one. Races to select sweep-oared boats are held in pairs (rowers have one oar each so can't row on their own, as they'd go round in circles). Every combination is tried; first, you race with one partner. It's your pair against the rest of the team, pulling together to try and come out on top. Then you go back to the landing stage and swap partners, working with someone you were trying to beat a moment ago, trying to beat the rest again, including your recent partner.

There can be all sorts of anomalies: You can win all your races except one, but if you go dreadfully slowly in that one poor race, your cumulative time can leave you languishing at the bottom of the rankings table. Two rowers may be the fastest overall combination, but the individuals may not go so well when racing in different combinations. It's a nightmare for coaches when results aren't clear-cut, and torture for athletes whose Olympic dreams hang in the balance. But that's how it's done, and often on that one day, key decisions are made about who is 'in' and who is 'out'. Other sports work similarly, some have even harsher methods.

The margins can be tiny. I have known brilliant athletes limp away with a sense of failure for the rest of their lives after coming out at the wrong end of the rankings. But those are 'the rules of the game': if you can't hack it, then clearly you're not made out to be a winner. The views of those not selected are dismissed because they are losers. No one who is selected is going to be daft enough to encourage suspicion about their own position and potential to be a winner. It's a self-perpetuating modus operandi. But is there a cost to both those selected as well as those who don't make the cut? Does this really help achieve our highest levels of performance?

Gladiatorial fighting in the Roman Empire retains to this day a glamorous, instantly recognizable heroic image, depicted in Hollywood blockbusters centuries after the actual events. Politicians frequently adopt the tactics of those encounters, using persistent metaphors about battles – at times, modelling themselves on those Roman gladiators in a bid to appear as heroic saviours. Many business leaders have taken on the gladiatorial mantle too, acting boldly (and at times brutally) to turn around companies on the precipice of collapse, or slugging away as huge giants battling to be the marketplace winner. History is peppered with epic business battles, such as Ford versus General Motors in the car manufacturing industry in the first half of the 20th century, Coke versus Pepsi in the 'cola wars' of the 1980s or Microsoft versus Apple at the turn of the 21st century.

We can find seeds of our preoccupation with winning throughout different aspects of history, whether that of politics, philosophy, sport or business. Re-examining some of these stories may help us review our current understanding of what winning means and consider whether that's useful for us now and in the future.

Victory and defeat, meaning and virtue

History books around the world usually focus on the winners from the past: military generals and political leaders predominate. When these winners are also the authors of what happened, we cannot help but see the world through their perspective. History literally tells us 'his story', a highly selective viewpoint of the (male) victors. As Caroline Criado Perez sums up: 'Most of recorded history is one big data gap.'[1] A simple common theme dominates this one-sided patriarchic narrative: the winners are the strongest and most powerful who defeat the weak.

We can easily see where our current association of strength with winning has come from through history. It reflects themes of domination and control, the language of imperialism. It's a binary world with only two states: dominant or submissive, colonizer or colonized. You win and rule, or lose and are defeated.

Tales of winning heroes have been passed down to us through some of the best-known classical literature, starting with epic stories such as Homer's *The Iliad* and Virgil's *The Aeneid*. Heroic characters are depicted battling through sieges and sackings and celebrating the greatness of the respective rulers and victors in these stories, retold by generation after generation of writers. These themes aligned with the politics of the time: kings and emperors trying to impose their dominance on other states and nations. Fighting and winning battles became the prevailing rhythm of politics and government, mirrored in culture and entertainment.

It has long been common practice in warfare that the winning army got to do what it wanted in the territory it had 'won'. That meant looting and taking whatever the victorious army wanted: wealth, harvests, women and property were all legitimate 'spoils of victory'. Similar principles still exist today. In some cases, winning still leads 'victors' and the strongest in society to feel they have a dispensation to behave how they want – an automatic waiver from customary behaviour, even permission to go beyond the law. These are basic examples of how easily winning can corrupt. Through history, there has been little recourse to justice. And even if there have been attempts in recent times, and at vast expense, to set up international tribunals for national figures who have committed some of the worst war crimes and atrocities, such as through the International Criminal Tribunal for Rwanda and the International Criminal Tribunal for the former Yugoslavia, it remains incredibly difficult to bring these powerful perpetrators to justice. Our easy love affair with battle-winning heroes began centuries ago, but why do we continue to accept it so easily given much richer perspectives of history? Previous generations had limited access to other views, but, today, modern technology, a broader range of authors and experts, and stronger streams of revisionist thinking should open up a much wider range of perspectives. People can look at what happened in the past, hear previously untold stories and recalibrate their view of the past to reshape their views of the future. But it would seem that alternative perspectives on history and politics are yet to reach the 'mainstream'. While schools, businesses and countries continue to hold focus events such as 'women in science' events or Black History Month, it's probably safe to conclude that the same old simplistic historical narratives continue to dominate.

History is dominated by the 'winners', and those who have benefited from the political and military events that feature so prominently remain in positions of power. They continue to define what winning on societal, governmental and intergovernmental levels will look like in the future. Where there are calls for change, they lead that change, all the time ensuring that they continue to come out as winners and bringing their innate biases to any attempts at social change. *New York Times* author Anand Giridharadas explains that this is why so many people feel that 'the game is rigged against people like them', and why he calls for more to be done to strengthen our shared democratic institutions as the best way to effect change in a context of equality.[2]

The proliferation of widely available channels of information offers opportunity to previously unheard voices. Of course, it also creates opportunity for 'fake news'. But this challenge shouldn't put us off finding a richer and more accurate view of the past to inform what we do in the future. We need to engage with a challenging, questioning approach, and a mindset that isn't looking for simple answers.

While battles for power and strength dominate the history books, there is another thread of thought through history. Philosophers and other thought leaders have always been searching for greater meaning to life and a broader understanding of individuals and societies. Ancient Greek philosophers famously contemplated what constituted success, fulfilment and human happiness. Many struggled with the military might and material wealth valued in society and longed to explore deeper ideas of what life was about.

Aristotle and the Stoic philosophers concerned themselves with defining 'virtue' and debated whether success or 'happiness' should be focused on the individual or the collective, whether success was a physical (material) or spiritual experience, temporary or eternal. The Stoic philosophers rejected the notion that bodily and material goods contributed to human happiness. In *Nicomachean Ethics*, Aristotle goes through all the things that you could mistake for the purpose of your life – glory, money, honour, fame – and explains why they will never be sufficient, stating that only 'human flourishing' (eudaimonia) can bring fulfilment. The Stoics believed in the *pursuit* of happiness rather than the achievement of happiness itself, since the outcome is not within our control. They may well have laid the early roots of modern sports psychology's mantra to 'control the controllables' and focus on the 'performance process' that you are responsible for, rather than on results and outcomes beyond your control. This perspective will play a part in how I redefine winning later in the book.

These philosophers typically brought longer-term thinking to the shorter-term social norms that they saw around them. They extended concepts of time by referring to the 'afterlife' or the perspective gained at the end of life on earth, something we see echoed in concepts of spirituality among many religions. Ancient Greek has two words for time: *chronos*, a quantitative concept of chronological or sequential time, and *kairos*, referring to 'defining moments' in time as a more qualitative concept.

On the Indian subcontinent, Buddhism emphasizes a spiritual and non-material way of life where success is defined around devotion to meditation. Hinduism similarly places a strong emphasis on meditation as a way of connecting with one's inner 'soul', moving away from any earthly or material form of virtue. In Asia, ancient thinking based on Confucius sees virtue as a more social and collective concept. Transcendence in Chinese culture comes from the wider society, the group, rather than belief in a god. Ubuntu philosophy, with its origins in ancient Africa, believes in a completely social view of humanity focused around a universal bond of sharing that connects all humanity.[3] These approaches have been absent in many Western cultures, though there is an increasing interest in these ways of thinking in response to the challenges of burnout, stress, dehumanized workplaces, climate change, social injustice and inequality.

Christianity is full of contradictions. The Bible contains stories of traditional battles for power and dominance, and the history of Christianity comprises endless battles to defeat other religions and increase its own wealth and power. But the teachings of Christianity also show that reward comes through eternal life in heaven, not material wealth, social status or political power. An early subversive thinker, Jesus challenged many of the social norms of his time. Mark's gospel describes a scene where the disciples argue over who is the greatest, competing with each other for personal success, echoing the struggle for status and recognition in Jewish society back then. For the disciples, seeking greatness was a natural, noble and worthy pursuit. But Jesus turns this on its head: 'Anyone who wants to be first must be the very last, and the servant of all.'

The rejection of the material world is common in the theology of the major religions. In Islam, the Quran shows the Prophet Muhammad guiding his followers on what constitutes a good life and what would be rewarded with eternal paradise. Success is described in terms of how the followers live their lives, unrelated to wealth, health or happiness in this life, with rich rewards coming in the hereafter. The Arabic word for success is *falah*, heard every day in the call to prayer, *hayya alal-falah* – literally, 'hurry to success, come to prayer'.

The philosophical dilemma about how we define success in life is as old as it could be and comes with a substantial body of thought to keep in mind as we question what winning means in our lives today.

Sporting philosophies

An obvious place to visit as we trace the history of winning is the ancient Greek Olympic Games. These Games first took place in 776 BCE in honour of Zeus and were held every four years until well into the fourth century. The Greeks believed the Games had their roots in religion and that athletic competition was tied to worship of the gods. The ancient Olympics comprised a broad festival that included sport, literature and religion. Celebrated for bringing peace and harmony, the different Greek states came together, laying down arms, if at war, for the period of the Games.

The original focus was on running races, but the Games expanded over time to include wrestling, boxing, pankration,[4] horse racing and chariot racing, and jumping and throwing. Most of these sports mirrored military battles. Many were life-and-death encounters. Athletes in combat sports had to indicate their surrender by raising their index fingers; some died before they could do this.

Winning had huge prestige. The winner received a crown of olive leaves cut from the sacred tree at Olympia. No medals were given out. Only the winner's name was recorded. Coming second or third meant nothing. The winner was allowed to set up a statue of himself to commemorate his success, often had victory songs specially written for him and could receive privileges such as free board and lodging or theatre tickets for life. Olympic victors became popular heroes with huge followings of fans. Winning, and the significant status that came with it, was central, despite the broader cultural and religious underpinnings, and reflected the dominant political and military narratives of the time.

Just before the turn of the 20th century, the Olympics were revived by Baron Pierre de Coubertin and coloured by his own sporting and educational philosophy. He particularly admired the ancient practice linked to the Games of the sacred Truce, which had created a temporary ceasefire between city states. He believed that in modern times too, the Olympics could promote peace and understanding across cultures.

The Olympic Truce was renewed by the International Olympic Committee (IOC) in 1992, and further reinforced by a United Nations (UN) resolution in 1993, drawing on the ancient Greek tradition. The International Olympic Truce Foundation was founded a few years later to promote these peaceful principles, and each host city is encouraged to incorporate the spirit and principles of the Truce. There have been a few historic moments relating to the Truce since, such as when the North Korean and South Korean teams marched together at the 2006 and 2018 opening ceremonies, and attempts by host cities to engage younger generations in understanding and supporting the principles of the Truce. Otherwise it has struggled to have any greater or longer-term impact on world politics.

De Coubertin's approach was also greatly influenced by the social consequences he saw around him following bitter defeats in the Franco-Prussian War. He saw the Olympic Games as a vehicle for a kind of military training that addressed the mind as well as the body, where sport could be a 'source for inner improvement' and social reform.

On a visit to Rugby School and other British public schools, de Coubertin had seen the role that sport played in education, building 'social and moral strength' and developing impressive young men who would know how to 'fight well'. While his approach is still full of battle metaphors, de Coubertin included moral and ethical values alongside physical strength. He emphasized the importance of 'how' you win and lose, rather than simply valuing the outcome, a shift away from the ethos of the ancient Games. This outlook is memorialized in the phrase that he is most famous for, 'the important thing is not winning but taking part', first said during the 1908 London Games (drawing on a speech in London by the Bishop of Pennsylvania a few days earlier). It later appeared on the stadium scoreboard at the opening of the 1932 Los Angeles Olympics and forms the essence of what is now called the Olympic creed: 'The important thing in life is not the triumph, but the fight; the essential thing is not to have won, but to have fought well.'[5]

The phrase 'it's not the winning that counts; it's the taking part' has entered common parlance. It is typically used in two distinct and contrasting situations. Firstly, it is used when an act of extraordinary kindness and generosity becomes the greater story, rather than who won or lost – such as those occasional moments when one competitor helps another who has fallen mid-race, even though it's at their own cost. Higher principles come into play, as a higher human value of respect and friendship trumps winning. These are some of the most iconic moments of the Olympics, unrelated to winning, such as when American Abbey D'Agostino stopped to help New Zealand runner Nikki Hamblin cross the finish line of the 5,000 metres track race in the 2016 Rio Olympics after a devastating collision. Secondly, and more commonly, the phrase is used to mock those who lose. It is cited as fake sympathy, derisory sarcasm or contemptuous consolation for those who didn't make it to the winners' podium. It directly contradicts the phrase's original meaning and reinforces the dominant attitude that it's only the winners who count – anyone who thinks otherwise is, well, a loser according to a self-justificatory logic.

De Coubertin aimed to enshrine the Olympic principles as a philosophy and guiding way to live in the Olympic Charter. Every competitor at the Olympic Games still receives a participant's medal (though it's rare to see photographs in the media of these medals being held aloft). There is also a special Pierre de Coubertin medal, an award given since 1964 by the IOC to athletes who demonstrate the spirit of sportsmanship in the Olympic Games or give exceptional service to the Olympic movement. Technically, it is seen by the IOC as the highest award within the Olympics, but most people haven't heard of it, and it generates few headlines.

The Olympic Charter sets out three Olympic values: excellence, friendship and respect, intended to reinforce the values of Olympism and the importance of how sport is played rather than the results. The Paralympic values build on these with their four values: determination, inspiration, courage, equality. These are strong values but how deeply are they embedded within the sporting world, grassroots or elite, let alone acknowledged within the commentary we hear and the reports we read? I can't remember them ever being mentioned in all my years of competing (in fact, coaches specifically told me not to give competitors too much respect, fearing that I might not be as 'ruthless' in the race if I did).

The Olympic motto 'Citius, Altius, Fortius' (faster, higher, stronger) – perhaps a more naturally heroic sporting mantra – is generally better known. First proposed when the IOC was created in 1894, de Coubertin believed these three words represented a 'programme of moral beauty'. We seem to have slipped a long way from that. Breaking barriers in sport and beyond undoubtedly retains an inspirational aspect, the thrilling experience of watching or exploring the limits of what is possible. But this can tip over into a desperate striving to be the best at all costs, to beat everyone around you in order to prove your own worth. This is far from inspirational or life enhancing. At what point does the earnest desire to be the best you can be become an obsessive drive to be the best whatever it takes? Echoed across the business, educational and political world, this tipping point is crucial to how we define and pursue success.

One area with a strong tradition of ethics and values is the world of martial arts. They date back thousands of years, traced to ancient civilizations in Egypt, Greece, China and India. A clear combat element is combined with an equal emphasis on emotional and spiritual wellbeing. Their underpinning philosophy comes first, whatever level you are training or competing at, novice or elite. This contrasts with Olympism, where the values and philosophy are applied patchily and inconsistently, and rarely visible above results.

Many sports are waking up to the need to create an environment with strong guiding principles and values. That includes developing an athlete as a whole person, and supporting their physical, mental, emotional and spiritual health and wellbeing needs equally. Sustainable performance, athlete retention, mental health challenges and social media pressures demand improvements in these areas across the high-performance sporting world. Coach development plays a crucial role. Are coaches continuing past practice or given the space and exposure to introduce new perspectives? A more holistic approach requires a belief that wellbeing is essential to results and part of valuable broader gains off the field of play. That requires a brave rejection of the dominant, inherited narrative of results, results, results.

A brief history of winning in business

If sport reimagined combat, the birth and growth of the business world further developed the competition for primacy in society. Business and trading have been part of our history for as long as we have had records. What is mainly recorded in business history? It's the winners: the heroes who built great trading empires and created vast wealth.

The concept of business can be traced back to the eighth century BCE in India with early organizations called *shreni*, the first firms that could independently enter into contracts or own property. By 960 CE, China's Song dynasty saw the advent of gunpowder, printing presses and the first partnerships and joint stock companies to resemble our own modern capital structures, set up on a primarily competitive basis. By 1500, government-backed firms, like the Dutch East India Company and British East India Company, began building global trading empires and floating stocks and bonds on new exchanges as their goods moved round the world.

By the end of the 18th century, the Industrial Revolution was under way in Europe and the US, drastically changing how economies grew. Agricultural economics had remained little changed for centuries, but the Industrial Revolution enabled output to increase year on year, with huge ramifications. Growth became the main aim, a goal that has run through the history of business ever since and provided the dominant definition of success. Still today, most businesses' aims, strategies and economic survival are tied up with growth, as I explore further in Chapter 7. Until well into the 21st century, there was little opposition to the concept that business existed to do anything other than maximize profit and grow.

The Industrial Revolution brought great social change through the spread of education and the beginnings of public debate about greater equality. With that came new ways of considering what life was about. Economists debated free market economic theory and the 'rules of capitalism', building on the work of Scottish philosopher and economist Adam Smith and his magnum opus *The Wealth of Nations* (1776). Politicians tried to grab onto these ideas to deliver increased prosperity and win more votes.

Scientific management, also known as Taylorism (after its founder, Frederick Winslow Taylor), began in the 19th century, based on the principles that a manager's job is to increase efficiency in a production system. It has proved stubbornly enduring and its roots underpin the dehumanized workplaces we see struggling today to engage employees to meet the very different demands of the modern business world.

By the 20th century, the US, 'the land of the free', saw the birth of the 'American Dream'. The term was coined by James Truslow Adams in his 1931 bestseller *The Epic of America* and was based on an ethos of possibility, hope, and a belief that 'life should be better and richer and fuller for every man'. Its roots go further back to the thinking in the Declaration of Independence 'that all men are created equal, that they are endowed by their Creator with certain unalienable Rights, that among these are Life, Liberty and the pursuit of Happiness'. Adams went on to say explicitly that it is not 'a dream of motor cars and high wages merely', but winning in life became increasingly synonymous with material success, epitomized so vividly by F. Scott Fitzgerald's novel *The Great Gatsby* (1925).

The language and philosophy of the American Dream form a strong thread through the American psyche, though it has faltered increasingly in recent times. Its aspirations failed to materialize in past generations, and the effects of globalization increasingly isolated many who hoped and dreamt of better. Despite repeated promises of a better life by successive American presidents, the reality of continuing social constraints, gross inequality and racial and social discrimination in American society has seen many 'lose out' on the life they wanted, and a growing realization that we can't all be winners in the way that the American Dream seemed to promise. Similar social and economic traits and experiences can be traced across the developed world.

The last century of history and politics

As business and industry developed in the West through the last century, it combined with politics and the military to take warfare to a new level of aggression and devastation. Peace treaties continued to be negotiated on a win–lose basis, ensuring the next war was never far away.

Reeling from the savagery of the First World War, David Lloyd George of Great Britain, Georges Clemenceau of France and Woodrow Wilson of the US met in Versailles in 1918 to discuss the peace treaty. The mood across the countries who had 'won' was to 'make Germany pay', an extremely popular slogan in Britain at the time. The Treaty of Versailles was not negotiated but imposed by the victors, immediately laying the foundations for the Second World War and ongoing disruption in the Middle East. The First World War is one of many wars that may in one sense have been 'won' in the short term. But looking at the dire political events that ensued, it is hard to describe this moment as victorious or successful for any of the countries involved in the longer term.

The aftermath of the First World War saw the first moves to create new means of international cooperation, first through the establishment of the League of Nations, and then through the UN and NATO (North Atlantic Treaty Organization) after the

Second World War. It was a bold attempt to improve international cooperation within a framework that could last, and to make it easier to cooperate than not. Of course, these organizations were founded by the 'victors' with good intentions but also the most power (the five permanent countries of the UN Security Council remain the same decades later: the US, the UK, Russia, China, France), and have remained dogged by zero-sum game thinking and power struggles. The biggest challenges of the 21st century are inherently global, whether protecting the planet or fighting a health pandemic, yet it's hard for these international institutions to play their full potential role.

Just as industrialization changed warfare drastically in the First World War, so technology changed it again towards the end of the 20th century, as threats and conflicts developed in a way that conventional armies were not prepared for. Winning in wars is now harder than ever to define. However many battles were reported as being won in the Afghanistan and Iraq wars in the 1990s and 2000s, however many times victory was claimed by politicians, the reality on the ground overturned those statements time and time again. Success in conflict requires an ever more diverse and adaptive approach, yet many politicians still find it hard to move away from talk of simple victories over the 'enemy'.

The allure of the heroic narrative is embedded in mindsets and often reinforced in the physical structures of politics too. Inside the UK government's 'mother of parliaments', MPs (Members of Parliament) sit on opposing benches, the distance of two sword lengths apart, with a spiked metal mace lying between them. Members choose which side they are on. The act of changing from one party to another, 'crossing the house', is seen as an act of extreme treachery, betrayal and weakness. In this world, sticking to one's party come what may, even if going against one's values and beliefs, is 'strong', winning behaviour.

The famous weekly session of Prime Minister's Questions (PMQs) is all about combat at the despatch boxes. Every Wednesday at midday, the leader of the opposition and MPs across the House of Commons can hold the prime minister directly to account. Each week, the session is characterized by cheering and booing, shouting and finger-pointing. Political journalists and analysts give their verdict on 'who won PMQs', the prime minister or the leader of the opposition. Political analysts even score each leader with marks out of 10. More emphasis is given to the leaders' rhetorical performances and the relative strength shown by the two leaders than to the substantive issues at stake.

The set-up of British politics makes great television: it's a modern gladiatorial contest. The media report on the winners and the losers. But it's hard to see this binary contest helping any government to find the best way forward 'in the national interest' (to borrow a phrase that echoes rather hollowly through the debating chamber) or to tackle sensibly any of the main complex global challenges of the 21st century.

This combative language and thinking plays into an easy nationalist narrative, and many versions can be found around the world. Nations are still looking to 'win' politically and economically at the cost of their neighbours. This fundamental narrative undermines the ability to build effective cross-boundary, supranational coalitions, and underpinned the bitter Brexit debate in the UK. The language of winning and conquering continued throughout Britain's membership of the EU as prime ministers from both sides of the political divide returned from summits and negotiations waving the agreed treaties as papers that showed how Britain had won the negotiations against its allies. No surprise then that many of the British public continued to see their European neighbours as the enemy, rather than the reality of them being the UK's largest trading partners and peaceful allies for over 70 years.

It is noteworthy that in the UK and the US, both known for a strong binary system, strong beliefs prevail about the weakness of coalition governments and their undesirability. Coalitions are weak in a world where strength is about swift, easy decision-making rather than a collaborative process of sharing multiple perspectives to find the best collective way forward. The continuing British bias away from coalition government or cross-party cooperation undoubtedly constrains possibilities of pooling the best ideas across politics to address the complex issues of the 21st century.

Governments thus end up focusing on daily micro-battles that they are trying to 'win', and struggle to effectively tackle global issues ranging from trade to crime, migration flows, climate change, health and security.

Why considering history matters

Our perspective on what winning means sits deep in our psyches, influenced by thinking from the earliest events we learn about in history. We cannot develop new ideas fit for new times unless we better understand the ideas that went before. Looking back, we can see the narrowness of the narrative told by the victors. But we can also see how the realities of life, business and war have changed immeasurably over time.

Recent times have seen some shifts, such as the #MeToo movement, which campaigns against sexual abuse and harassment and famously brought down Hollywood mogul Harvey Weinstein. Campaigns like this, where different voices are heard and now listened to, show an important change in what's socially accepted behaviour from our leaders, and are triggering increasing culture crises for leaders in organizations and public life.

There is an increasing mismatch between the way our political and cultural systems grew up and the world in which they now exist. No one nation can 'win' at climate change; no one country can 'defeat' terrorism, or a global pandemic, on its own. As many philosophers have argued through the ages, none of us can 'win at life'. Part II shows us how this deep-seated cultural obsession with winning threads through our lives in many different ways and often holds us back from fulfilling our potential.

Part II

How Our Obsession with Winning Holds Us Back

*Winning at all costs comes at a price:
collateral issues of rivalry, arrogance,
selfishness and a lack of humility and generosity.*

Anthony Salz (*Salz Review:
An Independent Review of Barclays' Business
Practices, 2013*)

Chapter 4

From Monopoly Memories to the Greasy Pole

Real-Life Encounters with Winning

I still remember the tension sizzling in the air. After several hours of tense and at times tantrum-provoking play, my friend's brother, Thomas, rolled the dice and moved his old boot slowly along the board. He could already see where it would end up, though part of him still wanted to deny it would happen. My friend and I had made the same calculation and were holding our breath. Thomas quickly reviewed his escape options: his body temperature was rising, the light hairs on his arms standing on end. His emotions surged up inside him, and his view of the board narrowed as the primitive, reactive, survival-motivated part of his brain took over the rational part. As he shuffled the old boot onto the edge of Park Lane with a chunky red hotel on it, he stood up and ranted increasingly tearfully about how unfair it was, how his sister and I had cheated. He finished by throwing the board up in the air, sending all the houses, hotels, and 'chance' and 'community chest' cards flying.

Let's consider our earliest experiences of winning – maybe family games, school exams, music competitions or football tournaments. Our experience of what winning means is shaped hugely by our environment and upbringing: what gets rewarded and who our parents and teachers declare to be the winners. This is where we start to develop questions that form our own philosophy of winning. Is winning about school league tables, parents' expectations or media verdicts on what constitutes success? Can we have won if no one else sees us win? Is winning about beating a previous personal best or about beating an opponent? Is it defined by others, or can I define what success looks like for myself?

Stories of winning are often told with the intention of setting standards for us to reach, whether related to school examinations, work promotions or sports leagues. Winning quotes are held up and cited by business leaders hoping to inspire greater performance in a sales team, coaches hoping to rally a team to win a match, or parents hoping to inspire a son or daughter to come out top in an exam. It can seem an easy and logical pattern to follow. I, too, have felt keen to fall in line and follow suit. The trouble is that time and time again, this approach doesn't lead us where we want to go. Or if it does, it entails untold suffering along the way.

Childhood encounters

Our first encounter with winning and losing, and battling and negotiating, often comes early in life within the first 'team' we ever encounter – our family. We quickly learn about values, who has power (and who doesn't), and how we can best get that chocolate biscuit we want! It quickly shapes our relationships with others. Our home environment, parents and brothers and sisters play a huge part in how we first experience 'winning' and what value gets attached to it. These are our first opportunities to choose to compete to win or to explore how we might cooperate or collaborate and reach a different outcome.

Sibling rivalry is often depicted in TV dramas, books and films as a world of 'winners' and 'losers', governed by a zero-sum game mentality. This can be an early introduction to a binary perspective, typically when an older child feels that he or she can only win at the expense of a younger sibling or lose out to them. The first-born child is used to having the mother's complete attention – then a sister or brother arrives and 'steals' some of that time. The first child can spend a lot of time and effort fighting to 'win' the parents' time, attention and love in a battle that is ultimately always lost. The parent can never give undivided attention solely to one child once another has arrived on the scene.

It's a huge period of adjustment until each child finds a way (hopefully) to 'share' the parents' time, to work out a way to play together and enjoy games together. As any parent knows, this is not easy to achieve, but we also seem to see few examples of what it looks like around us. TV dramas, news features, books and films seem to focus much more on the Cain and Abel stories of bitter rivalry than on ways to adjust and create a different dynamic.

At playgroup or nursery school, children go through the whole process again, working out how to get all the best toys or all the attention of the adults. Then, realizing this isn't possible, they can either spend their time and energy fighting for the toys and attention they crave, or find another way of navigating their environment.

Home and school experiences shape how that 'winner–loser' narrative develops, and whether a short-term, competitive, zero-sum game mentality gets embedded or different ways of thinking are nurtured. School life is often punctuated by competitions, awards, stars and scoreboards, teaching children what matters. How many of us can remember competing to know the right answer at school, wanting the teacher to call on us and not our fellow pupils, and hoping that they get the answer wrong if the teacher calls on them instead of us? Because if they do get it wrong, we might have another chance to show how smart we are – their failure could help us succeed. Potential friends and collaborators become opponents and enemies.

In British schools, children are typically rewarded with stickers, gold stars or house points for doing things well, obeying the rules, being quiet in class, being kind to others. The problem is that the acts themselves are often quickly forgotten. At the end of the week, the sticker, gold star or house point chart reveals the 'winners' and the 'losers', and the actual gains from each commendable activity or behaviour are forgotten.

My seven-year-old son worked out the easiest way to get house points was to open doors for others in school and did this with huge energy and enthusiasm, racking up points along the way. To a certain extent, this was great. It's a good way to behave, but he didn't understand why it was good beyond winning the most points for himself on the class chart, or notice how it made him and others feel. When, the next year, he no longer got points for opening doors, he naturally stopped (well, until we had a little chat which I hope may have encouraged him to open a few doors again from time to time for different reasons!).

Some schools are missing a trick in what they emphasize – is it learning how to be the winner of the class chart at the end of the week, or is it understanding your impact on others through being generous, supportive and kind? Sometimes, it feels easier to demonstrate good behaviour through awarding a sticker; as a parent, I can definitely see the allure. But there are limitations. Short-term it can create good behaviour. But external motivations, providing extrinsic rather than intrinsic rewards, don't explain the long-term benefits or instil a deeper, lasting value.

Collaboration is increasingly talked about in schools, but where does it sit in the hierarchy of reward? Do examples of collaboration (or living according to the values of collaboration) ever outweigh or come close to the level of recognition given to those who come top in academic tests, musical examinations or sports competitions? Reward systems teach pupils what has real value, how much the mission statement on the wall actually counts and what success is really all about.

When I ask friends and interviewees about when they first encountered winning, they often pause and then gasp. A surprisingly high proportion widen their eyes, raise their eyebrows and say: 'Oh, God! Monopoly!' There then follows a stream of memories of being bankrupted by siblings and close family members whenever that green board with red trim came out.

Described by Wikipedia as 'part of international popular culture', the game of Monopoly is based on a competitive premise with the goal of driving your fellow players into bankruptcy.[1] Winning is defined by others losing, preferably disastrously. It sets up an early childhood experience of a zero-sum game world where collaboration is not just irrelevant, but undesirable. Success is based solely on others losing and suffering as a result of your deliberate choices.

Many other board games work on a similar zero-sum game basis, where there can be only one winner and that winner's success is demonstrated through the losses of the other participants. Cooperation is to be avoided at all costs if you want to be that winner. The clear way to success is to focus on yourself and do everything you can to outwit and, if possible, destroy your opponent.

I definitely had some 'Monopoly moments' in my childhood too, and not just when that rectangular red and white box came out. Other elements of school and family life taught me to think that there could only be 'one winner' and to have a voice I had to try and be that winner by having the final say through having the best (or perhaps the loudest) argument. There was little space for alternative arguments, for building on each other's views and understanding different perspectives. There tended to be only 'winning' and 'losing' arguments. This prepared me for academic success at school, university and, thereafter, an Olympic training environment. But it left me less well equipped to manage other aspects of school, university and sport, and, later, work and family life.

At school, there were clear categories of winners and losers: the academic types, the sporty ones, the musical ones. Many were excluded from any or all of these. There was always a clear sense of who was top of the class and who was bottom. Anyone who saw the world differently tended to fall to the bottom. There was no time for different perspectives or ideas; there were exams to be passed.

This continued at university if that was the path you chose (with of course the university you went to signifying success or failure in itself before you even started studying). Winning was clearly defined by grades and marks, rather than students doing a course that inspired them, stimulated them to go out into the world and make a difference or create something new. The same logic continued seamlessly in the world of work, where people compete for promotion, bonuses and senior positions.

But we limit what we learn and how we develop when a winning-obsessed mindset focuses purely on the outcome of arbitrary tests, exams or interviews. As we see in the next chapter, narrow, short-term metrics distract us from focusing on where we can do our best work and make our best long-term contribution to the world around us.

First encounters with the 'will to win'

I was not particularly sporty as a child, despite what followed. I wasn't in the top few in my class at sport and was quickly categorized as a 'non-sporty' type. This definition of success was based on who could run fastest, largely determined by whose physical development was most advanced: either the oldest children in the school year or those whose families spent their weekends being active.

This categorization of 'sporty' and 'non-sporty', with the sporty ones being the 'winners' on school sports days and praised by the teachers during sports classes, dominated my experience of school sport. I was one of the youngest in the year and could see that I was often the weak link in hockey games or, worse still, volleyball games (my absolute nemesis). The funny thing was, I wanted to be good. It wasn't the case that I didn't care, even though school reports suggested I had a poor attitude and put in little effort ('Class 4A: Physical Education: Catherine at times adopts a negative approach to PE resulting in a lack of effort'). I just didn't know how to get better and escape the 'non-sporty' label. Nor did I feel any route was open to me to work that out.

Once you have dropped out of regular exercise or sport when young, it stops being a healthy part of life, and many never go back. Worldwide, governments and sporting organizations are trying to find ways of keeping children active in their teen years or re-engaging them if they have stopped. The first wave of initiatives tended to focus on offering more activities, thinking about the type of activities that youngsters are interested in. It's only now with further research that more is understood about the 'experience' of sport and the importance of the culture and environment where that activity takes place. The role that 'winning' plays in that culture has a huge effect on what children take from their early experiences of sport and can determine whether activity becomes a lifelong healthy habit. We all start off life moving to the extent our bodies allow and pushing the boundaries of our movement – we should consider what happens in our lives to stop that natural process from being part of daily life growing up.

I feel extremely lucky to have encountered the sport of rowing at university, which certainly changed my relationship with sport for life. Armed with the knowledge that I wasn't sporty and didn't like getting up early, I had no intention of taking up a new sport, especially not one that was so physically demanding and practised close to dawn. But chance events led newly formed friends to ask me to 'sub' into their novice crew halfway through the first term (after some bribery involving the college bar).

The first early morning was an uplifting experience, though it probably didn't look at all successful to the onlooker. I was quite hopeless in the boat that first time and even managed to break the spoon of the old wooden oar I was gripping and clumsily failed to manoeuvre out of the way when our boat drifted close to the bank. But it was clear that nobody minded, that we were all beginners together, and a new oar was quickly fetched by our coach. The emphasis was on learning and fun. No one had rowed before and that was levelling. The sport involves a lot of coordination and timing, so as beginners together we were all helping each other to work that out.

While I didn't fall in love with the early alarms, I quickly began to look forward to the early morning mist over the river, the clatter of oars and chatter of the novice crews zigzagging their way down the river, the exhilaration from the mental and physical exercise and the energized camaraderie with my crewmates. The feeling of connection underpinning our interdependence as we worked together within the boat was a new and thrilling experience. I had zero aspirations to be an Olympian; it never even occurred to me. I still wanted to do my best in the crew and learn as quickly as I could. We wanted to acquit ourselves well in the end-of-term novice race, although regardless of the result, we were already planning to continue the next term because of the fun and friendship.

I am so grateful to have been introduced to rowing, the challenge of trying to synchronize effort, the frustrations when not pulling in the same direction and the only option open to you is to adapt and try again. You can't 'opt out' once in a boat, as I had ended up doing on the school hockey pitch or volleyball court. You have to keep moving and making the best contribution you can. You also can't just analyze robotically what's required. It's critical to tune in to the water beneath the boat. That means being completely 'present', sensing the movements of the rowers either side of you and the river running underneath, as you search together for those elusive moments where it all 'clicks' and the boat takes off and flies along. It's a great metaphor for collaboration and teamwork in any environment.

A few years later, racing and winning started to appear more regularly as I started on the path towards the British Olympic rowing team. I quickly learnt the rules of being a 'serious', 'dedicated' athlete. Winning came first; enjoyment much lower down the list. One of the most common phrases used by multiple coaches was 'you can enjoy yourself on the podium' – that is, don't expect to enjoy yourself until and unless you win. The two were inextricably, and dangerously, linked. I regret not questioning that logic sooner, though I doubt I'd have dared to voice it. Clearly, within the team, it was all about rankings: who was top and who was bottom. No one wanted to be bottom. Some people were referred to as 'winners', others as 'perpetual losers', even within the British team, the best in the country. I quickly felt fear and desperation, as the new girl on the scene, to be associated with the former and not the latter.

This wasn't easy. The whole women's rowing team were often seen and described as losers in those days. Back then, no women had won any Olympic medals, and only a few had ever won medals at the World Championships. That seemed to define us in the eyes of others, a burden that we all had to take on. We felt a desperate need to prove that we could be winners too. But what did that really mean and how could we make it happen?

When I just squeaked into the Olympic team for Atlanta in 1996, it felt like a far-off pipe dream had incomprehensibly become reality.

When I looked back on my woeful school sporting achievements, I couldn't believe where I was now. But I was surprised and confused about being in a team where everything seemed to reinforce that the women were not very good, certainly not as good as the men, and at times openly the butt of jokes in the men's squad. We tried to show that we were different and could win, but so much around us seemed to undermine what we were trying to do.

No sports psychologist was available to the women's team, and the men's coaches openly talked about how the women's team didn't seem to have a 'winning attitude'. I wasn't really sure what that was and thought about it a lot, tormenting myself about whether I had one or not, agonizing over whether I could develop one or whether it was innate.

I can remember our crew being granted the incredible opportunity of a talk from the coach and psychologist who had worked with a crew that had won a gold medal at the previous Barcelona Olympics. They talked a lot about this winning attitude and asked us all: 'Do you have the will to win? Do you *really* want to win?' It was clearly essential, and I felt that this must be something profound that I hadn't found yet. I tied myself in knots, with imposter syndrome quickly rearing its head:

> I think I have it, I want to have it, but how do I really know? What if I haven't? What if I'm kidding myself? Who am I to think I have it? What if I think I have it, but I don't really, and others in the race have it more?

This mythical 'will to win' was held up above us, just out of reach. But time spent thinking about that seemingly elusive will to win took our focus away from all the things that would have made us faster. For a whole host of reasons, we didn't perform well at that Olympics.

A year after my first 'failed' Olympic experience, a new sports psychologist joined and started to use different language. He talked about developing a 'performance mindset' and never once asked about my will to win. He did ask about my capabilities and strengths and how I could use them and play to them more. He did ask about my commitment to deliver my best in training and racing, and my belief that I could develop and improve each day. It started to open up a new way of thinking. This was the beginning of redefining what success looked like for me as a sportswoman. This time it went far beyond just the outcome, and yet at the same time it helped to achieve the best outcome.

We associate the will to win with sport, but the concept is just as present in most non-sporting contexts. We encounter the language and desire to 'recruit winners' into teams at work when leaders are hiring. We hear the same easy language within the strategy and goals of so many teams and organizations. It seems so positive and easy to say, 'Let's all be winners', 'Let's make sure our team is the winning team.' The challenge is, though, to develop a common view of what that actually means, what 'winning behaviours' might look like, and understand the wider impact of always trying to win on the bigger picture of what you want to achieve.

In the workplace, hierarchy often provides a constant visible chart of the winners and losers on a daily basis – whose views count most, whose value is greatest in the company. When I joined the Civil Service, everyone was identified in terms of their grade and whether they were in the Fast Stream or not. These judgements brought such bias about each other's value and affected who was given space to speak in meetings and whose views were ignored. Business leader and author Margaret Heffernan sums up the damage that hierarchy has brought to organizational life:

> For decades, managers imagined that corporate ladders were motivating and that dreams of climbing them would drive superior performance... The outcome was a failure to share ideas... Great ideas and vital concerns all get trapped, lost or paralyzed in power struggles and turf wars.[2]

Later on in a career, there can be a sense that it's too late to win. If you haven't reached a certain level by a certain point, that's it. In fact, that can be the assumption in life more widely. This is a phenomenon which Rich Karlgaard challenges, highlighting our illogical cultural worship of early achievers and the severe costs of underrating 'late bloomers' in the workplace and beyond.[3]

Reflections on real-life winning

At home, school, sport, work and beyond, we have all had multiple encounters with winning across our lives. It's worth reconsidering these with a curiosity to look beyond the labels and assumptions. What was developed and strengthened in our mindsets and behaviours as a result of these experiences, and to what effect? What might have been overlooked or undervalued?

We have considered how we may have experienced this obsession with coming first personally. In the following chapters, I look across society at some examples of how winning plays out across education, sport, business and politics in ways that are often taken for granted but which warrant closer examination and questioning if we are to create better ways to succeed.

Chapter 5

Who's Really
Top of the Class?

The Impact of Trying to Win in Education

The psychologist Madeline Levine recounts the story of a 10-year-old boy sitting quietly on the sofa in her office, legs not quite touching the floor. She asks if he'd ever thought about what he'd like to do when he grows up. Without hesitating, he sits up and says: 'I want to run a start-up.' He doesn't even know what a start-up is, but he does know in great detail what he needs to do to become hugely successful in running one. He charts the next 15 years of his life. He will apply to the most competitive high school to increase his odds of going to Stanford. Then he will need to become an intern and hopes it will be at Google. He is intent on being a 'winner'. His parents, teachers and community all encourage this way of thinking without realizing that they might actually be reducing his future chances of success.

Madeline Levine goes on to describe how 'in the enclaves of privilege in this country [the US], part of the culture is more and more centred on a narrow notion of what success looks like and how to attain it. Money is overvalued, and character undervalued.' The 10-year-old on her sofa is the logical outcome of this approach: 'He wants to be a winner, but knows nothing about the kind of work he's signing on for.'[1]

I can remember a surreal conversation with a local mother who wanted to share her concerns over her *two-and-a-half*-year-old son's future prospects. She told me:

I'm worried about my son. We keep trying to teach him how to hold a pencil, but he's not interested. I don't know what to do. He'll never get into [x] school unless he can. And if he doesn't, who knows what'll become of him in the rest of his life. We have had a tutor recommended who we are desperately hoping will get him through his upcoming entrance interview.

This conversation about a child preparing to compete at the age of two and a half to get into a top London private school really stunned me. Parents worry from the birth of their child that if the child doesn't get into a particular preschool, they won't get into the right junior or prep school, so the best secondary school will be impossible to reach, then the best universities are out of the picture and everyone's lives will be ruined. It's an exhausting, draining game to play for those families with aspirations and access to good schooling. Many families are not even in this game.

Despite recognizing its narrowness, I can still feel trapped by this game of schooling that parents and children seem forced to play. There is a sense that if you do well, if you can 'win' the schooling game, then your life is set forever. But if you 'lose' at the schooling game, you are blighted forever. This is often one of the first experiences, endorsed by parents and teachers, that teaches children supposed criteria for success in life.

Measuring and ranking in education

Many countries still have rigid systems of testing and narrowly charted education paths, which bear no resemblance to lifetime experiences or the attributes needed in the modern workplace. Employers are crying out for more creativity, innovative thinking, collaborative working and complex problem-solving skills in their workforce. World Economic Forum reports confirm this shift in what the future workplace will need. A few countries include greater collaborative working and fewer exams within education, notably Nordic countries and the Netherlands. But many countries still offer no alternative to a one-size-fits-all competitive approach that produces verdicts of success and failure based on narrow measures from an early age.

The pressure of comparison dominates this world, with success measured in both absolute terms – school grades – and relative terms – how your child compares to the next. Margaret

Heffernan, lecturing at a business school, and Benjamin Zander, a conductor teaching music, both experimented with giving their classes an A automatically from the beginning, in order to try and escape from this negative preoccupation with comparison. Despite it being a class about setting up businesses, where grades were close to irrelevant, Margaret Heffernan's MBA students were not happy. After years of being conditioned to get grades and judging themselves by whether they were better or worse than their colleagues, 'they didn't just want to learn; they wanted their success assured by the relative failure of others'.[2]

In conductor Benjamin Zander's music classes, he gave out As at the beginning of term, keen to create new 'possibilities' for his students. Previously, class after class would be in a permanent state of anxiety over the measurement of their performance and so would take no risks with their playing. But the 'art of music, since it can only be conveyed through its interpreters, depends on expressive performance for its lifeblood... it is only when we make mistakes in performance that we can really begin to notice what needs attention.'[3]

Critics and defenders of the established system (often those who have done well themselves under the narrow success criteria and therefore feel loyal to them or even dependent on them to justify their success) cry out that standards might drop. Zander found the opposite. Instead of lining up with the standards to use against his students, he was now lining up with his students in their efforts to perform to the highest possible standard. Zander didn't want his students to limit their learning to doing what would please their teachers, or to how much they could get away with, but wanted them to explore much further with the teacher alongside them. 'Giving yourself an A is not about boasting or raising your self-esteem. It... lifts you off the success/failure ladder and spirits you away from the world of measurement into the universe of possibility.'[4] The music analogy highlights how artistic excellence is not supported by making performers compete to win. It's not such a leap to imagine the same in other worlds, such as business and politics. Our countries end up led by those who are the best at winning political campaigns, but not necessarily the best at running a government, and businesses are led by those who have done well at being promoted, but may not be the best leaders.

In many countries, education has turned into a game that operates on the same basis as sporting leagues. Both pupils and teachers quickly learn the rules and work out what marks out the winners from the losers.

If we go back to its roots, the word 'education' comes from the Latin word *educare*, which refers to 'bringing up'. *Educo*, taken to mean 'I educate', literally means 'I lead forward, I raise up' (*e-duco*). What a great basis for education – leading forward and lifting up others, echoing Benjamin Zander's teaching approach. There is no sense here of winners and losers, competition, rankings or metrics. How has the language of education in many major countries, such as the UK, the US, Japan and China, become governed by targets and league tables?

In the UK, schools are increasingly seen as 'businesses' within a competitive educational marketplace (in public and private sectors). Complex chains of academies are ruled by CEOs, not headteachers. Managers from the private sector are encouraged by the government to move into education to raise performance and transfer business methods of driving results into schools. Yet it's not clear if these practices are actually effective in business organizations, let alone applicable and transferable into the world of education.

What has this emphasis on measuring meant in practice for teachers, pupils and the world of learning? In the UK, the US and Japan in particular, competition was placed at the heart of education to improve the quality of children's education, ensure a good return on investment of public money and close the 'achievement gap' between different parts of society. The seductively simple logic flows that all the schools will want to be at the top of the league tables and will strive to improve, and so education will advance. Good intentions for sure, but how has this played out in reality, and how is the concept of 'winning' affecting how and what the next generation is learning?

It's not hard to find primary or secondary teachers in the UK and the US leaving the profession because they feel trapped in a bureaucratic game of numbers and metrics. It's a world away from what they entered the teaching profession to do: inspire the next generation and unlock their potential. Headteachers can feel particularly ensnared. The narrative and rationale behind the metrics that come from the government are so positive: it's about improving standards, increasing mobility, tracking progress. How could anyone stand against those intentions? But the impact looks so different. Staff time is diverted to pursuing targets and rankings, which can be held against them in a number of ways, such as reducing funding or public blacklisting. There is an emphasis on short-term improvements in the metrics, while worrying longer-term trends are ignored – such as dipping staff morale, teacher retention and teacher and pupil wellbeing.

Increased testing, measuring and chasing exam targets each year drives particular thinking and behaviour. Time is diverted from anything that isn't directly measured and fed into rankings. This affects broader learning – for example, subjects such as art, music, PE, social studies and history are at a disadvantage compared to subjects that get measured, principally English, mathematics and science subjects. Within the testing of those subjects, teachers start to focus narrowly on the particular skills required by the test, rather than the broader learning processes and mind-expanding experiences. Professor Jerry Muller looks in depth at the American No Child Left Behind policy, designed 'to close the achievement gap with accountability, flexibility and choice so that no child is left behind'. Like many others, Muller highlights that 'students too often learn test-taking strategies rather than substantive knowledge'.[5]

Pupils are discouraged from taking subjects they may love but do not excel in, seen through the lens of examination requirements. I am not sure anyone really addresses the 'why' any more: Why do we go to school? What's the purpose? And yet it would be such a useful question to consider – it's hard to find that it's just about achieving a string of grades. David Boyle exposes the damage from pointless target cultures across our public services in *Tickbox*, and describes his suspicion that many schools that top the league tables 'got there by excising anything creative from the curriculum and shuffling off responsibility for their more difficult pupils'.[6] British educationalist Ken Robinson's 2006 TED Talk *Do Schools Kill Creativity* was the most watched TED Talk of all time at the point of his death in 2020, so this isn't new information. Robinson worked with government education bodies in the UK and the US. But our education systems seem slow to adapt and our leaders obsessed with meaningless metrics to prove themselves. When the stakes are high and these tests become the chief criteria by which schools are evaluated, the desire to win at this game also drives deeply dysfunctional and, at times, corrupt behaviours. Examples include reclassifying weaker pupils as disabled or with special needs to remove them from the assessment statistics, or excluding such pupils or moving them to another school. In some cases, cheating occurs, where teachers change answers or 'lose' low-scoring tests, or pupils look for ways to improve their results dishonestly.

Despite huge government efforts, hours of civil servants' time creating educational policy and decades of recording and publishing the metrics, it's hard to see any significant progress in the UK or the US towards closing the 'achievement gap' across the population, and the pandemic and other socioeconomic instability have increased the gap in many countries. Of course, no one wants to admit this, so more metrics are created in an attempt to demonstrate progress or obfuscate reality.

This approach has created students throughout the system who are thinking solely about the results, not the process or reasons for learning. The system has told students that they are 'earning' a mark or a grade: 'You do this, and you get that.' The reward isn't doing the work or applying the new knowledge acquired or adapting that knowledge for a new context. It isn't thinking differently or learning how to think; it's all about the mark you get at the end.

Benjamin Zander and Rosamund Stone Zander reflect on this:

> in most cases, grades say little about the work done. When you reflect to a student that he has misconstrued a concept or has taken a false step in a math problem, you are indicating something real about his performance, but when you give him a B+ you are saying nothing at all about his mastery of the material, you are only matching him up against other students. Most would recognize at core that the main purpose of grades is to compare one student against another.[7]

As rankings pit students against each other, they destroy the process of learning how to collaborate and cooperate with peers at the point when they are developing social understanding in their lives. Rankings reinforce the message that for one pupil to win, another must lose. Despite most work in organizations being in teams, the experience at school is one of pupils working mostly alone. The emphasis on 'relativization' – that is, defining winning through comparison with others – distorts the very act of learning and developing.

The focus on 'winning results' also leads to a narrower view of what constitutes education and an incentive to ignore whole areas, such as developing critical thinking, self-control, how to cooperate, collaborate and be creative, and the arts in general – all of which are much less easy to measure but offer increasing value to the modern workplace that requires creativity, innovation and an ability to manage uncertainty.

In Karen Arnold's research into valedictorians, high school success was a good predictor of college success, but it wasn't a predictor of career success. While many had good jobs, none of the valedictorians she studied went on to lead the world or change the world. Arnold realized that what made these students good at school – obeying the rules and being compliant and learning what was required for exams, but no more – did not help them in the world of work, where the rules are much less clear and it's useful to think beyond obvious categories and do things differently.[8]

This competitive educational approach also puts huge and constant pressure on our self-esteem. As Alfie Kohn explains:

> The desire to be better than others feels quite different from this desire to do well. There is something inherently compensatory about it. One wants to outdo in order to make up for an impression... of personal inadequacy... one wants to be stronger or smarter than others in order to convince oneself at some level that one is a good person.[9]

James Carse's *Finite and Infinite Games* describes the paradox of short-term finite winners, where 'the more we are recognized as winners, the more we know ourselves to be losers' because of this need to win in order to justify ourselves. Winners of titles, trophies and wealth are reliant on comparison with others and the audience who will applaud and endorse their victory. This leaves them stuck in the winning trap: 'Winners, especially celebrated winners, must prove repeatedly that they are winners. The script must be played over and over again. Titles must be defended by new contests. No one is ever wealthy enough, honoured enough, applauded enough.'[10]

This is the breeding ground for insecure overachievers, often common in elite sport as well as top law and management consultancy firms and other elevated positions across society, bringing warped views of human worth and compulsive comparison into the worlds they lead. Interestingly, the qualities found in fierce, competitive cultures are close to the destructive impulses seen in neuroses. This doesn't feel like the best way for us to be successful.

Harmful judgements flow from these systems of standardized education – whether a child is 'academic' or not, 'bright' or not, 'high potential' or not – regardless of the evidence that children develop at vastly differing rates, and that potential could exist in many useful fields beyond simple class subject categories. The grades and measuring suggest that intelligence is immutable, that it can be reduced to a single number and that children can be ranked in a linear order. But we know that isn't true. It makes no sense to assume that the ones who are succeeding in the system have the talent, and the ones who aren't succeeding aren't talented. These narrow definitions of talent leave a vast and untapped pool of diverse thinking and unexplored potential among us that could benefit employers and society if acknowledged and supported.

Where there are selection systems within schools, and streaming is a common one, children receive a clear message about who are the winners and losers. Although the intention of being in the bottom set may be to encourage children to improve, the reality is that a 'not academic' label quickly becomes shorthand for 'loser' in the schooling world. Such labels can be damaging, and when quickly accepted by the child can become tragically self-fulfilling. Those who 'lose' at an early age may believe they can never succeed. And the lack of enjoyment of the arbitrary win–lose game may lead many to avoid such experiences again, leading society to lose out on precious talent, innovative thinking and other potential contributions.

A child gets sucked into a virtuous or vicious circle where the best pupils get taken more and more seriously, are explicitly identified as 'gifted and talented' and are therefore invested in and supported differently. The students who are less good get less and less. Knowing this, it's not surprising that parents become pushy and families become stuck in a self-perpetuating though ultimately pointless world of trying to support their child to 'win' at this game, regardless of whether it will equip them well for the future.

'Tiger parenting', where parents will go to any lengths to push their children to high levels of academic achievement, developed out of this world. Tiger parents are associated with Asian cultures where success in education (defined as high exam grades) brings cultural status and honour to the family. However, it comes at a cost. In South Korea, for example, social and family pressures on students are extreme, and although exam results are good, student suicide rates are worryingly high.[11]

The need to 'win' has been found to drive academia in similar ways. 'Impact factor measurement' and other metrics encourage academics to pursue high rankings as the first priority and good academic research as the second.

The competitive nature of rankings discourages academic collaboration, yet this is the lifeblood of progress. Many of the discoveries and new research areas in the 21st century come from academics combining ideas and bringing together two or more previously separate fields of study. Collaboration and multidisciplinary thinking could start much earlier if we freed ourselves up from rigid measuring regimes and reconsidered what we value and nurture, and how we 'bring up' the next generation.

The same logic is often applied to our work careers and a narrow, linear depiction of what is required to progress and be 'successful' at work. However, radical changes are reshaping this, driven by the rise of widespread entrepreneurism, the impact of technology, digitalization and artificial intelligence (AI) as well as determined attempts to reframe our careers, such as the 'squiggly career' concept coined by Helen Tupper and Sarah Ellis. Our education system needs to catch up with these shifts.

Learning mindsets

A fundamental assumption underlies how many schools are set up: that a child's innate talent and ability can be identified, tested and proven in quantitative terms. This is the basis on which governments set tests, determine curricula and view children's achievements.

It shapes the development of children's mindsets, drives their thinking and behaviour, potentially for a lifetime. Working out what really matters to a parent or teacher are key moments in the development of a child's mental approach. We have learnt a lot about the importance of a child's mindset for their ability to learn, based on research by US psychologist Carol Dweck.[12] She discovered that a child's view of their own ability determines how open they are to learning new things and challenging themselves. Dweck coined the term 'growth mindset' to describe those who do not set a limit on what they are capable of and are not afraid of failure, enabling them to learn broadly and effectively. Those with a 'fixed mindset', however, are fearful of failure. They place a ceiling on what they believe they can achieve, leaving them less able to deal with difficult areas of learning. This way of thinking naturally sets the path for how you might manage more or less effectively challenges and unpredictable events later in life.

There has been criticism of Dweck's thinking and research on how powerful a growth mindset can be in exploring our potential. In fact, there are many other factors in our environments, our personality traits and our experiences. But it's clear that how parents and teachers praise, define success and talk about achievements with children hugely influences children's views on what matters in the world. A focus on winning and fixed outcomes rather than the process of learning, applying effort and working with others all reinforce beliefs that certain narrow, arbitrary outcomes matter most. The labels we give to success or failure early on impact our subsequent development over the long term at school and beyond.

Motivation

When education is a competitive game of winning results, grades, house points, prizes and league tables, this also has a major impact on motivation and resultant performance. Teachers celebrating the 'winners' demotivate the rest at the same time, albeit unintentionally. We have all experienced it. When the winners are heralded and given prizes, the message to the rest is that they are not good enough. Some will be spurred on to do better next time, but usually there is more disappointment than joy or celebration if you look at the experience of all those involved. Too many pupils leave school with a deep-rooted sense of failure in their studies, and more damagingly, they may conclude, before even embarking on their adult lives, that they are failures as people too.

By focusing exclusively on external markers and extrinsic rewards (grades and marks), schools teach pupils to overlook their intrinsic drivers. This not only limits their chances of success, but also their experience and appreciation of learning, and what should be a joyous experience of exploration and discovery.

Intrinsic motivation within education involves learning to think in different ways, to love language and numbers, to unpick puzzles and design new ones, to use one's imagination – skills needing a long-term way of approaching and thinking about things. Exams and tests rarely reward 'divergent thinking' – that is, coming up with multiple options and solutions to issues – but require 'convergent thinking' – that is, one single answer that can be summarized on a marking sheet. Yet every day we see that our adult lives do not work on a right/ wrong basis; there are often no expected answers and leaders need to think creatively and innovatively. Schools rarely test for creative and innovative behaviour, collaborative skills or ability to challenge the status quo (doing that can get you expelled!). Yet I come across multiple organizations crying out for their staff to work more collaboratively. One organization I worked with had 'challenging the status quo' as one of their key behaviours and values, and couldn't understand why they couldn't get anyone to do it.

This is even more perplexing in our current world, where AI is increasingly taking over straightforward and predictable jobs. Humans can bring value in areas that require being creative, having ideas, innovating, building relationships, collaborating across boundaries and thinking about things in a different way.[13] Those skills need to be part of daily life in the classroom. Historian and educator Sir Anthony Seldon has long called for schools to move away from 19th-century 'factory' school thinking and embrace 'entrepreneurialism, active learning and creativity', and to explore how AI could transform and personalize pupil experiences.[14]

Psychologists Teresa Amabile and Beth Hennessey conducted a series of experiments to explore which aspects of an education system kill creativity. They came up with the following ways:

- having children work for an expected reward;
- focusing pupils on an expected evaluation;
- deploying extensive surveillance;
- setting up restricted choices;
- creating competitive situations.[15]

Each of these is characteristic of most education systems across the world. Most are visible in the workplace too, and are just as damaging there. Psychologist Daniel Pink sets out three keys to motivation: autonomy, mastery and purpose.[16] All three are restricted in many school experiences as well as many workplaces.

Learning about success and failure

A system dominated by rankings and grades labels failure visibly and creates a fear of failure at all levels. Pupils cannot be allowed to fail, because that would mean failure for the school, which could come at a high cost in terms of income, funding and other critical factors that schools need to survive. Yet the research about growth mindsets tells us that failure is essential to learning. We all learn that naturally at an early age, before we go to school. No toddler stands up and walks the first time they try.

There are numerous inspirational stories of sporting champions who have failed significantly along the way to success. Basketball star Michael Jordan is famous for a quote immortalized in a Nike advertisement: 'I've missed more than 9,000 shots. I've lost almost 300 games. Twenty-six times I've been trusted to take the game-winning shot and missed.' The message is clear: success requires embracing failure. Thomas Edison, the inventor of the light bulb, made the same point: 'If I find 10,000 ways something won't work, I haven't failed. I am not discouraged, because every wrong attempt discarded is another step forward.'

Yet this spirit of success through failure is strangely absent in many schools, or, worse, the point is missed or manipulated. There is an accepted narrative which includes a limited amount of failure, but not too much and only as long as it leads to ultimate success, measured in terms of simple results, often without any wider long-term meaning or social benefit. Athletes are invited into schools and written about in the media with stories that generally fit this model. The emphasis is all on the outcome and the glorious victories that ensue. Any hardships along the way are justified by the outcome. Yet failure doesn't work like that in life and our experiences don't always follow that model.

There are brilliant top-level athletes who experience failure and, however hard they try, don't come home with an Olympic medal – maybe because they weren't quite good enough on the day, maybe due to luck or natural physical disadvantage or other reasons beyond their control. But we tend not to hear their stories. We seem to shy away from accepting or acknowledging the reality that sometimes we aren't good enough and that's normal. A business school dean commented to me that there were 200,000 start-ups at the time in London, of which 95% would fail. Business schools always studied or invited in people from that 5%, and rarely from the 95%. But surely this only limits their learning about start-ups and sets false expectations. As in schools, the ones who succeed are praised and rewarded, with the assumption that the rest are somehow less talented, less hard-working, less worthy. Where we define success narrowly, we risk losing out on vast amounts of talent and potential.

The entrepreneurial mantra to 'fail fast' can then seem impossible to navigate given our early experiences of avoiding failure at all costs. Harvard business psychologist Amy Edmondson explores this phenomenon of what it means to fail well in *Right Kind of Wrong*, in which she helps us develop a more intelligent relationship with failure.

Philosopher Alain de Botton laments how we are setting ourselves up for crushing disappointment by deciding that 'an ordinary life is not good enough, you have to be extraordinary'.

It makes no sense for us all to want to be like Mark Zuckerberg or Lionel Messi and view anything less as 'not good enough'. But that's the story of what winning looks like that we are often presented with throughout life. The pressure of expectation means that we are setting up children to expect their lives to be amazing when, in reality, they are more likely to be ordinary, and 'an ordinary life is a good life'. The obsession with being an 'against-the-odds winner' breeds a deep lack of self-acceptance and what de Botton calls an 'epidemic of mental unwellness'.[17]

I always feel uncomfortable about playing a part in this warped narrative. I am allowed to tell my story to business conferences, school assemblies and sports events. I can mention the failures that I had along the way because my story ends with Olympic and World Championship medals. My fellow rowers who didn't make the team, or who made the team but didn't win a medal, aren't asked to share their story, join a speaker academy or speak to audiences. Yet they have a great story to tell, a human story we can all relate to: they gave their all; they explored what they were capable of; they coped with enormous pressure on a daily basis; they learnt how to push themselves and how to cope with pressure; and they supported their teammates and built lifelong friendships. Those who didn't win a medal still competed at the highest level and played a crucial role in some of the most epic Olympic races. Great races require everyone to play their part, not just the winners. The tactics, mind games and performance details beyond the outcome can be fascinating. But we typically just focus on who came first, ignoring all the other interesting stories in those races. Arguably, they have a more important and more common human experience to share. They had all the qualities the winners often had – discipline, focus, commitment and much more. Yet it simply isn't possible for everyone to come first, and we need to be able to manage that and acknowledge the other gains that come from the pursuit of excellence.

Those who may not have been fastest were still athletes that I learnt from and had the utmost respect for. They dealt with huge challenges along the way with dignity and enormous mental strength, and ultimately had to face the fact that they couldn't recover from an injury in time, that they simply weren't quite strong enough by a fractional amount or that some other factor beyond their control played a role in them not quite reaching the top. Our Olympic rowing squad couldn't survive without more people than there were places; that was necessary to provide a high standard of rowing for everyone to learn and develop. They all have a great story to tell.

British Olympic hockey medallist Annie Panter explains what I remember being naively shocked to realize for myself: it makes no sense to make heroes only of those who come first.

> You see people who don't win a medal, have never won a medal, who define everything that I value in an Olympian, or who were better or more talented, but their time wasn't right. But you see people who win a medal, and maybe they don't have all the values, and have all the things you valued... but their timing was right.[18]

Rugby sevens player Tom Mitchell builds on this further from his own position of having won silver and then finishing fourth in Tokyo:

> As someone who has been fortunate to have come home with a medal and without one, any youngsters should know that hard work and following your passion are worthwhile in their own right. Don't get me wrong, achieving your goal feels great, and not achieving what you set out to get is painful for a while. But both outcomes contain emotions that only last for a while. The deep sense of fulfilment that comes from pursuing a passion and dedicating yourself to it lasts much longer.

Ocean rower Roz Savage, the first woman to row solo across three oceans, adds further perspective as she reflects on her own classic story of endurance and resilience. She has led a course on courage at Yale and given talks around the world. One day, she was listening on the radio to an account of how migrants crossed the Mediterranean in rickety boats, with poor equipment, woeful supplies, no navigation instruments. Should they make it across to Europe – and many don't – they are put in detention centres or worse. Their courage and resilience is second to none. Roz suddenly realized that her own story isn't so different from theirs, but the end result couldn't be more different. She is paid to stand on a stage and applauded for her resilience, while they are detained in the most terrible conditions, marked out as losers socially, just because of where they were born. We might reconsider more carefully the stories we value and why.

Reflections on winning in education

How we define success in our early years shapes our mindsets and behaviours for life, unless we choose to reshape them. Re-evaluating what winning means in childhood is not about limiting children's ambitions – quite the opposite. It is about creating an environment that broadens the possibilities for all children and expands their potential future contributions.

Sport is often seen as a model of how we learn about and replicate what winning means. It offers us heroes and role models who epitomize what winning is supposed to look like. Let's turn there next and take a closer look at the reality of winning in sport.

Chapter 6

'It's All about Medals'

Truth and Myth in
High-Performance Sport

Golfer Thomas Bjørn found himself thinking 'Is that it?' when he won his first victory on the European Tour in 1996 at the age of 25. He received the Loch Lomond World Invitational trophy and beamed throughout the media interviews that followed. He then went to the locker room to collect his things and when he stepped outside, he found himself alone. 'I felt empty. It was my first victory on the tour, and it had been great during the prize ceremony. It was the biggest dream of my life. But then you are alone. I felt flat.'[1] It's the side of winning that we don't all see, that isn't splashed on billboards, but is nevertheless real.

In the classic sporting film *Chariots of Fire* (1981), Harold Abrahams is asked by a friend shortly after winning the 100 metres final in the 1924 Olympics, 'What's wrong?' He replies, 'One day you are going to win and find that it is pretty difficult to swallow.' Swimmer Mark Spitz crashed mentally after winning seven gold medals at the 1972 Olympics, as he realized the effects of winning were not lasting; he struggled to recreate a life after swimming. Victoria Pendleton described how she felt 'empty' and 'numb' receiving her first Olympic gold medal in cycling. Having just become world heavyweight champion, Tyson Fury woke up the morning after he knocked out long-time boxing world champion Wladimir Klitschko and felt that 'there was just a void'.[2] These stories clash uncomfortably with traditional expectations of what glorious winning looks like. At first, we want to find excuses: it was the effects of pressure, the stress, the emotions riding high after a tense period of competing. But there is more at play here.

A deeper look at winning and losing

British and Irish cyclist Michael Hutchinson points out that those watching the winners often feel more joy than the winners themselves. Expectations set by coaches and teachers that 'winning is what is most fun in sport' can set athletes down a path of not expecting or looking for joy along the way. It also creates a thought process that sets up many winners to fail when their experience of the 'thrill of victory' does not match their expectations. Many winners talk predominantly of relief. Steve Redgrave, after winning Great Britain's only gold medal of the 1996 Atlanta Olympics, spoke starkly of the pressure in a famous interview after his race. There is no joy whatsoever in this interview, minutes after winning an Olympic gold medal, and it ends with the now famous and rather sinister comment: '[If] anyone sees me go anywhere near a boat, you've got my permission to shoot me.'

Hutchinson delves deeper into the reality of winners' emotions:

> The more you've already won, the more relief is dominant. The pure joy of victory is the most transient emotion there is. For most of those competitive enough in spirit to make a career out of something as trivial-yet-difficult as sport, the pure joy phase of their careers is probably a fading memory by the time they're old enough to vote. It tempers into feelings of achievement, then to satisfaction, and finally to a whooshing relief that they made it, that all those days, weeks and years ruled by total perfection in the utterly trivial have not been a wasted life.[3]

Olympic champion rower Tom Ransley reiterated the relief that followed a starkly dehumanized experience of competing in the Rio Olympics where he felt like 'a machine, merely executing its function' as he sat on the start line:

> To win is to enact a series of rehearsed procedures, it is muscle memory, and should feel like the only possible outcome. Any other result is failure. That's why most images of the big winners show only relief. Pure escape. It is over. It is done.[4]

In his autobiography *Open*, Andre Agassi describes his feelings after winning a long-awaited grand slam, exposing the chimera of winning:

After two years of calling me a fraud... they lionize me... But I don't feel that Wimbledon has changed me. I feel, in fact, as if I've been let in on a dirty little secret: winning changes nothing. Now that I've won a slam, I know something that very few people on earth are permitted to know. A win doesn't feel as good as a loss feels bad, and the good feeling doesn't last as long as the bad. Not even close.[5]

If that's how some of the winners feel, what about the others? First, let's look at the silver medallists, those who came closest to winning. Five-time British Olympian Katherine Grainger described winning her third silver medal in Beijing as 'like a bereavement'. Fellow teammate and rower Annie Vernon won her first Olympic medal in that same crew and talked of being 'left with regrets that you take to your grave'.[6] There was huge pressure and expectation for this crew to win and become the first British women's rowing crew to win Olympic gold. They had won the last three World Championships in the three years preceding Beijing and led for 1,750 metres of the 2,000 metres Olympic final. It was heartbreaking to watch; the reactions from the crew and the journalists, commentators and pundits were universally negative, and the crew cried their way through the medal ceremony. No wonder one study shows that the stress caused in silver medallists appears to limit their lifespans.[7]

British taekwondo Olympian Lutalo Muhammad sobbed into his father's arms after winning a silver medal in Rio and told the BBC: 'This is the lowest moment of my life.' Six months afterwards, he said: 'I think about what happened in Rio literally all the time. It hurts to my core. And it's something I will never get over.'[8]

Comedian Jerry Seinfeld has mocked society's approach to the runner-up:

I think if I was an Olympic athlete, I would rather come in last than win the silver... you know, you win the gold, you feel good. You win the bronze, you think, well, at least I got something. But you win that silver, that's like congratulations, you almost won. Of all the losers, you came in first of that group. You're the number one loser.[9]

What about the rest? Interestingly, bronze medallists buck the trend. One study shows that they were happier on the podium than silver medallists. In their case, the 'relativization' and comparison aspect of winning – that is, your result depends on how you do compared to others around you – works in their favour. Silver medallists typically regret 'not winning' gold, whereas bronze medallists compare themselves with those who come fourth and end up counting their blessings and feeling much happier.[10] Studies into 'silver medal syndrome' have fascinated researchers for years. Their findings reinforce the importance of the criteria we use to define success and create our goals from the outset.[11]

Behind those on the podium are endless tales of failure and low self-worth. Canadian rower Jason Dorland described the devastation and numbness following his crew's sixth-place finish in the Seoul Olympics: 'To go to the Olympics and not come home with that medal meant failure. It meant that all those years of training were for naught.'[12] British Rower John Collins spoke in an interview *four* years after the Rio Olympics about how returning from that Games without a medal had 'haunted him in ways that he could never have foreseen before'.[13]

Think of the simple visuals on the news when the British Olympic team flies home. The gold medallists are flown back first class by British Airways, disembarking by the front steps for a photo opportunity with the awaiting press. The rest of the team travel back in economy class and leave by the back steps, unnoticed by the waiting press, trying to hide, often feeling embarrassed or ashamed. If we assessed the performance rather than just the result, then there would have been brilliance, drama and inspiration across all the passengers, but our obsession with rankings immediately devalues so much of that.

Michael Hutchinson contemplates the reality of how it feels for those who don't win:

> it's hard to know what they think, because no one really asks. The personal satisfaction of having done their best, having done something they enjoyed? Crushing disappointment? Both? It's a doubly difficult question, because while success is normally quite easily defined, failure is more nebulous.[14]

Hutchinson points here to the external validation involved in who are the winners and the losers, and how this colours athletes' experiences. Others determine in print or online whether or not you gave your all, without having the faintest idea what was going on inside your head in the heat of competition. The advent of social media has only increased the number of external judgements, and it was to these that Australian Olympic swimming champion Cate Campbell fell prey in the aftermath of the Rio Olympics.

Campbell went to Rio as the 'undisputed favourite' to win the 100 metres freestyle final race. She was the reigning Olympic, world and Commonwealth record holder but went on to finish in sixth place. Tormented by the 'keyboard warriors' who leapt to judgement after she 'choked', she was still struggling to come to terms with the experience two years later. She wrote an open letter describing 'a surreal experience' on her return from Rio: 'I went into the Games as one kind of role model and came out... a very different one... Australia's poster girl for failure.'[15]

Campbell's experience demonstrates how perilously easy it is for an athlete's identity to be closely bound up in winning. It's not a surprise when an athlete trains to be the best they can be, seven days a week, most weeks of the year, in a training environment geared around measuring and assessing their worth. But there is a critical line between an athletic performance and the self-worth and value of that athlete. Despite the extreme commitment and effort required to perform at the highest levels, athletes and coaches must make a deliberate effort to separate individual worth from athletic results. Once that dividing line is lost, then the psychological balance is tipped regarding what winning means. It's no longer about being the best in the world at boxing, rowing or cycling. It's no longer just about being the best technician at your sport and stretching the limits of what is humanly possible within your chosen sport. Winning becomes inextricably linked with your self-worth, your self-esteem and with justifying your existence.

This has characterized the experiences of British double Olympic swimming champion Adam Peaty. He spoke publicly about his mental health battles and admitted: 'I always used to think success and happiness were defined by the gold medal or the world record. I try not to live by that any more.'

The construct of our identity is a critical component of sports psychology. When I first made the GB rowing team (long ago), I was excited to have made the step up to Olympic level from university- and club-level rowing. But it came as a shock to see that the women had part-time coaches and poor equipment. At training camp, the women's crews had to go out in the afternoons when the wind was strongest and the water roughest, making it hard for us to work on improving our technique. Our coach's launch had an engine that frequently broke down, further disrupting our training. When I raised this with the management, I was brushed aside and told that the women's team was not the priority because we didn't win. 'Who are you to have views on this? How many World Championship or Olympic gold medals do you have?' The answer was of course none. It wasn't the lack of physical equipment or support that affected me most; it was how I was silenced and humiliated. My lack of winning results equated to having no voice. It was a hugely demoralizing experience that had a lasting effect.

I experienced the clear message that losing represented a loss of personal worth in other ways too, notably the dreaded 'airport ticket moment' on the way home from each competition. The British rowing team travelled together as one large group to international rowing events. On the way out, we'd collect our tickets as we arrived at the airport, full of excitement and nervousness about the weekend's racing opportunities. Collecting the ticket home was a different experience. The team manager held all the return tickets and the only way to get one was to go to him. He would stand prominently near the departures desk. There was an unspoken but clear order in how they were given out. The winners usually collected theirs first – laughing and joking, buoyed by their victory, medals jangling in their pockets, they received their tickets with a merry pat on the back. Those who had lost waited their turn, hanging around awkwardly. It was like an additional punishment for failing to win. I already felt low after a disappointing race, frustrated with myself, frantically searching to understand the reasons for the poor performance and find the solutions to going faster next time. I really didn't need any additional reasons to feel bad. These interminable moments seemed to reinforce that this wasn't just a poor sporting performance, but that my own personal value had somehow diminished over the weekend. Tickets aren't handed out like that any more, but looking back, it reminds me how small cultural norms can be hugely damaging – in this case distracting self-belief and emotional energy away from the task of going faster next time.

By my second Olympic Games in Sydney 2000, where I finished ninth, I felt a total failure, embarrassed to speak to people who had come to watch. I felt ashamed of the losing result, regardless of giving my utmost and having raced harder than probably any race I have ever raced before or since. There were a whole host of reasons for the poor result – there always are: some visible, some less visible, and some within our control, some beyond our control. No matter how hard we pulled in those Olympic races, our effort wasn't making the boat go faster. That's the beauty and horror of sport, that elusive X factor that determines whether timing, effort and teamwork click or jam. Following Sydney, I sank into a deep pit of personal despair for over a year; that went far beyond how good I was as a rower into the deep recesses of my mind where I considered what self-worth I might have.

The challenges of athlete welfare

If athletes become solely defined by results, when those results don't materialize or simply come to an end, moving on to something else becomes hugely difficult. Regardless of whether an athlete has a winning or losing record, the lack of investment in developing a future after sport has led to a crisis in athlete welfare and transition that is only now slowly being addressed. For a long time in high-performance sport, and still in pockets today, coaches, clubs and the wider sporting environment have not accepted their responsibility for their athletes' wellbeing beyond sport.

The BBC State of Sport survey in 2018 highlighted how 'more than half of former professional sportspeople have had concerns about their mental or emotional wellbeing since retiring.'[16] In research by EY, 40% of athletes surveyed were bankrupt within five years of retirement, a similar number were divorced and two-thirds admitted to mental health challenges.[17]

The UK government sponsored a year-long review of athlete welfare, led by Baroness Tanni Grey-Thompson, with a report on the *Duty of Care in Sport* published in 2017. This report addresses the 'challenging questions about whether the current balance between welfare and winning is right and what we are prepared to accept as a nation', stating that 'winning medals is, of course, really important, but should not be at the expense of the Duty of Care towards athletes, coaches and others involved in the system'.[18]

Athletes interviewed for the review and in the media frequently talk about falling off a cliff edge as their highly structured sporting life comes to an end. If athletes have become defined by their sport and their voice in the world has come to depend on their sporting output, they can feel silenced or crushed.

Worse still, experiences of abuse and maltreatment continue to be uncovered. For example, revelations from gymnasts across the world are shocking. An avalanche of gymnast abuse stories was triggered largely by Netflix's powerful *Athlete A* documentary, released in 2020, just months before the first edition of *The Long Win* was published, contributing to an environment where leaders started to face up to the dark side of a 'win at all costs' approach in sport. A two-year (then) QC-led review in Britain, the Whyte Review, recorded shocking examples of physical, emotional and sexual abuse.

Let's look at how success has become defined so narrowly and in such a short-term way. The media clamour for instant heroes, rarely willing to show the ups and downs of athlete journeys and the longer-term path of progress (including failure) over time. Funding and sponsorship is usually based on world rankings of the current year or the league performances of the last season. Coaches need results in the short term to keep their jobs. These factors push athletes and coaches even further into focusing on the short term and shutting out anything beyond sport.

Coaches and sports directors usually mean well in wanting to protect their athletes from what happens in the rest of their lives, keen to reduce distractions from outside interests. The narrative of the elite sport environment is one of pain, sacrifice and commitment to winning, revolving around a narrow logic of: 'I love my sport. My sport is everything in my life. Nothing is more important than my sport and succeeding in it.'[19] But the impact on athletes can be far more complex over time, setting them up to struggle with both performance and wellbeing while still competing and then again when transitioning to a different life when their performance career comes to an end.[20] Kitrina Douglas' research highlights the importance of allowing athletes to develop a 'multidimensional identity and sense of self' through developing alternative stories that go beyond the circular narrative given above.[21]

I can remember the suspicion of certain rowing coaches towards my ongoing postgraduate studies. Some saw a distraction, a threat. To me, this was a lifeline. I clung on to it as a precious link to life beyond rowing. Something that I could control and that wasn't measured by sports scientists or subject to daily ranking. Studying was my best hope of providing a tiny sliver of balance in my life. Rowing always dominated; my studies always came second. That was made clear to me and I accepted that. There was no other way. But I worked hard to hang onto my studies, which I believe helped me manage my mental health, particularly in periods when my performances dipped. That was also crucial for me when navigating the transition into a career after sport.

In the UK, the role and engagement of 'lifestyle advisors' in the English Institute of Sport, who support Olympic and Paralympic athletes to prepare for life after sport, has increased with the growing recognition that this is a crucial element of athlete performance, welfare and support. Culturally, it still tends to be seen as 'soft' support that comes second to 'hard' training. Such support still generally gets fitted around 'real training', rarely vice versa, which risks undermining the very support that is being offered.

The number of high-profile athletes speaking out to share mental health struggles, from tennis player Naomi Osaka to cricketer Ben Stokes to gymnast Simone Biles, is helping to change attitudes towards mental health in sport and facilitate greater support, but there is a long way to go in sport, as in the workplace, to normalize mental health challenges and create environments where mental wellbeing is prioritized.

The postponement of Tokyo 2020 threw a huge spanner in the works and disrupted the lives of Olympic and Paralympic athletes. The certainty of knowing the time and day of your Olympic final years in advance was removed in one fell blow by the sweeping effects of COVID-19 pandemic. It was a testing time for athletes and coaches. It was also an opportunity for them to develop in a different way and contemplate the wider meaning in their sporting journey. For all of us, the expected heroes of 2020 – Olympic and Paralympic champions and UEFA Euros champion footballers with medals and trophies – were superseded by nurses and doctors with stethoscopes. For a brief moment, there was a shift in perspective and values inside sport and beyond. It's a shift worth considering in the long term.

The winning imperative in sport

How did sport develop to be what we witness today? The word 'sport' comes from the Old French *desport*, meaning 'leisure', with the oldest definition from around 1300 being an activity that offers 'amusement' or 'relaxation', 'entertainment' and 'fun'.[22] It can also mean 'consolation, solace, a source of comfort' – things no longer associated with the word today. Over time, sport divided into two areas: firstly, recreational sport, continuing that original sense of sport as leisure, as a hobby, as recreation; secondly, competitive sport, pushing the boundaries of what's possible, focusing on who's the fastest, the strongest, the best – increasingly exploited by the juggernaut of business. The commercialization of competitive sport has seen it come to be worth billions globally. Huge international sponsorship deals allow brands to reach millions of spectators and associate themselves visibly with heroic feats of winning.

The commercial and structural realities mean that most elite sports teams and organizations need to win in the short term in order to survive, either to qualify for government-related funding or to attract commercial sponsorship and broadcasting contracts. As Michael Hutchinson sums up when referring to the GB cycling team: 'This is the sharp end of a team. The aim is for the team to win medals, not to help any given individual make the most of themselves. It's Darwinian.'[23]

The situation in Olympic sport in Great Britain reached crisis point with the disastrous results in the Atlanta Olympics in 1996, where the British team won only one gold medal. Thirty-sixth place in the medal table represented a national humiliation. Britain needed to find a way to win again, so a new system was put in place providing consistent funding support and investment, and a focus on developing a new 'winning mentality'.

Funding was offered to Olympic sports under simple criteria: you win medals, you get funding; no medals, no funding. Public statements from UK Sport, the agency set up to oversee the funding and change in performance of the British Olympic and Paralympic team, boldly announced that there would be no more funding for sports teams who got knocked out in the first round or athletes who failed to deliver medals. It was proudly described at the time as a 'no compromise' policy, indicating the difference in mindset that would see Britain change from being 'plucky losers' to 'heroic winners'. From then on, it was all about results. After all, that's what sport's about, isn't it? That was where, it was assumed, things had been going wrong.

Since then, Great Britain has achieved stunning success in terms of medals won. Twenty-nine gold medals in London 2012 and second place in the medal table in Rio 2016 (even though the Olympic Charter is explicit in its section on 'solidarity' that competition is between individuals and teams, not between countries). By the measures above, that would prove that the system had succeeded gloriously and hit on a winning recipe. But it hasn't been quite that simple. The number of medals won had been closely monitored. But how those medals were won had hardly been considered or reviewed. Culture was a little-discussed concept in the early days of turning around Olympic performance. But soon there was talk of bullying, a lack of psychological safety, and stories of abuse, harassment and depression started to hit the press with greater regularity. With a number of high-profile allegations around cultures of intimidation, a 'toxic atmosphere' and 'culture of fear' in sports ranging from cycling to bobsleigh, there was criticism of a stark absence of leadership, cultural frameworks or value-based systems.[24] Internationally, we have seen the same phenomenon – high-performance sporting cultures achieving great things but hiding toxic cultures that enable abuse, cheating and corruption.

The revelations have caused governing bodies and other sports organizations to realize that it does matter how success is achieved and to recognize their responsibilities in this area. A number of teams are openly changing their language and approach. Great Britain, Canada, Australia and the US have all started to articulate various moves away from a medal-focused approach, though it remains a work in progress. The US Olympic & Paralympic Committee changed their mission statement in 2020 to focus on athletes achieving 'sustained competitive excellence and wellbeing', introducing upfront the need to consider wellbeing alongside results. The Canadian Olympic team stated 'the life skills and experience obtained through athletic preparation, competition and teamwork are far more valuable than any medal ever awarded', but continued to face a huge crisis of abusive cultures across Canadian sports.[25]

In 2022, the Australian High Performance Sport System launched a new strategy to 'win well', attempting to integrate a vision of more diversity within sport as a longer-term objective and oversee a closer integration of high performance and participation levels in sport. UK Sport also talked about 'winning well' without clarifying what 'well' meant, and continued to use medals as the main funding criteria. They used the language of 'medals and more', though the 'and more' part was ill-defined, leading to feelings of scepticism across the high-performance sporting community. These steps show how difficult it is for sporting leaders to step out of existing powerful narratives or reform systems based on a 'win at all costs' approach.

A shift will take time and continuous effort by coaches, leaders and athletes, who together create the sporting cultures in which they strive to become the best they can.

Cheating in sport

When winning is seen as the single aim in sport, 'the only thing that counts', then the costs that athletes are willing to incur increase. The desire to win has led to some deeply unpalatable behaviours far from our ideals of what sport could and should represent, the philosophy that Baron de Coubertin tried to define and any definition of success that could last in the longer term. The darkest side of a 'win at all costs' culture leads to cheating, whether in the form of financial doping, match-fixing, physiological doping or deliberately subverting the rules.[26] Some cheating is condemned more strongly than others.

While doping infractions are almost universally denounced, football fans and sponsors seem to accept regular diving and attempts to pull the wool over the referee's eyes on a weekly basis.

The vexed question of financial fair play has challenged European football clubs desperate to win the Champions League title, which brings the most lucrative rewards in football. UEFA's Financial Fair Play Regulations continue to cause controversy. In England, both the football Premier League and Premiership Rugby provide examples of how difficult it is to set any rules on financial fair play that will not be bent, ignored or manoeuvred for the sake of winning next season's league.

Within the Paralympic movement, there are increasing challenges over the classification of disabilities of competing Paralympic athletes, alongside accusations of athletes manipulating the classification process and the portrayal of their own disabilities to gain competitive advantage. The authorities face the dual requirement to get a grip on these issues and win more medals at each global competition.

Taking a closer look at the rule book, it's clear that anyone who tries to divert the golden rule that there can only be one winner may also be deemed a cheat. Back in 2016, the British Olympic triathlete Alistair Brownlee chose to help his exhausted and badly dehydrated brother Jonny over the finish line at the Triathlon World Series in Mexico. There were two contrasting reactions: firstly, an emotional, instinctive reaction from those watching, who were moved by the sight of sibling love triumphing over the desire to finish first. Secondly, consternation from the authorities that the desire to win had not come above all else. The International Triathlon Union (ITU) subsequently changed its rules to prohibit such assistance, so when two British triathletes, Jessica Learmonth and Georgia Taylor-Brown, crossed the finish line hand in hand at a World Triathlon Olympic qualification event in Tokyo in 2019, they were disqualified for breaking ITU competition rule 2.11.f, which states 'athletes who finish in a contrived tie situation, where no effort to separate their finish times has been made, will be disqualified'. A brilliant athletic performance by two athletes at the same time as a close bond and supportive relationship between competitors is clearly forbidden by the rules.

The costs of cheating are high, with some more visible than others. Huge long-term damage has been done to individuals and the wider reputation of sport, from the appalling abuse of athletes in what was the German Democratic Republic (East Germany) to the countless drug-fuelled winners of the Tour de France, to the systematic state-sponsored doping of Russian athletes. British Olympic swimmer and campaigner Sharron Davies has been tireless in publicizing the long-term consequences of doping and the wider misogyny endemic in sport, which continues to adversely affect the access and experience of half the world's population.

The negative ripples from cheating are evident across sport and society, and last generations. Disgraced multiple Tour de France winner Lance Armstrong admitted after one of the biggest doping revelations in sport that 'my ruthless desire to win at all costs... is a flaw. That desire, that attitude, that arrogance.' One of the most famous, breath-taking and damaging examples of an obsession with winning at all costs came in the form of Ben Johnson in the 100 metres final in the Seoul Olympics of 1988:

> Here were the seven fastest men on earth, and with them an eighth who made them look slow. Marvellous, yes. Marvellous in a slightly frightening sort of way... Ben Johnson seemed to be running away from his own humanity. Two final floating strides with his right index finger pointed at the sky... His head lifted high, neck arched to the sun, an instant icon. Victory. But at what cost?[27]

Ben Johnson revelled in a glittering glory that lasted 55 hours. For the rest of his life, he lives in shame, and the damage he caused the reputation of his sport also endures. Johnson has suffered from bouts of depression ever since that race, and when interviewed in 2011, Richard Moore described how 'the pain of his defeat remains etched on his face, his anger unconcealed', still desperately hanging onto the fact that he went faster than anyone else for a few seconds, despite being fuelled by steroids.[28]

Outside the Olympic world, cricket saw a ball-tampering scandal involving the Australian team during their tour of South Africa in 2018 that shocked the world. The governing body, Cricket Australia, commissioned an independent review by The Ethics Centre in Sydney to understand what had happened. It concludes that a culture of winning 'without counting the cost' was to blame. In the report, the players describe feeling part of a machine 'fine-tuned for the sole purpose of winning'. The leaders are held to account: 'The leadership of CA [Cricket Australia] should also accept responsibility for its inadvertent (but foreseeable) failure to create and support a culture in which the will-to-win was balanced by an equal commitment to moral courage and ethical restraint.'

As one Cricket Australia staff member puts it: 'We are obsessed with being number 1 but it's fool's gold. We should be striving to be the sport that every Australian can be proud of.'[29] Somewhere along the line, the need to win took over from the wider purpose of being a sport that 'every Australian could be proud of'. The review also drew parallels between the cultures in sport and banking, highlighting insufficient emphasis on building and sustaining the capacity for ethical restraint alongside the drive for performance.

There are many more stories of cheating driven by the desire to win, whatever it takes. Most of the gains are short-lived but the damage can be widespread and lasting.

Grassroots sport

We have spent most of this chapter looking at examples from elite sport. That's where the most visible role models are seen and where the extremes of winning and losing play out. But it is of course important to consider winning in the context of grassroots sports.

Schools, clubs and teams around the world often try to copy elite athletes, so it's no coincidence that the same issues are present: an obsessive focus on winning at all costs, the denigration of losers, attempts at cheating and an undervaluing of balanced cultures.

Research undertaken by Sport England to understand why so many women did not take part in sport uncovered a number of barriers. Successful elite athletes were too distant to feel relatable, and poor school experiences had a lot to answer for: 'a lot of girls leave school with a very bad feeling about sport. There's always been that attitude of "you're either a natural or not."'[30]

Keeping children engaged in sport through their teenage years has become an urgent challenge for countries across the world. Severe increases in obesity, diabetes and low fitness levels are causing huge pressures on healthcare systems. Drop-out rates are particularly high for girls, disabled children and minority groups.

I have heard countless stories of coaches and teachers preaching that the purpose of school sport lies in beating the school on the other side of town, and that it doesn't matter how you play, as long as you win.

A preoccupation with 'identifying talent' in youth sport is not just damaging for young people's early experiences of sport; it's also hugely inaccurate. Research continues to prove that successful junior athletes and successful senior athletes are largely two disparate populations. Increased efforts to identify future talent have meant that sport has stopped being fun. Yet studies show that sport needs to be fun for children to carry on. In one study that looked into the causes of fun, winning came 48th in the list. When asked what made sport fun, the top four answers were: trying hard, positive team dynamics, positive coaching, and learning and improving.[31]

Linda Flanagan, American journalist and former cross-country coach, investigates in *Take Back the Game* how the youth sports industry capitalizes on parents' worry about their children's futures, selling the idea that more competitive play is vital, leading to overspecialization, increased risk of injury, egregious behaviour by coaches and parents, and reduced access to sports for low-income families.

There's no doubt that more is demanded of parents, school and club coaches, and countless volunteers who make sport happen. Many are grappling with issues of duty of care in sporting organizations that have only recently woken up to their responsibilities. Beyond obvious safeguarding priorities, there is also a need for greater expertise in developing emotional resilience, leadership and wellbeing alongside technique and physical fitness in sport. Too many youngsters have been turned off or excluded from sport, and it is essential that we start to understand the reasons better and galvanize the collaborative effort required across society to address these.

Reflections on the reality of winning in sport

It doesn't take much to see that the sporting world is far from a gilded arena where the secrets of high performance have been cracked, success is golden and the winners glow forever. Whether finishing first or further down the field, the reality of winning certainly seems distinctly less shiny than traditional positive images might suggest. If 'winners' can feel flat and empty, and 'losers' worthless, then surely things need to change in our sporting environments? Crossing the line first seems to bring only a brief sense of fulfilment for many, unless linked to something deeper and more meaningful that goes beyond that moment. I return to the importance of a broader and longer-term perspective in the redefinition of success in Part III.

It's clear that sport has significant untapped potential to be a far more effective driver of physical and mental health, a more positive means of exploring human potential and a more powerful force to unite communities. There is significant scope to develop sporting success that lasts beyond the finish line, to reframe what winning means in order to improve *both* performance and wellbeing of athletes in the future and to explore more fully the potential of sport to create positive social change.

Business often looks to sport to provide the models and metaphors for success to copy and learn from. In the next chapter, we turn to consider how those winning analogies play out in a business environment.

Chapter 7

'It's All about Being No. 1!'

The 'Will to Win' in Business

'Can you help us win?' This is the first question I am often asked when invited to work with companies. I usually respond by asking: 'What exactly do you want to win and why?' Sometimes there's a pause, even a little confusion. Sometimes questions fly back: 'Isn't wanting to win enough?' 'Isn't that what it's all about?' Others assert the apparently obvious, self-explanatory goal to be no. 1 in the marketplace, to be best in sector, maybe to win an industry award. Some reply with percentages of growth or amounts of profit, others with coming top of a 'best employer to work for' survey. If my questions are still being tolerated at this point, I go on to ask: 'Why do you and your company deserve to be no. 1?' 'What positive difference to the world will you make by being the best in your sector?' Clear, meaningful answers are all too rare.

I enjoy exploring how much of a sense of purpose exists within a company. What are the fundamental goals and motivations from which the daily mindsets, behaviours and conversations flow? All too often there is a primary focus on competition and rankings, which fuels winning-obsessed behaviours based around egos, status and short-term reward. I use various team development activities to explore these behaviours. Before the activity, participants have usually heard a range of speakers discuss leadership, organizational culture and how to build high-performing teams. There is usually a strong consensus about the qualities, mindset and behaviours characteristic of a top business leader. When I reference the need to adopt a learning approach, challenge assumptions, listen to others and reflect, everyone nods sagely. But minutes later, when we move on to a team exercise, something completely different happens.

Almost without exception, participants leap into whatever task I set them and assume that it's competitive and that the point is to 'win', often without considering the views or experience of others around them. The decision that 'it's all about trying to win' is made without actually considering what they are trying to win and without me stating that the objective of the activity is to win. Just the act of splitting a group into teams seems to create a sense of inter-team competition as the first instinct, rather than cooperation or collaboration. An unspoken assumption is that borrowing an idea from another group is cheating, and that a group's own past experiences will show them the best way to do things.

It is worth reflecting on how we learn about what cooperation means. As we saw in chapters 2 and 5, we develop assumptions about whether we perceive cooperation as positive or negative. All too often, cooperation has been mis-defined in school as cheating. Time and time again, sharing information and discussing answers with others is forbidden behaviour through childhood, and remains uncomfortable as adults unless consciously rethought.

Over the course of the exercise, some begin to realize what the task is really about. There are some 'aha' moments when team members suddenly recognize the unhelpful impact of their assumptions. Often these come when I pause the activity for a few minutes and allow participants time to reflect. They start to notice that their unconscious thinking may have led them to certain behaviours, such as blocking collaboration or ignoring others' ideas. Often these are deep-seated behaviours, perhaps learnt in school, university or the workplace, where they seem to be the behaviours you display if you want to be successful, get promoted, become a leader.

These team activities are a great stimulus for discussions about the way we approach working life – how task-focused and results-driven we can be, rather than being people-focused and culture-orientated. Another conversation usually develops around how often we simply try and do the same thing harder and faster to improve, rather than exploring and trying out alternatives. We stifle opportunities to innovate because of a compulsion to 'win' (even when that is not set as the goal) and quickly assume we are competing against our direct colleagues, concluding that we should not share anything to help or support our colleagues.

After the activity ends (sometimes without a 'product' or 'result', which can be intensely frustrating to those conditioned to do things in order to 'achieve' a 'result'), a vibrant debrief ensues. Here the aim is to stimulate different ways of thinking and challenge existing norms. I try to lead the debrief around the process of what happened, the mindset and behaviours that led teams in a certain direction. My focus is on 'how', reviewing the impact of mindsets, behaviours and interactions, but often it's really hard for participants to shift their focus away from the outcome. In the modern workplace, we are out of practice at analyzing our own thought processes, reviewing our interactions with others and learning in order to adapt 'how' we work. We are hard-wired mainly to calculate results and keep a tally of wins and losses.

Despite key aha moments, it can be hard to process the implications of the exercise to the point where participants recognize a need to change their thinking. It often feels easier and more familiar to switch back to working out who 'won', who was the 'best', and trying to find out what the 'result' was.

The language that participants use in the debrief brings the conversation back incessantly to 'results' and 'win–lose' talk. 'We won really' is a common phrase, even though teams may not have achieved the objective (which wasn't framed around the result in any case but about how to work out the best ways to improve). Despite not achieving the aim of the task, and not answering the questions about how they went about it, some participants remain focused on extrapolating some sense of meaningless victory over others, even sometimes making up criteria for winning.

Protestations of 'you cheated' are frequently aimed judgementally at teams that did better or who maybe approached things differently. This from people who earlier signed up to the idea of growth mindset (as discussed in Chapter 5) and agreed that growth mindset thinking brings significant benefits to organizations.

Many have learnt from workplace experiences not to welcome others doing things differently, creatively or collaboratively. Voices with alternative suggestions during the activity are often unheard or (un)consciously ignored. But if those voices with some of the best ideas are not heard, or if hearing new ideas from a wider pool of colleagues is not a behaviour associated with winning and strong leadership, then that has huge implications for workplace culture. Companies will struggle to develop the diversity, innovation and engagement needed to fuel the collective performance of their organizations.

Although I (genuinely) never set up these activities so that teams cannot collaborate, once placed into teams, a default assumption is nearly always that the teams must be against each other and definitely should not share any good ideas or strategies they come up with. There can even be a strong sense that they would be happier for other teams to fail, as it might make their own team look better. That cannot be a healthy default mindset driving the behaviours and culture inside organizations.

Sometimes participants start blaming me for allowing other teams to 'cheat' or for 'tricking' them through the way I set up the exercise. It's as if they need to find a way to justify that they are in some way still 'winners', even though (and perhaps because) it has been revealed that they misunderstood or made misassumptions about the activity. There is, at times, an unspoken need not (to be seen) to have 'lost'.

Astonishingly, the language of 'who really won' can persist throughout the day and even beyond. Regardless of how many times I explicitly state that the purpose of the activity is to learn about themselves, to see how their actions are guided by assumptions that they aren't aware of and to re-examine how they think and behave, there can be a pervasive underlying assumption that at the end of the day, it's still got to be about winning. Where we could be moving on to a deeper understanding of how our mindsets shape our behaviours and what is required to change our behaviours, we are still discussing who won an activity that didn't require winning.

Significant time is required to unpick what is happening in these activities and open up entrenched thinking. Often that can be hard when participants and sponsors of programmes are keen to move on and cram in more knowledge, theory and content, rather than allowing the serious time and space required for participants to reflect and adapt the way they think and behave. In practice, significant change within leaders in the workplace is achieved in too few leadership programmes. Part I showed us the deep and historic influences in our own lives that entrench how we think about winning. Behaviour change does not happen easily or quickly. It requires constant reflection and clear intent to challenge our own assumptions and create an alternative approach together.

Once the debrief is finished, I usually plan to move on to another aspect of team performance or another activity. But some are still waiting to be given a clear result on the best outcome of the exercise and an explanation of who the winners are. Even after it's been shown *not* to be about winning and, instead, that the objective was to work in a different way and that the results would have been far better had that happened, the question that hangs explicitly or implicitly is: It can't really not be about winning, can it? As if winning is so engrained that it's hard to accept any other reality. (My greatest fear after marshalling all the arguments in this book is that readers will still turn around and say, yes, there are some fair points, but 'it's still about winning really' and look for reassurance from others around them...)

The 'banter' around winning is curiously persistent and distracts from more effective behaviours and useful interactions. There is power play and a motivation to self-protect within it. We search for language that helps us feel that we belong and are safe, that fits in with those in positions of power and authority. Yet this banter holds us back from learning, blocks cooperation and collaboration, and closes down new ideas and alternative views. Although it can feel comforting and familiar, it usually takes us back to an unhelpful, limiting place in our mind.

The winning mentality in business

The language of heroic winners and mighty battles that filled our history books for centuries transferred across seamlessly to the business world and a string of heroes from Jack Welch to Richard Branson, from Jack Ma to Elon Musk. It's a world of heroes, of superhuman efforts and power that revolves around a macho narrative: talk of 'the big boys', 'those who can cut it', 'those with the balls to take the big decisions'. It's a self-perpetuating narrative that is self-protecting for the leaders who propagate it. Any who challenge it are quickly dismissed as 'losers', 'weak and disloyal', simply unable 'to hack it at the top'.

Internal competition is a strong factor in company cultures dominated by a short-term competitive desire to win. This is often reinforced through a variety of means: forced distributions of performance evaluations, employee-of-the-month programmes, promotion processes, contests between departments for prizes, and published rankings of individual or team performance. Each of these defines success for one person or department at the cost of another. Recruits who clearly take this approach are often chosen; or it's made clear to them, explicitly or implicitly, from day one that this is how things work if you want to do well. But research by Jeffrey Pfeffer and Robert Sutton at Stanford Business School found that the costs of internal competition are severe and borne not just by those that lose in each case, but by everyone with a stake in the organization.[1] Except for work environments where there is little interdependence or need for learning and adaptation, Pfeffer and Sutton conclude that the widespread use of competition cannot be justified.[2]

Fundamental questions are increasingly being asked about this way of operating in business. The global financial crisis in 2008 turned the spotlight on the way the leaders inside financial institutions were thinking and behaving. No one could fault their determination to win within the simple business metrics of profit and growth. But the commitment to win on these terms contributed to some extraordinary decisions and risk-taking by many highly paid professionals. It's one of the clearest examples in the early 21st century of how a drive for massive *wins* can lead to enormous *losses*, and not just financial ones.

The costs of a 'winner takes all' culture go way beyond the balance sheet. Yet it's only recently that companies are being urged to take a broader perspective – taking account of our communities, societies and environment through ESG (environmental, social, governance) responsibilities. Going back to the early days of management consultancy, driven by companies such as the Boston Consulting Group, Bain & Company and McKinsey, the basic analytical tools for business strategy left out people, community and culture. This has yet to be fully redressed.

Despite a booming consultancy industry specializing in creating ever more sophisticated strategies, there has been a trend towards focusing on the short term, with the fast pace of change seen as justification for this. But when you stand back, the opposite seems true. The bigger societal and global challenges we face require us to think long-term, now more than ever. As we see later, businesses that focus on purpose and connect with a long-term mission are seen to outperform those that are reactive to short-term trends.

In company strategies I've come across, 'winning' remains the top-choice adjective. It is seen as shorthand for company goals and good annual metrics, gaining market share and beating your key competitors. I remember a meeting at the office of a global strategy management consultancy to discuss an organization's strategy update. The consultant shared their staple one-page six-step approach to strategy. It all made sense; there was nothing earth-shatteringly original or unusual. As the group started to look through it and apply it to the strategic challenge in question, I found myself staring at the wording of the PowerPoint slide on the screen. I scanned the text several times. One word leapt out at me. I counted the keywords that appeared more than once on the page, to check I wasn't biased in what I was seeing – there were terms like 'strategy', 'results' and 'change'. But my counting and recounting confirmed that what clearly appeared more frequently than any other words were 'win' and 'winning'.

The heading contained it: 'Creating a winning strategy'. The next level of detail described a six-step process to create that winning strategy. Two of the six steps then contained it in their headings: the first was 'Define the winning aspiration'; the third was 'Define how to win'. The next level of detailed bullet points beneath that layer contained it twice more: '[determine] the purpose of the organization, defined in a winning manner'; then '[determine] core capabilities required to win in the chosen playing field'.

I was curious as to how conscious the consultant's choice had been to use 'win' and 'winning' so often, but when I asked him afterwards, my question was dismissed scathingly:

Because business is competitive. Because our clients work in a highly competitive environment, where it's all about winning. It's no good having a nice strategy if it doesn't win at the end of the day. Our clients' competitors are not going to take their attempts to increase market share and profits lying down, so you've got to be out to win.

This was emphatic, based on deep belief and certainty, said with a full stop at the end. No question mark in sight. But I was left full of questions as I walked to the lift. What did that really mean? What were they trying to win? Was it simply 'all about winning'? If it's such a given, why does it need repeating so many times? What else might end up in the strategy if they didn't have 'winning' as a constant focus? What other more specific words were not being considered because 'winning' was used every time? What if his clients beat their competitors but the whole game changed when a new disruptor entered their marketplace? Is it fun to work in organizations like these?

Metrics and growth imperative traps

Business strategies are based on a rhythm marked by quarterly results and shareholder reports. This need for quarterly reporting was meant to increase scrutiny and avoid financial crises in the future. The intentions may be positive, but the reality is a little different. Firstly, within large companies, an industry now exists purely to produce reports, update slide decks and add in new figures. As soon as one quarter ends, the report starts for the next quarter. Secondly, huge amounts of time and energy in organizations are shifted onto short-term markers. Long-term decisions easily get pushed down the line and are quickly forgotten. No equivalent demand exists for long-term thinking to balance this out. Thirdly, this cycle tends to drive relatively short CEO tenures in many cases. Fourthly, areas of the business that are less easy to measure and don't change on a quarterly basis – for example, culture – become deprioritized and overlooked.

Andrew Hill, *Financial Times* management expert, describes the assumptions across the business world that everything can be measured and that

> anything that does not submit to mathematical evaluation need not be managed or is simply unmanageable... [There is a] tendency to pay more attention to hard facts, targets, outcomes and initiatives than to soft factors that are equally, or sometimes more, important. Big data is hard. Culture is soft. Financial goals are hard. Non-financial targets are soft. Gender quotas are hard. Workplace inclusivity is soft. '[STEM]' subjects are hard. Humanities are soft... Machines are hard – very hard. Humans are all too soft... Too frequently, though, when a balance of two approaches would be best, the hard solution wins out as soon as pressure is applied. In the classic tussle between long-term sustainability and short-term returns, too many directors and executives still obsess about hitting close-range targets. Purpose makes way for profit. The demand to compete overcomes any impulse to reap the benefits of collaboration.[3]

The short-term metric-driven focus is reinforced by external pressures from the media and other market observers taking a daily view on the winners and losers in the stock market. Companies are driven to make compromises and focus on the short term purely to survive. The short-term win–loss narrative quickly becomes a self-fulfilling prophecy.

Short-term metrics are typically based on targets. Targets are usually intended to give clarity, motivate and raise performance. But over time, they can miss out important areas of work performance. Targets typically focus on outcomes, not the ways and means of getting there. Where bonuses and promotion depend on targets being met, behaviours increasingly bend over time to meet the target. This might mean not helping a colleague who asks for assistance, or actively obstructing a colleague's work because your bonus will be bigger if you reach your target better than they reach theirs. When internal sabotaging starts to happen, performance starts to suffer, the workplace is not a fun place to be, collaboration is out of the question and engagement levels start to drop. In some cases, cheating and corruption set in.

In a study of white-collar criminals, one of the inmates, a former business leader, explains: 'It was not about right or wrong, but what helped us meet our business goals. No one got rewarded for being compliant, but you got punished for not meeting your targets.'[4]

Jerry Muller explains the outcomes of metric distortion on innovative and creative thinking: 'Trying to force people to conform their work to preestablished numerical goals tends to stifle innovation and creativity – valuable qualities in most settings. And it almost inevitably leads to a valuation of short-term goals over long-term purposes.'[5]

Target-driven cultures suit particular personalities. If unchallenged, companies and recruiting managers recruit those who respond well to target-driven rules, reinforcing certain mindsets and behaviours. This can inhibit the development of more diverse teams. Teams lacking in diversity are shown to be less good at adapting, learning and developing new ways of working to improve company performance. If a short-term winning-obsessed culture undermines efforts to increase team diversity, this then leads to lower performance, in contradiction of its proponents' claims to be driving performance.

It is common sense that when winning is based on seeking the same goals and following the same rules, people become more alike, striving to beat each other's records. Unique characteristics, by definition, cannot be easily ranked and measured. Conformity increases. Diversity gets lost.

Business metrics often centre on growth. Growth is good, so winning equals growth, and quickly this leads to a belief that an organization that hasn't grown must be failing. The mantra that a company should grow because 'growth is good' can be heard inside businesses, inside government and inside newspapers' financial pages. But is growth the right thing for every company, and is it the right thing to do for our communities and societies long-term?

When I'm coming into a company to develop their teams and culture to help them 'grow', I always ask: 'Why is growth the right thing for this company?' It's often another 'lead balloon' moment. The response can be a blank look and an awkward silence. Sometimes senior executives look at each other to see who will answer my question; most answers include the phrase 'because growth is good'. It reminds me of that tempting remark that harassed parents use to shut up their children during that phase of asking endless 'why' questions: 'Because it just is.' It's never good when said to a four-year-old, and it's no better when said to an adult in the workplace.

Sometimes, the answer to why growth matters is attributed to someone higher up the hierarchy. The executive team or the board has decided that the company should grow by x%. Growth is frequently cited as the only way to survive. Short-term and locally, that may be the case. But the question of the impact of growth on employees, on society and on the environment should be central when developing a growth-based strategy.

Of course, it's no surprise that growth is the game that businesses want to follow. On a simplistic level, growth seems to promise greater wealth and profit. The economic language of the Western world is obsessed with growth. The key metric of gross domestic product (GDP) remains the main means of judging economies across the world. Most countries seem trapped in the narrative of growing GDP as the means of solving their problems and demonstrating success. Yet this measure ignores huge chunks of our lives – such as health and wellbeing, happiness and equality – and disregards any impact on the natural environment. David Pilling explains in *The Growth Delusion* how crude GDP is as a measure of the economy:

> GDP likes pollution, particularly if you have to spend money clearing it up. It likes crime because it is fond of large police forces and repairing broken windows. GDP likes Hurricane Katrina and is quite OK with wars. It likes to measure the build-up to conflict in guns, planes and warheads, then it likes to count all the effort in reconstructing shattered cities from the smouldering ruins... It doesn't deign to count transactions where no money changes hands. It doesn't like housework... and it shuns all volunteer activities... It can count a bottle of Evian in the supermarket but not the economic impact of a girl in Ethiopia who trudges for miles to fetch water from a well.[6]

Our standard means of measuring the economy have never focused on 'how' that growth was being created, nor have they measured rising inequality, global imbalances, long-term standards of living or environmental damage. Economist Joseph Stiglitz describes the 2008 global financial crisis as 'the ultimate illustration of the deficiencies in commonly used metrics'.[7]

Constant economic growth makes little sense. It requires a limitless appetite for stuff, material goods, a never-ending cycle of consumption. And if never-ending consumption and creating more and more goods isn't a sensible end in itself – and certainly it is one with huge environmental implications – then what else are we trying to achieve through it? Growth isn't always bad, just as competition isn't always bad. But a narrow obsession with growth above all else, as the only measure, is not a good definition of success. If winning the GDP game comes at the expense of things that matter to us – happiness, clean air, sound minds – then it's surely a hollow victory at best and hardly a game that we should be so obsessed with winning at all costs.

As in the worlds of education and sport, an organizational system based on incentives, targets and narrow metrics drives particular ways of thinking and behaving. Though nearly always unintended, such systems in business can lead to individual and systemic corruption, serious large-scale environmental damage, increasing inequality in society and, on an individual level, burnout. In Margaret Heffernan's analysis: 'our love affair with competition, the belief that contests will identify and elevate the best has produced a social structure that not only doesn't deliver prosperity but [creates] its opposites: volatility, stress, corruption.'[8] Who is winning here? What is the prize? Let's pause and take stock of how an unquestioning desire to win has had some seriously counterproductive outcomes for business and beyond. Then we can start to consider a different approach.

When winning underpins the culture

Culture is often defined as the 'way things are done round here' and indicates what really matters in an organization. At a superficial level, culture is described in value statements placed on websites and reflected in desired behaviours assessed on appraisal forms. But it exists more powerfully, at a deeper level inside human experiences of the workplace. It's the sort of thing you notice within an hour of visiting any business or organization. Who speaks first in a meeting?

Do the more senior people in the office have reserved parking spaces near the door? How are visitors greeted when they come into the building? What are the pictures about on the walls of the office and what does that tell us? These 'cultural artefacts' reflect how an organization is experienced by those who work there. They tell us whether hierarchy dominates, which people are most valued and what behaviours are acceptable in practice.

Once you become a 'cultural observer', you start noticing all sorts of things: When do people speak up in meetings and who speaks most? What are the things that get ditched when the pressure's on? Which behaviours prevail when deadlines are looming? What gets measured (and is therefore seen as most important)?

The cliché that 'culture eats strategy for breakfast' was coined by Peter Drucker, one of the early management gurus back in the 1970s, and it still resonates today. Drucker's quote highlights the gap between what is planned in boardrooms and C-suites and what actually happens on the ground. Organizations that focus on strategies, targets and all the measurable stuff can easily overlook the human experience of working in that environment, which ultimately determines how the grand strategies get implemented.

A culture based on winning at all costs, where meeting targets is the prime aim, can produce toxic behaviours and a workplace full of fear. There are numerous examples of how a toxic culture can lead to business disaster: from the episode of false accounting at Enron to the emissions scandal at Volkswagen to all the various culprits of the 2008 banking crisis. An unbalanced culture, singly driven to provide results in the form of profit, can start to cut corners in order to 'hit the numbers'. Along the way, a culture where people are not supported to challenge decision-making or raise questions of ethical restraint enables this path to continue. It may deliver results and hit targets brilliantly in the short term, but it can lead to long-term catastrophe. A desperation to win, and to win big, leads to an outcome that feels a long way from any definition of success.

In the case of Volkswagen, targets were given to engineers to design a diesel engine that would hit performance and price targets while emitting only a certain amount of nitrogen oxide. Meeting the target would result in money and promotion, but the engineers could not meet it. So they did what engineers do if they want to win: solve the problem and meet the targets set. They put their minds to engineering a solution – in this case, brilliant software designed to defeat emissions tests. Cars on the road were emitting up to 40 times more nitrogen oxide than was recorded in laboratory tests.

Volkswagen's CEO, Martin Winterkorn, was criminally indicted in the US on charges of fraud and conspiracy. It is easy to condemn those involved, but it is more important to understand how that level of corruption was possible within such a large, well-established, reputable company. Why was no one overseeing the decisions or being held accountable? Why were there no checks within the system to challenge the solution? Why did no one within that department feel a need to question what they were creating? Why did they feel they had to win the challenge whatever the costs involved? Why did no one understand the culture that short-term targets were fuelling? How could short-term targets be allowed to outweigh, and ruin, the long-term reputation of Volkswagen?

One of the cultural characteristics of these cases is always that simple but crucial lack of voice to speak up for those who might spot things going wrong. It's the questions that are asked, or not asked, in a company that play a huge role in the culture, the language that is dominant, the narratives that are seen as strong or weak. In their comprehensive work *Speak Up*, Megan Reitz and John Higgins interviewed over 150 leaders to understand conversations in their organizations. They explored how accountability was communicated, how easy it was to challenge decisions, discuss risks or compare short-term and long-term outcomes:

> Speaking up and listening up matters in our organizations. Without it, you might only hear about misconduct and wrongdoing when it appears on the front page of the newspaper. It is vital for innovation and adapting to this latest age of upheaval. It is essential to motivation and engagement.[9]

The 2013 Salz Review investigated the conversations and culture at Barclays, which was based on a 'deeply entrenched commitment to winning' in the lead up to the financial crisis:

> the interpretation and implementation of 'winning' went beyond the simply competitive. It was sometimes underpinned by what appeared to have been an 'at all costs' attitude... Winning at all costs comes at a price: collateral issues of rivalry, arrogance, selfishness and a lack of humility and generosity.[10]

Over at the RBS, CEO Fred Goodwin was known for his competitive nature.

Fred had to win, he always had to win... He had to win every single counter – it didn't matter how big or small. He had to dominate. RBS had a very strong bullying culture. Everything in that bank was competitive.[11]

Goodwin launched a series of ambitious takeover bids, starting with the NatWest bank (three times the size of RBS) and continuing with an Irish mortgage provider, an insurance company, a car company, a train company and a US investment operation with the world's largest trading floor. Not satisfied with that, he set up a consortium in order to launch a hostile takeover of Dutch bank ABN AMRO. It was a race based on being bigger, better, richer. Anyone mentioning due diligence was dismissed as a loser and a wimp within Goodwin's macho winning narrative. But in February 2008, RBS announced a loss of £24 billion, the largest annual loss in British corporate history, and had to be bailed out by the British government.

In examples like this, winning has provided a cover for poor behaviour and inappropriate practices. Self-delusion and a misperception of reality has led some business leaders to think that everything is OK if a company is winning, hitting profit targets and delivering to shareholders. That the end justifies the means. In business, as in sport, cases of bullying and intimidation, fraud and corrupt behaviour have emerged from organizations previously considered to be 'winning organizations'.

Even the gem in British industry, Rolls-Royce, was forced to pay £671 million in penalties after a long-running bribery scandal concerning how the company went about pursuing and winning valuable contracts abroad. And high-street retailer Tesco was prosecuted by the UK Serious Fraud Office after vastly overstating its profits in a period where it was fighting tooth and nail to look competitive against its fiercest supermarket competitors. The short-term focus improved figures of course, but resulted in a devastating slump once uncovered.

Another area of cultural damage comes from a focus on rewarding individuals rather than teams. Winning is often seen as an individual challenge. The intentions of motivating others through winning seem well meant, aiming to motivate and raise performance. But the consequence is that teamwork is devalued and deprioritized, and collaboration becomes non-existent.

What's the human experience inside organizations following short-term winning strategies? There are widespread challenges of motivation and productivity across the developed world. A Gallup survey of the global workforce suggests only 13% of employees are engaged in their jobs; in the UK, it's only 8%.[12] Burnout is a challenge for many HR (human resources) directors and senior executives of some of the most prestigious companies. The taboo of mental health issues is slowly being broken down, but it is unleashing stories of misery and abuse that show the depths to which corporate cultures have sunk in some cases. Assumptions are still made about using extrinsic rewards to motivate employees despite an increasing body of research revealing this as hugely flawed, mirroring what we saw in the case of motivation in education and sport.

The application of metrics to workplace talent further undermines opportunities to develop cognitive diversity and unlock a broader base for developing people and improving performance within companies. Employees continue to be categorized as 'top talent' or 'future talent'. As with school grades, this demotivates and excludes the rest of the workforce, who are indirectly categorized as 'low talent' or 'without talent'. These arbitrary categories have many unintended consequences on workplace culture and are usually riven with bias. They can also be based on false assumptions about 'high-flyers' and the false allure of 'star performers'. A study by Thomas DeLong and Vineeta Vijayaraghavan shows that these assumptions are harming organizations who mistakenly 'downplay average performers because they lack the lustre and ambition of stars'. They conclude:

> in our collective twenty years of consulting, research, and teaching, we have found that companies' long-term performance – even survival – depends far more on the unsung commitment and contributions of their B players... Companies are routinely blinded to the important role B players serve in saving organizations from themselves.[13]

Shifting away from meaningless categories, metrics and box-ticking is an important opportunity for organizations of the future. Career success and workplace performance need to be viewed in a much more diverse and pluralistic way, creating a different employee experience and investing in people beyond their job titles.

Reflections on winning in business

So many latent assumptions still dominate the business world, including the assumptions that the priority must be to win, that targets and outcomes are the best way of ensuring success and that competitive environments get the best out of everyone. But taking those assumptions for granted holds us back, worsens business performance over the long term and prevents us from exploring better ways of organizing how we work.

There are no easy answers, and life can seem so much more complex for CEOs of the 21st century than their predecessors. Leaders have to balance challenges of social responsibilities and shareholder returns, sustainability and employee engagement, environmental impact and community support, and for companies on a global scale, issues of customization and mass production, globalization and localization. But that's even more reason why simple competitive narratives and metrics focused on 'being no. 1' are inadequate. As I set out in relation to Long Win Thinking, we need to move beyond this finite thinking to develop a more meaningful sense of purpose over the longer term, a focus on a diverse, collaborative culture, and the prioritization of people over tasks and targets.

What we see happening in our schools, on the sports field and in the workplace plays out in a remarkably similar way, and has even greater consequences on the global stage of international politics, which is where we're headed next.

Chapter 8

'It's All about World Domination'

Global Winners and Losers

On the eve of the US invasion of Iraq in 2003, President George W. Bush addressed the US, stating 'we will accept no outcome but victory'. But did victory follow? President Bush tried to claim that it did. He delivered a now-infamous speech aboard an aircraft carrier in 2003 in which he declared an end to major combat operations in Iraq and announced: 'In the battle of Iraq, the United States and our allies have prevailed.' Yet the American role in Iraq was far from finished. It would be another seven years before President Obama finally ended the combat mission, in 2010, and around 150,000 civilian deaths and nearly 5,000 military deaths had occurred since Bush's speech aboard the aircraft carrier. When we look back at the Iraq War, it's hard to see a clear-cut victory, and the costs of any temporary and narrowly framed victory were sky high.

Looking at other conflicts, even going as far back as the First World War, it's actually hard to see clear winners if we take a close look, even though this world of warfare defines itself by victory and defeat. Who won the Cold War? Who won the wars in Korea or Vietnam? What about the invasions of Iraq and Afghanistan in the 1990s and early part of this century, or the fight against ISIS (Islamic State of Iraq and Syria)? Again, there are no obvious winners, and a lot of disastrous unintended long-term consequences.

Who can 'win' the battle against terrorism? This sort of language appears regularly in political speeches, but this is not a finite war that is ever won or lost. As for the other key issues of our time, we have yet to win the battle for climate change, inequality, security or poverty despite various political attempts to 'win' on all these fronts.

Faced with the COVID-19 pandemic in 2020, politicians predictably wheeled out the language of 'winning' and 'beating the virus'. But it's hard to see how that mindset of winning, together with the competitive comparison of different nations' data, did anything to help address the real issues; more likely, it distracted from a more effective joined-up response.

National leaders have returned time and time again from international summits on trade, refugees, climate change and security only to announce to their electorates how they fought for a better deal for their country, for their citizens. But it's a nonsense when each leader returns from the same summit with the same message. They can't all have won at the others' expense. But they rely on the fact that citizens of one country don't see the other leaders saying the same things simultaneously in the neighbouring country on the news. Too few leaders are courageous enough to return from a summit and speak of collaboration, compromise, support for others. Those that do find it hard to realize gains from changing the narrative, as their electorates are so used to the old ways of thinking.

If looked at through a narrow, 'power-focused' zero-sum game, it is not in any government's short-term self-interest to challenge its powers and its centuries-old governing style. But the issues confronting governments and international organizations have changed. Current ways of governing are proving woefully inadequate to deal with the big global issues of our time. In this chapter I look at how a narrow focus on 'winning' can mislead on the biggest stage of all.

Mindset and language in global politics

There are different systems of winning in elections, whether it's first past the post, as in the UK, or proportional representation, as across most of Europe. Whatever the system, it sets up winners and losers. That's what we see; that's what the media coverage depicts. But where there are winners, there is a cost – often greater than the winners want to believe or admit.

What is success for politicians? Do they set out to win votes and power? Or do they set out to change the world for the better? They need the former in order to achieve the latter, but if their aim is to win votes in the next election, then a politician's focus can start to fix on the short term. Changing the world for the better requires a different way of thinking, a new capability and fresh approach to tackle the real issues before them, from terrorism to climate change to global health. There are few quick or easy wins on any of these issues.

There is an increasing tension between politicians being elected for the short term yet with predominantly long-term issues to manage. Their election and survival depends on doing well individually and as a political party in the short term. Party identities are often formed in explicit opposition to another party and set of individuals. Soon, politicians find that their existence and survival is based on opposing others. If an opposing politician has a better idea about a subject, it makes it almost impossible to support the idea. That defies common sense and is certainly not in any wider interest.

We probably hardly notice it, but this ongoing culture of 'winning battles against others' creates a mentality where cooperation and collaboration are seen as weak and undesirable. It becomes doubly hard for countries to work together to tackle the biggest global challenges of our time, despite the fact they cannot be addressed by any single country alone. The same applies on an individual level. If you make a mistake as a politician, the last thing you can do is admit it. Every human being on the planet makes mistakes, yet as we saw in Chapter 1 when we looked at the traditional language of winning, politicians (reinforced by the media) have developed this narrative to a stage where it's strong to be right and weak to be wrong.

This plays out disastrously on the larger governmental scale. Time after time, we see the delusion that winning must mean carrying on against all reasonable evidence. There are many cases of a 'sunk cost' bias – a government has invested so much in a policy that even though it has been proven to fail, it ploughs onwards rather than admit any fault or mistake. The poll tax in 1980s Britain was a classic example, where the government carried on implementing the tax long after it was seen as unworkable and had remarkably little public support. The project failed horribly and had to be withdrawn at vast cost.

In the years following the 2016 Brexit referendum, promises of what Brexit could and should deliver kept UK politicians clinging to their original promises, even though there was less and less evidence as time went on that these could be delivered. They stuck to their position regardless of changing information, just as their opposition, those who wanted to remain, continued with their predictions of economic collapse. No one knew what was possible, as it had never been done before, so it was inevitable that some initial promises would not work out. But no one was able to admit that then, nor have they since. Trapped in a win–lose binary world, politicians were unable to adapt their views to knowledge gained after the referendum. Each side remained laser-focused on 'winning the argument' and making the other side look stupid, not on finding the best solutions or understanding each other's perspective.

UK government departments offer a classic example of how a competitive culture set at the top – where government ministers jostle for positions and power – sets the tone for siloed departmental cultures. There needs to be collaboration across departments to tackle the complex issues facing them, from obesity to pandemics, from security to immigration, and from energy to environmental protection. But all the structures, incentives and accountability continue to revolve around each individual department. Cross-departmental working remains a huge effort against the tide. I can remember, when I was working in Iraq, arguing with a colleague from the Ministry of Defence (MOD) about how we needed to align our objectives so that we weren't working against each other. I pointed out that we were, after all, working for HMG (Her Majesty's Government). He looked at me in great puzzlement and said: 'You're mistaken. I work for the MOD. My targets are set by the MOD, I am reviewed, paid and promoted by the MOD, my allegiance is to the MOD.'

House of Commons committees and reports frequently highlight insufficient cross-departmental working as a cause or contributing factor to poor outcomes in various policy areas. Cross-government units are typically seen as a solution. But having been a co-director of one, I can confirm that the reality of cross-government units is a chimera. These units are set up to demonstrate a joined-up response to a recommendation, while the key incentive and power structures remain the same. When things get difficult, or interesting, the departments simply behave individually and take back control.

There are examples of political leaders – such as Nelson Mandela in South Africa, President Barack Obama in the US and Prime Minister Jacinda Ardern in New Zealand – who have tried to put more of an emphasis on compassion, partnership and collaboration in their language, thinking and politics.

Mandela outwitted the game of oppositional politics through his mindset, behaviour and ways of relating to others. During his long prison sentence, he used empathy and humility to outthink his 'opponents' and 'out-emote' them. When he said that the best way to defeat an enemy was to make him your friend, he managed to change the game of power that others were playing.

Obama and Ardern each veered away from traditional heroic, oppositional language in response to national disasters or terrorist attacks, choosing to reach out to all communities rather than blaming one particular part of society. Jacinda Ardern went furthest in trying to change the political narrative to be more inclusive, believing in compassionate governance and attempting to use wellbeing to displace GDP as the central measure of progress. Following a terrorist attack on Christchurch, Ardern avoided threats of vengeance, tightened gun laws and focused on support and empathy for the victims, using inclusive language to emphasize that these Muslim victims were 'brothers, daughters, fathers and children... were New Zealanders. They are us.'[1] Ardern repeatedly articulated the notion that compassion is strength: only by looking after each other can we build strong communities, and thereby a more resilient society and economy. While these leaders remain a minority, and are typically dismissed as 'weak' in the eyes of the all-conquering hero-leaders, they offer our societies an alternative approach.

Winning in international diplomacy

The battles that pepper our history books continue to this day: states fighting other states to gain more territory, power and wealth. It's a primitive zero-sum game that is hard to break. The international institutional framework struggles to address cross-border problems. Whether it's tackling environmental matters or a global health pandemic, it's hard to see that the necessary international structures exist to ensure effective action and the scale of engagement and collaboration required to address the big global questions of our time.

During my diplomatic career with the Foreign and Common-wealth Office, a large amount of my time was spent trying to change mindsets from a zero-sum game mentality – where one side can only win at the cost of the other – to a 'win–win' mentality – where a solution can be agreed where everyone compromises yet everyone gains and there is a step forward in the overall situation. (Or even a 'win–win–win' mentality as the Japanese like to say.)

As much as we pored over complex, technical briefs ahead of a negotiation, progress relied more on the mindsets of those in the room that we were negotiating with. Whether it was about persuading the bitterly opposed political representatives of the ethnic groups in Bosnia to work together to agree reforms to move their poor, war-torn country forward, or trying to persuade the

Spanish and Gibraltarians to work together more cooperatively at the border, the common challenge was shifting mindsets. Many of our political issues can be seen through the prism of psychology and should perhaps be considered more in that vein. It's not about who has the best idea: no one individual or country has the monopoly on the best ideas. We need systems to find the best new and innovative solutions to emerging issues. Political power alone is being proven increasingly ineffective at tackling the tough global issues we face.

The world is changing and requires a different approach. The concept of 'enemies' has evolved as part of that. Back in the 19th century and beyond, there was always a clear enemy. There were distinct periods of fighting and usually a clear outcome, with a winner and a loser. In a simple, less interconnected world, the winner typically gained in power and wealth and suffered few costs through winning. Today, in our complex, interconnected world, winning a battle doesn't have the permanence it used to have. It can come at far greater cost, not just financially but in social and environmental impacts which affect the 'winner' as much as the 'loser', if it's even clear who is the winner. In current conflicts, fighting can be unpredictable and never-ending. There may be no physical fighting and it is not always clear who the enemy is.

The US were wrong-footed many times in the Iraq conflict because of the unpredictability and unconventional nature of al-Qaeda, a loose network that was able to reconfigure in real time and integrate globally dispersed actions. Similarly in Afghanistan, the US faced a far from conventional fight, and the numerous declarations of 'jihad' on the West in the early 21st century posed ongoing unpredictable threats.

Coalition forces found themselves fighting over and over again to 'win' back territory, only to lose it again, stuck in a never-ending vicious cycle of winning and losing, far from the simplistic concept of victory that they had set out to achieve. When victories were declared, these were quickly overturned, leaving the Western armies demoralized as their expectations of a short, sharp conflict and return home disappeared. The enemy could not be beaten, there were no clear lines on the map to show victory and defeat, and it became harder and harder to define what success could ever really look like.

Western military and political thinking continues to struggle to move on from what military strategist Edward Luttwak identifies as a strong 'materialist bias' in the way winning is defined. Measurable inputs and outputs (such as firepower, targets hit, numbers of aircraft available) tend to assume greater importance in depicting whether Western forces are winning or not, rather than looking at arguably more crucial, albeit intangible, human factors, such as strategy, leadership and morale.[2] In *Behavioural Conflict*, UK senior officers in the British Army and the Royal Navy, respectively, Andrew Mackay and Steve Tatham call for a major shift in the way government departments and military services think, in order to prioritize understanding behaviour and motivations in future military strategy.[3] The same applies to foreign policy and government policy more widely.

From working as a diplomat in the British Consulate and military HQ in Basra in 2008, I can remember the daily reports, full of numbers and metrics that the military would announce in the 08:00 morning meetings: the numbers of helicopters working that day, the weather forecast and predicted temperatures, and that day's operational targets. It gave a brilliant picture of control and clarity. As learnt over centuries, this is essential to organize large numbers of military forces effectively. But it was not always helpful for the chaotic task in hand – a complex, volatile and unpredictable world characterized by violence on the streets, no single enemy and no clear political parties or system in place.

The lack of alignment between military precision and sociopolitical reality created tension. When, as diplomats, we tried to summarize the political situation each day, it formed such a contrast to the precise military reporting. The goal of political reconciliation sounded so vague. It was impossible to say for sure who held which views or which local politicians supported us. Positions shifted all the time, and because of the hostilities, we did not have free access to talk to the local political leaders, as would happen in peaceful political environments. I could sense the frustration of military colleagues as I gave daily updates on the complex and fluid political situation. I can remember one military officer asking if we could predict a date when political reconciliation would happen. I couldn't even begin to answer the question and give the precise information that military colleagues valued so highly. But the pursuit of precision can be misleading. This wasn't a world of clear winners and losers; success couldn't be project-managed; there would be no day on which peace and victory could be declared.

General Stanley McChrystal, US Army commander in Iraq and Afghanistan, describes how the US Army had to reorganize itself psychologically and organizationally in order to become more agile. Old mental models about how the world should be run had been mechanistic, based on clear rules, demarcations, categories, standards and rules of engagement. New mental models needed to be messy, adaptive and self-organizing:

> Eventually, we all have to take a leap of faith and dive into the swirl. Our destination is a future whose form we may not find comforting, but which has just as much beauty and potential as the straight lines and right angles of the past century of reductionism: this future will take the form of organic networks, resilience engineering, controlled flooding – a world without stop signs.[4]

Global metrics

The pursuit of economic growth above all else, that competitive urge to beat another country's GDP, remains a key success metric for governments, as we saw in the previous chapter. But winning the GDP game has been at best a narrow and hollow victory for the wealthiest nations, and at worst a human catastrophe. The route to economic growth has seen a ransacking of biodiversity, unsustainable levels of consumption and CO_2 emissions which now threaten the future of our planet, to mention just a few of the still unfolding consequences.

Despite increasing evidence of these consequences, most governments continue along the same route, stuck in self-perpetuating governmental systems that are unable to shift in the way that McChrystal describes. Yet they are left more vulnerable to unpredictable challenges of the future, as COVID-19 and the pace of global warming have started to show.

Governments often claim to be active in protecting the environment, increasing social mobility and investing in the health systems of their countries. Yet a look at the bigger picture shows that their efforts are not succeeding. A different way of (co)operating is required.

Swedish environmental activist Greta Thunberg highlighted this in clear terms when, aged 16, she toured European capitals in 2019 to urge politicians to act credibly to address the crisis. In her speech to the UK Parliament, she criticized the UK's 'very creative carbon accounting':

Since 1990 the UK has achieved a 37% reduction of its territorial CO_2 emissions, according to the Global Carbon Project. And that does sound very impressive. But these numbers do not include emissions from aviation, shipping and those associated with imports and exports. If these numbers are included the reduction is around 10% since 1990 – or an average of 0.4% a year... The climate crisis is both the easiest and the hardest issue we have ever faced. The easiest because we know what we must do. We must stop the emissions of greenhouse gases. The hardest because our current economics are still totally dependent on burning fossil fuels, and thereby destroying ecosystems in order to create everlasting economic growth.[5]

Metrics once again dominate at the level of global politics, obscuring reality and misleading electorates. Of course, many disagree with Greta Thunberg's views; scientists and politicians continue to battle over the evidence. But trying to 'win' that battle and belittle an opponent's views distracts from the real challenge at hand to protect our planet. Does proving another's statistics wrong justify destroying our natural environment? Can we 'win' in the environmental crisis? Is it creating a new clever way of carbon accounting that makes a government look like it's taking action? Is it taking part in summits and spending weeks and weeks negotiating and arguing to ensure that one government isn't asked to take more action than another? Or maybe it needs to look quite different, and the first step is to realize that this is not a battle to 'win' at all.

Reflections on winning on the global stage

There is a desperate need for new ways of thinking on the international level, for the new mental models that McChrystal refers to, which can acknowledge more complex realities and wider possible solutions and move away from fixed wins and losses. Current systems of government are struggling to adapt to the challenge, obstructing efforts to do so while being eternally self-perpetuating. We should be discussing in more detail how to develop the structures, behaviours, mindsets and relationships needed to address the global issues of our time. There is of course no 'right' answer, but the status quo feels far from optimal. The 'winning' rhetoric of our politicians feels more misleading and meaningless than ever. We must demand better.

Our exploration of the worlds of education, sport, business and politics in Part II has shown how dominant narratives of winning distort our lives and societies, and hold us back. It has suggested some seeds of what a different approach might look like. Part III focuses on the development of that alternative: how we might embark on a different approach to defining success, for individuals and organizations, and how we might reshape the way we think, behave and interact with one another in order to generate the Long Win.

Part III

A New Approach to Winning

For the loser now will be later to win,
For the times they are a-changin'

Bob Dylan (*The Lyrics: 1961–2012*)

Chapter 9

Finding a Better Way

The Beginning of Long Win Thinking

This time it had to be different.

Experiencing my first Olympics in Atlanta 1996 had been an enormously formative experience. I felt optimistic that with greater support, better performances would come. But although we had decent equipment and a full-time coach for the first time, our training environment and culture had not moved on. I endured four brutal years of training with an old-school coach who only spoke in terms of 'winners' and 'losers' and believed that anything was permissible in the cause of 'toughening up athletes' and 'building champions'. I improved physiologically but finished ninth at the Sydney Olympics in 2000 and was left devastated. I found myself constantly searching for understanding: 'How had I trained harder and gone slower?' 'Was this result a true reflection of how good I was?' A logical extension seemed to be: 'This proves I must be a loser.' More worryingly, I started extrapolating this 'losing result' to my own worth as an individual.

How had I come through four gruelling years of training and lost so badly? Moreover, how had I got to a place inside my head where I saw this failure to move a boat backwards faster than the rest of the world as an indication of my (lack of) value to society? I limped on into the next year of training but lacked self-belief and felt hugely vulnerable. After another disappointing year, I decided to retire.

At the same time, the opportunity arose to join the diplomatic service at the Foreign and Commonwealth Office, a long-held career ambition of mine, from before the days of boats and oars. This change of career brought a hurricane of fresh air to my thinking.

Every aspect of my life seemed to change: what I wore, what I ate, what I thought about, who I spoke to. Working and functioning in a different environment, being recognized for my contributions, learning rapidly on a daily basis helped me feel alive and engaged again. I was seeing first-hand serious life-and-death situations play out that put my rowing career and anxieties around winning into considerable perspective. My voice and opinion were valued at work from the start, even when I knew very little compared with more experienced colleagues. I felt so boosted by this.

Right from day one of working, I had stayed fit. A few months in, I found myself not just enjoying each working day but also looking forward to training at the gym most evenings. I was joyfully setting myself tough sessions, pushing myself and constantly improving my running times across a range of distances. I had given up rowing, I was a retired Olympian, yet I was getting fitter and felt more positive about training than I could remember ever being.

I was still in touch with some of the rowers who were friends, and one in particular, Katherine Grainger. When we got in a boat together the previous year, after Sydney, it instantly felt remarkable. We connected straight away and, with our love of racing, had high aspirations to take women's rowing to the next level and show that we could perform consistently at the highest levels internationally. But in the year following Sydney, at the World Championships, we finished out of the medals, coming fifth. It had been a short season as both of us had taken too much time off after the Sydney Olympics – Katherine to relax, travel and celebrate her Olympic medal; me to try and get over the devastating result and experience of the Sydney Olympics and the four difficult years leading up to it.

Katherine had been upset and surprised when I announced my 'retirement' as we both really believed we could compete together successfully at an Olympics. I don't think she realized how hard I was finding it to believe in myself and move on from the Sydney experience. I had come to the painful but inescapable realization that I could not recover mentally by staying on in training in the squad. Stepping away was already starting to give me a whole new lease of life. Thoughts started to creep into my mind: 'What if?' 'Could I possibly?' 'What if I had another go?' I even found myself daydreaming about racing in Athens. For a while, I thought this was a natural part of the 'moving on' process. But after a few months, I realized the thoughts were persisting, and I started to envisage in ever more practical terms how I might yet get to the start line of the Athens Olympics.

Those thoughts stayed in the back of my mind for several months. It was not an easy decision. I knew that if I was going to return, I would need to clarify why I was going back and how it was going to be different. I did not want to go back to the same experience as before. I was curious about whether I could find a new approach.

I knew from the start that my return could not all hinge on winning a medal, however much that remained part of my motives. No statistical analysis, probability equation or cost-benefit calculations would make it a sensible idea to spend six hours training, seven days a week, 49 weeks of the year to try to win a medal against the world's best who are training just as hard. With the additional evidence of my places in previous Olympics, seventh and ninth, my prospects did not look good. Even if I moved on from past evidence (though it was hard to shake off), the reality was that I could get injured or fall ill at any point or simply make a mistake in a race. All these situations were humanly possible and would be certain to happen to at least one dedicated, talented athlete with huge potential however hard they trained, however committed they were. As much as I longed for a better result, one that I felt would do justice to my potential, success needed to be framed as more than just a placing, a medal and a photo on a podium. I couldn't go back until I'd worked that out.

I had been hanging on and surviving mentally in the previous Olympiad, battling to cope with being told daily that I wasn't good enough. I had survived it. I had been one of the last ones standing. There was nobody tougher. But there aren't medals for that: I was living proof. Being tough had not made me a better athlete, nor a better person, friend or crewmate.

I knew I had to find a different way of viewing and responding to situations and developing a different dialogue in my head. It wasn't easy (and it's still a work in progress, to be honest) but was hugely helped by a much broader perspective that came from my diplomatic work. This was showing me a much bigger world beyond the rowing lake. I could already see that sport had given me hugely transferable skills in teamworking, managing pressure, focusing on what's important and learning constantly. On a deeper level, though, there still needed to be a shift in my sense of self-worth and the self-destructive belief that the losing result in Sydney defined me as an athlete and person.

I knew that it was possible to have a different experience as an Olympic athlete and to improve on a much broader basis: not just working on technique, strength and fitness, but also actively working on my mindset, behaviours and relationships with others.

At that time, these were areas being explored much more proactively by athletes, coaches and psychologists across Olympic teams looking for performance gains in all areas once the limits of physical training had largely been reached.

The culture when I returned was starting to change. We were still all measured and timed regularly, but now with more room to work on improvements that might take time to yield benefits. A new sports psychology approach was spreading through the British Olympic team, with a rigorous focus on all the aspects of sporting 'performance' to provide the best way to improve 'results'. Results remained a useful indication of progress but couldn't reliably predict long-term future performance. The two needed greater separation. On a day-to-day basis, the focus needed to be on maximizing all the ingredients of going fast – communication as well as strength, collaboration as well as technique, recovery as well as maximum physical power, mental preparation as well as fitness – and developing these as more meaningful criteria for daily success. This might not make you go faster tomorrow, but would all be crucial to maximizing longer-term performance gains.

Ongoing momentum was forged in a way that wasn't entirely dependent on results. We were always looking to improve; there were always things that had gone well and elements that needed to change, regardless of the result. Our psychologist helped us to become world-class at improving. That became a measure of success. Win or lose, I was still the same person focused on improving from one day to the next. This helped offset the rocky ups and downs that come from a sole focus on results. It also provided a more stable and enjoyable approach to training and performance.

The military have long been seen as leaders in human performance and leadership. The extreme situations they face and the need for adaptability have seen significant changes in how Western armies recruit and train. As an example, the US Marine Corps train and select their officers over a 10-week process. The course involves 20 mini problem-solving challenges and the candidates are assessed on qualities such as how they manage pressure, how quickly they understand tasks and how well they delegate. No part of the assessment looks at their ability to complete a challenge successfully. As Simon Sinek explains: 'They know that good leaders sometimes suffer mission failure and bad leaders sometimes enjoy mission success. The ability to succeed is not what makes someone a leader. Exhibiting the qualities of leadership is what makes someone a leader.'[1] This shows us how definitions of success in high-performance and high-stakes environments can and should expand to prioritize mindset, behaviours and relationships, communication and collaboration.

Another difference I saw on my return to row at a third Olympics was the different perspective I brought. I knew that I would only be back for two years until the next Olympics and would then continue with my diplomatic career. I wanted to enjoy those days, not have the uncertainty and unlikelihood of a winning result cast a negative shadow over them. That wasn't easy, and of course some days it was a grind and the old ways of thinking persisted inside my head (and in others' minds). But I was aware and grateful that my return to rowing brought more time in one of the places I have always felt most at home – in a boat, on the river, whatever the weather. I had definitely lost sight of this joy in the previous four years through the singularity of the focus on results, results, results and the sense of constant failure within the binary win–loss paradigm.

Regardless of the savage training, regardless of how fast or slow I was going, regardless of how exhausted I was, I loved being out in a boat, sensing the water moving beneath the hull and my crewmates moving alongside, seeing the seasons turn around us. Tapping into that was so obviously an important criterion for success, and I wondered how it had been overlooked previously?

My perspective had broadened exponentially having started a career outside rowing. I had addressed the taboo of 'life after rowing'. I knew it didn't mean I was disloyal or not dedicated to rowing, as it had felt previously. It was inspiring to contemplate an exciting future rather than an inevitable void after the Olympics, and this helped me to grasp this last opportunity to have another go in Athens.

I was due to start planning my first foreign posting and had succeeded in securing a diplomatic posting to Bosnia that would start in October 2004, within weeks of the Athens Olympics. Irrespective of whether I got selected for the Athens Olympics, or what results I achieved, I knew I had a life waiting to take me in new directions. (This also brought the slightly unusual benefit that when I wasn't training, I was studying Serbo-Croat to prepare for my upcoming first posting to Sarajevo. It seemed like madness to most people around me, but I loved it.) It gave me a broader identity than 'just' athlete. On those days when my performances weren't quite where I wanted them to be, when it felt like I was struggling to keep up and dropping in the pecking order, that broader sense of who I was kept me on track and able to regroup for the next day.

My decision to return wasn't made through a spreadsheet and cold metrics; it was driven by self-discovery, a passion for learning and a willingness to take some risks. It involved finding out what might be possible for someone who had not been sporty at school, had come seventh and ninth at her first two Olympics but still believed more was possible. I didn't know if I would achieve anything other than falling flat on my face, but I was curious to try and create a different experience and, still with some trepidation, I went back.

I performed well throughout all the winter testing and enjoyed working on many areas of performance that I had not been able to previously. I was doing well until the last set of final trials, the main point of selection for Olympic crews. Tricky crosswind conditions during a race in my weakest discipline, the single scull, combined with persistent shoulder pain saw me fall out of the top set, and as a result I dropped out of the coach's calculations for World Championship crews that year. In effect, it was game over.

I felt devastated, largely because I had not been able to show what I was capable of. But through all that frustration and exhaustion, it was a very different feeling from the one I had after Sydney. I was extremely disappointed and upset but didn't feel that drop into nothing, that fall into a void of worthlessness. I knew that I had tried everything, had raised the bar of what I was capable of physically and mentally, and had gained so much from finding a way to go back and try. I also knew that in a few days, I could pick myself up, phone the Foreign and Commonwealth Office HR department and be back at work, and that that was OK. In fact, it was more than OK; it was a great prospect.

A few days later, just as I was about to do that, I received a call from the chief coach, who needed me to take part in some further seat racing trials as they did not have enough numbers due to a couple of people having injuries. Suddenly, I found myself back in the mix. And somehow, I found myself back on the overall ranking that came out of that – the top four were to go into a quadruple scull, the next two athletes were to go into a double scull, and those ranked seventh and eighth – Katherine and myself – were to be put in a pair.

None of the coaches wanted us to form a pair again, having fallen short of the medals in the 2001 World Championships. We knew we had somehow secured an unlikely and therefore incredible second chance for a project we both still believed in. Within just a few weeks, we went to race at the first international regatta of the season, though strictly under the proviso that if we didn't win a medal, the coaches would break up our crew for good.

We went and returned with a World Cup silver medal; despite the caveat, we raced with a freedom and thrill, having been given this second chance against the odds. The same criterion was set for the next World Cup race, and this time we won. We collected a bronze at the third race and found ourselves selected to race in the World Championships in Milan in August 2003. We would collect something way beyond that medal too.

We arrived in Milan full of optimism and eager to race. But things didn't go smoothly. A number of unpredictable events threw us off track. Along with our boat being damaged early on in the week, there were weather disruptions and injury challenges. We got ourselves back on track in the semi-final, but in the course of that race, Katherine injured her back so badly she could barely get out of the boat afterwards. We weren't sure if the medics would let her race the final two days later, so a lot of stressed conversations between our coach and the medics followed over the next 48 hours as they worked out the best way forward. Katherine spent a lot of time lying on the floor, icing and stretching, with me often lying next to her, helping with the stretches or reading my book to keep her company.

The night before the final, at the last hour, the medics gave us the all clear to race. We felt a huge surge of joy and relief. Normally, I'd be feeling extreme nerves the night before a big race and moments of wanting to run away. I've heard athletes often talk about feeling as if they have a gun to their head. This time, I felt enormous gratitude and happiness at having the opportunity to race the next day. All thoughts of the outcome of the race had gone out of our minds, along with thoughts of our coaches and support team. No one talked about medals or winning. It was simply a chance to go out and do what we loved doing, and to try to deliver 250 of the best rowing strokes that we'd been visualizing over the last few days while lying on the floor.

Katherine and I pushed off for the final, excited about going to race in our beloved pair. We had a good warm-up, the boat was feeling relaxed and we were enjoying being back out in it after two days of stress and lots of lying flat and stretching. We even managed to see the funny side of a rather embarrassing practice start that saw me nearly steer us into our main opponents. We coolly lined up for the race.

We were firmly in the middle of the pack through the race, slipping a little behind the leaders at halfway, but always in touch. Of all the races I've raced, this was the one where we stayed 'in our bubble' most, mentally in the present moment throughout, focusing on the stroke we were on, building one to the next, immersed in our rhythm and race plan, not thinking about finishing positions, expectations or results. As we started our sprint to the line, at a point when our bodies were full of lactic acid and our lungs were gasping in oxygen to feed our muscles, the boat lifted up and felt light, as if flying along for little effort. I was so immersed in the moment that I barely realized when we crossed the finish line. As I sat recovering, Katherine shouted at me to look at the big screen beside the lake. I turned around and saw us on it, front and centre.

On a day when I had honestly barely thought about winning, I had won on the global stage. We had gone faster than the rest of the world on a day when it counted in the eyes of everyone watching. The journey of the months leading up to this seemed hard to fathom. I had gone from initially being dropped after final trials in April to becoming a world champion four months later. I had been part of the first-ever British women's team to win the World title in the coxless pairs event.

It was an unbelievably sweet moment to stand on the rostrum and hear the national anthem, but while others were starting to see me as an athlete in a different light, what it confirmed for me was really exciting. What I had won went way beyond that moment on the podium. I had found the beginnings of a better way to define what success means and a way to go about it. It was the beginnings of a new perspective, a new approach and what would, over time, become a new way of thinking, which I have come to call the 'Long Win'.

Long Win Thinking: The 3Cs of Clarity, Constant Learning, Connection

Long Win Thinking has emerged from stories, research and personal experience. I have taken thinking from across psychology, philosophy, anthropology and organizational studies and combined it with my own experiences, ranging from the Olympic frontline to the high stakes of international diplomacy and the inside view of leadership teams and boardrooms. All of this has fuelled my ongoing learning about what really helps us individually and collectively to be at our best, and what holds us back; how we can make a positive difference to the world around us and stand a better chance of being fulfilled and successful. It offers a way of tuning in to our thoughts, actions, relationships and impact at a deeper level.

There are three key areas underpinning Long Win Thinking, the 3Cs:

- Developing Clarity about what matters to us, clarifying plural success criteria over the long term and defining the experience we want to have along the way – this is about more than short-term metrics and finite outcomes. Clarity is about developing an emergent broader 'why' in our lives, a sense of purpose and a view on the impact we want to have on others and the world around us.

- Developing a Constant Learning approach to everything we do and defining success through personal growth rather than external results (which also helps us maximize those results) –this enables an ongoing focus on the 'how', the way we do things. It balances out the overwhelming focus on 'what' we do at work and at home – the endless to-do lists, deadlines and checklists of achievements that often control the way we live – and ensures we keep growing and developing even when we fail.

- Developing Connection proactively, investing in our relationships as a priority in everything we do – this focuses on the 'who' in our lives: our colleagues, partners, friends and others in our networks, as well as those we have yet to connect with. How are we actively looking to develop our connections with others, as opposed to comparing ourselves against others, so that we can move away from a competitive zero-sum game approach to life?

Clarity, Constant Learning and Connection are not finite activities to be ticked off. They are not key performance indicators (KPIs) to be project-managed via Gantt charts or flow charts. They are open-ended and ongoing themes to help us develop how we think about the world and see ourselves within it, and how we connect with others.

The 3Cs approach keeps us on track to grow our 'mindsets' and mental models, change and adapt our 'behaviours' as we develop, and build more meaningful 'relationships' to create opportunities to work together to achieve what we cannot achieve alone.

As David Brooks explains in *The Social Animal*, success isn't so much about what happens on the surface level of life; rather, it's about what happens one level down in 'the unconscious realm of emotions, intuitions, biases, longings, genetic predispositions, character traits, and social norms' that influence us and which we can then choose to perpetuate or challenge.[2] Long Win Thinking is aimed at embracing and developing the full spectrum of factors that influence how we define success and then pursue it.

I have found that when success is defined by narrow, short-term, temporary outcomes (such as targets, quarterly or annual results, crossing the line first, standing on a podium, league table positions) and non-human terms (such as bonuses, profits, medals, rankings, spreadsheets, certificates), and is fixed and imposed by others (such as bosses, partners, managers, coaches, parents), then our individual and collective performances and experiences are severely limited.

The 3Cs offer a broader, more expansive, more ambitious way forward to explore what's possible together. Over time, we start to see how what we are building and aiming for are not fleeting moments, trophies, short-term gains. Instead, we are building and aiming for meaningful experiences, lasting positive impact, and memorable stories that connect us, and which long outlive the trophies.

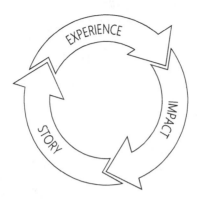

Each of the three themes, Clarity, Constant Learning and Connection, has shone out as essential in every organization I have worked with. Discussions, conversations, meetings and workshops have uncovered what leaders have really wanted to achieve and the deeper issues holding them back. These thought processes combine to form a new long-term approach for individuals, teams and organizations, and a means of escaping the traps of doing things the way they've always been done and overfocusing on short-term, temporary goals.

Not all workplaces, sports clubs or schools are set up to acknowledge the need to approach things differently; nor are they geared to support us as we develop our mindsets, beliefs, behaviours, habits and interactions. Despite that reality, these areas are nearly always within our own spheres of influence to try out, practise and develop.

Working on the 3Cs requires proactive choices and deliberate action. When we open ourselves up to finding the 'why' in our lives, to learn and connect more deeply with others, it brings fun, mastery and meaning to what we do. Together, these three areas can help us connect with ourselves and others around us and counteract the pull towards a narrow, limiting, short-term focus on winning at all costs.

In the following chapters, I look at Clarity, Constant Learning and Connection in turn, exploring how these can help us to escape our obsession with coming first and instead put Long Win Thinking into practice. This is not a definitive how-to manual or formulaic prescription. Rather, it sets up new rivers of thinking for us to redesign success for ourselves, with lots of questions to help us continually explore our potential and expand our ambitions. These themes are then illustrated further in the real life leaders' stories in Chapter 13.

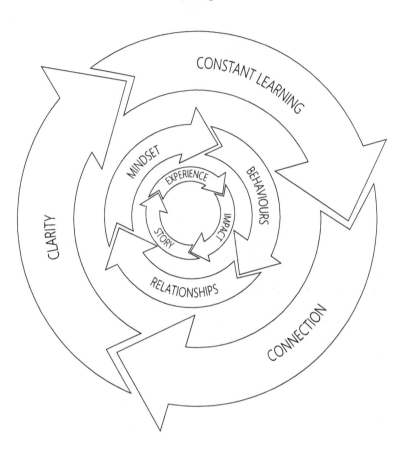

Chapter 10

Redefining Success

The Role of Clarity in Long Win Thinking

What could success look like?

Nervous friends wanting to protect me from repeating the devastating experience of Sydney had urged me to think twice about returning to try out for Athens: 'Don't go back to rowing, it's done, move forwards in your life.' It was vital that I set this up to be a step forward. My aims included medals for sure, but I couldn't stop there. By all reckonings, medals were highly unlikely, so there needed to be other gains to make that were at least as valuable.

Developing Clarity about what matters is an emergent, ongoing and dynamic process of thinking, listening, understanding and developing meaning. There is no fixed end point; it's not another metric to tick off. It's not something decided by someone else that feels abstract or irrelevant to our daily lives. It's an ongoing exploration of what's possible for ourselves and those around us, individually and collectively.

Two concepts are the heart of clarifying what matters: 'purpose' and 'perspective'. Both create a deeper focus on the 'why'. They are closely interconnected:

Purpose: what really matters?

Questions can be a huge help in developing our thinking. Instead of going into automatic pilot or simply following the logistics for the day, questions can help us tune in to what matters most. Rather than focusing on the day's long to-do list, ask yourself about the difference you want to make to your family, team, community or society, now and in the future. Articulate the things that drive you, that you care about, that energize you. Remember your strengths and how you can bring them to the day ahead. Consider the longer-term impact or legacy that you are working towards. Focus on what you can do today that will move you a step closer to that. What might your actions and choices mean to you when you look back on them later in life? These sorts of question help us connect better to ourselves and the world around us.

'Why' questions start in our own minds. We need Clarity about ourselves before starting to consider the external world and how we best fit in and contribute to it. Such questions can be simple yet are not easy to answer. Don't save them for rainy days but make them part of daily language, conversations and thoughts.

Let's look at two questions in a little more detail to support our thinking on this:

What gets you out of bed in the morning?

I'm not talking coffee, alarm clocks or young children. I mean: How do you feel when you wake up and think about the day ahead? Do you know what you want to get out of the day? (It doesn't need to be endless productivity!) What do you look forward to each day? What will make it a worthwhile day when you look back on it later? There is an extraordinary dynamic that we awaken in us by answering these simple questions that connect us to what matters to us.

When I ask people how often they ask these simple questions of themselves, let alone of colleagues, the answer ranges between never and rarely. I used to ask myself this every day when I was training as an Olympic athlete. Partly because when the alarm clock went off, the first thing I was aware of was the messages to my brain from different parts of my body saying not to get up. Everything ached: legs, back, shoulders, hips, arms. I needed a good reason to override those physiological messages and get out of bed. It wasn't enough just to ignore those messages and get up out of habit. I needed to turn up in the best frame of mind possible, ready to push my mental and physical boundaries that day, and to learn and stretch myself.

Asking this question daily became part of my thinking, and this continued after I retired from sport. I have definitely had times when I've not been sure I've had a good enough answer. But by realizing that, I was able to start to understand why and address the need for change. Questions like this tap into who we are and help connect that to what we do. They activate a different part of our brain from merely considering the logistics of alarm clocks, train times, electronic calendars and all the other things on our to-do lists.

Asking these questions is not about psyching ourselves up to do Olympic training or achieving world peace, but about recognizing what we want out of each day and how we can contribute to the world around us. I remember the inspirational sports leader Dame Sue Campbell telling an audience of leaders that 'No one gets out of bed for a KPI!' This is echoed in London Business School Professor Dan Cable's finding that 'people do not move much by KPIs and reward/penalty. These cause small changes. People move in larger ways by noble purpose, emotional connection, experimenting with new things, and leading by example.'[1]

Behavioural psychologists have proven that being clear about what matters to us and how that links to a broader purpose outside of ourselves is a key motivating factor and natural source of creativity and resilience. If you don't understand what energizes and drives you, it's much harder to find work and create a life that will deliver that. It's also much harder to commit to any wider, collective team or organizational vision if you don't know what's important to you in the first place.

Once you have answered this question for yourself, consider whether you know what the answer might be for your fellow colleagues, teammates and family members. I would never want to work in a team where I didn't know. I care much less about the skills and qualifications listed on a colleague's CV. They tell me mostly about the quality of a person's early educational opportunities. But if I need to work closely and collaboratively in a team with someone, I want to know who they are beneath the surface, what makes them tick, what they really care about. Only then can we start to co-create an effective way of working together, understand our differences and harness the benefits of those, and play to our collective strengths. Finding out how colleagues would answer this question unlocks a powerful source of energy and Connection – like gold dust in the elusive search to increase performance and engagement in the workplace. It involves expanding management beyond purely 'instrumental growth, efficiency and alignment'.[2]

Having asked a question that takes us to the heart of who we are as individuals, we are then ready to look outside ourselves at what matters.

What is the difference that you want to make?

This question starts to help connect who we are in relation to the world around us. What wider impact do we want to have? What do we want others to experience when they work with us or are part of a team with us? What change do we want to see in the world and how can we contribute to that? Building layers of Clarity in this area helps us to develop meaning beyond the short term and, through that, invest in lasting motivation.

Whatever 'level' you work at, from chief executive to administrative assistant, job contribution does not depend on your pay scale. The famous anecdote about President J.F. Kennedy's trip to NASA (the US National Aeronautics and Space Administration) demonstrates this perfectly. On visiting the Space Center, the President met a man in a white coat and hat and asked him what his role was. The man replied instantly and confidently: 'I'm helping to put a man on the moon.' The President asked further about what he did, and the man explained he was a cleaner. He knew that he needed to keep the floors spotless to ensure that no dirt got into the engineering construction of the shuttle. Random pieces of grit in the shuttle's structure could prove fatal under the pressure of travelling through the earth's atmosphere at high velocity. What is often overlooked when this anecdote is retold is not just that the janitor knew exactly how his role linked to the bigger picture, but that he believed in, and cared about, the importance and relevance of his own work to that wider mission. How many employees in organizations that we know would answer like the NASA janitor?

It is the link between the individual and a bigger purpose that is so powerful. In their article 'How winning organizations last 100 years', Alex Hill, Liz Mellon and Jules Goddard look at organizations across sectors that had flourished for a hundred years, including the Royal Shakespeare Company, NASA and Eton College. Their research reveals: 'Most businesses focus on serving customers, owning resources, being efficient and growing – but the Centennials [companies that last 100 years] don't. Instead, they try to shape society, share experts and focus on getting better not bigger.'[3]

Undoubtedly the ownership and governance of these companies, which comprise a range of models, are critical to creating an environment in which a longer-term purpose is central.

Jim Collins describes purpose as the 'extra dimension' that marks out what enables companies to go from 'good to great'.[4] Steve Jobs, the Apple co-founder, was a strong believer in the power of purpose. This enabled him to withstand short-term pressures in the name of creating excellent products. The goal was never to beat the competition or make money, but to make something that he and his colleagues could believe in and that would transform customers' lives. The language used by companies embracing a Long Win view sounds different, feels different, uses unusual words in a corporate context. Steve Jobs and Steve Wozniak spoke about their work being 'dedicated to the empowerment of man' back in 1977. Apple continues to allude to empowerment in the language used to end press releases, stating that its 'more than 100,000 employees are dedicated to making the best products on earth, and to leaving the world better than we found it'.[5] Unilever's Sustainable Living Plan (2010–2020 – now the Unilever Compass for Sustainable Growth) set out to decouple the company's growth from its environmental footprint, while increasing its positive social impact in line with the UN's Sustainable Development Goals. Google's mission is 'to organize the world's information and make it universally accessible and useful'.[6] The language of these goals is about being better, not simply bigger. They are ambitious yet responsible, and inherently acknowledge and incorporate the 3Cs of Clarity, Constant Learning and Connection.

Whether it's Victor Frankl's classic 1946 work *Man's Search for Meaning*, Simon Sinek's business bestseller *Start with Why* or the mounting research on the power of purpose, there is no shortage of compelling arguments about the importance of knowing why we do what we do and working out what brings meaning to our lives (and what doesn't). Purpose also offers alternative language to the metaphors of war and the related bias towards control and domination of others that we have seen in narrow winning narratives.

In 2016, the *Harvard Business Review* in partnership with EY published the results of a survey examining 'the business case for purpose'. In the report, purpose is defined as 'an inspirational reason for being which inspires and provides a call to action for an organization and its partners and stakeholders and provides benefit to local and global society'; it is also noted: 'Purpose-driven companies make more money, have more engaged employees and more loyal customers, and are even better at innovation and transformational change. It seems to be easier to win the game when you care about the game.'[7] (Notice here also the unusual association of the concept of 'caring' being associated with business success, moving away from the language of domination, competition and fighting.)

In the report, Harvard Professor Rebecca Henderson explains that

The sense of being part of something greater than yourself can lead to high levels of engagement, high levels of creativity, and the willingness to partner across functional and product boundaries within a company, which are hugely powerful... Once they're past a certain financial threshold, many people are as motivated by intrinsic meaning and the sense that they are contributing to something worthwhile as much as they are by financial returns or status.

For a long time, many businesses existed to provide services or goods and meet the need of the customer. Systems, incentives, targets and structures within organizations reinforced short-term shareholder and customer pressures. But these 'systems' no longer work when employees make career and work decisions based on long-term purpose.

Research, legislation and initiatives are all increasing in this area. Companies that integrate ESG data are shown to make better investment decisions and outperform their peers. The B Corporation movement that started in the US in 2007 now exists in over 60 countries, offering certification for businesses on the basis of their social and environmental performance. Contrary to fears that purpose might distract or detract from business performance, it has been shown to enhance shareholder value, so it's becoming a win–win.[8]

In 2019, over 180 leaders of the US Business Roundtable, including CEOs of Amazon and JPMorgan Chase, changed their decades-long creed of 'shareholder primacy', urging companies to prioritize protecting the environment and supporting workers' wellbeing alongside the pursuit of profit. Their statement refers to 'long-term value' and 'service' to others. The UK Institute of Directors launched a manifesto on corporate governance in the same year, including a call for businesses to have a clear purpose statement. Also, in 2017, the British Academy published a report titled *Principles for Purposeful Business*, describing its widespread research into why purpose should come before profit in business. The UK government passed the Public Services (Social Value) Act in 2012, which requires public sector organizations to think about the 'social value' that can be generated through the companies they choose to work with and expands the definition of what success and criteria for winning tenders looks like beyond purely financial metrics. In 2013, the G8 set up the Social Impact Investment Taskforce and then a broader steering group. The language of 'social impact' and 'return on social investment' now permeates throughout every sector of society (though sometimes with an overfocus on creating more metrics rather than more meaning).

It's not hard to find reasons that support purpose-led business, so why is it taking so much time to change mindsets? Businesses are stuck in a gap between 'knowing' and 'doing'. Corporate purpose is rapidly becoming a global phenomenon but action to put this into practice is puzzlingly slow. Although US economist Milton Friedman's notion that a firm's purpose is 'just making money' has largely been discredited, the alternative is not yet understood with as much Clarity. As we shift from a superficial, material priority to a deeper cause, a different cultural shift is required to change mindsets, behaviours and relationships. We need to translate these findings and reports about the case for purpose, and the purpose statements that exist, into different ways of thinking, working and connecting with each other. CEO and author Robert Phillips has noted that although many leaders see the value, socially and commercially, of their enterprises being purpose-led, they are prevented from making this a reality by cultural or operational factors in their organizations. Phillips describes purpose-led business as a series of lasting relationships, based on commitment and expectations, with all stakeholders of organizations.[9] He points out the trap of accounting for purpose through metrics, which, as we have seen in previous chapters, are too easily created or skewed.

My work takes me to annual conferences and strategy awaydays where a company purpose or mission may be discussed, typically arranged on an annual or six-monthly basis. These are usually fine gatherings in splendid venues with well-meaning discussions and a great lunch menu! But that's not how meaning and purpose work. These events can, at best, be a useful first step. If discussions on purpose are not part of what happens thereafter, then those meetings are pointless. If the 'why' is not part of the daily workplace, in the live exchanges and decisions made within the real-world pressures we all face, then purpose is not leading the business.

On one occasion, I was asked to work with a team to help develop their purpose and culture. The first thing I did was to ask why the team existed, how it contributed to the wider organization's purpose. They were a core part of the business and were able to tell me what they did, yet found it difficult to articulate why they did it. When it came to how their team fitted into the purpose of the company, the HR manager informed me that the company hadn't yet worked out its overall purpose and had delayed that because of changes to the leadership team, so we would have to go ahead without that. It's a strange logic to apply to an organization. How could we build a sense of team purpose, ways of working and culture without being able to connect and relate that to the bigger picture? Of course, even though the company had not set its official purpose, it was indirectly communicating its attitude to purpose by leaving its employees to work in a vacuum, make assumptions about the company's purpose or, most likely, switch off from the greater value and purpose of their work together.

We all have stories of attending meetings without knowing why we're there or working on projects without understanding how they fit into the bigger picture. Every time we do that, we limit ourselves and undermine what's possible.

We can see examples of purpose being explored innovatively and inspirationally across the sporting landscape, particularly in team sports. At the top level, most teams can't improve through training harder or longer. The drive to make a team more than the sum of its parts leads sports teams to explore all possibilities, including how purpose impacts on performance. Certain teams and clubs have gone above and beyond to build a different mentality and culture, and a deeper sense of purpose.

The New Zealand All Blacks rugby team provide an example of an incredibly successful team who have closely linked their identity to their country's history, traditions and culture over a long period of time. 'In answer to the question, "What is the All Blacks' competitive advantage?", key is the ability to manage their culture and central narrative by attaching the players' personal meaning to a higher purpose.'[10] The All Blacks idea of 'leaving the jersey in a better place' for the next player brings an incredible sense of purpose, perspective and humility that underpins their sustained levels of high performance. The All Blacks mantra 'better people make better All Blacks' ensures investment in developing players so that they can contribute beyond the rugby field, knowing that this will enhance their sporting performance too.

The British women's Olympic hockey team, nicknamed 'the history makers', embodied this inherent sense of purpose at the 2016 Rio Games. They won an incredible Olympic gold medal in a tightly contested final match against the favourites, the Netherlands. There was little technical difference; if anything, the Dutch were slightly better. But the British team dynamic created a different response to the twists and turns during the match, which ended up in a penalty shoot-out. It was this that separated the two teams in the end. The British team's culture was rooted in a wider meaning behind what they were trying to do, which helped them optimize their performance in that match. Over many years they had developed a purpose-driven culture based around a mission to 'create history and inspire a generation' – no mention of winning or medals there. But it was that wider mission that inspired them to perform at the level required to win gold in Rio.

The FIFA (Fédération Internationale de Football Association) Women's World Cup in 2023 saw an extraordinary awareness across all the teams, whether from the UK, Nigeria or Australia, that their greater purpose lay beyond the scoreline. Losers and winners consoled each other after hard-fought matches, all connected by a shared opportunity to be pioneers for women's sport. All the teams seemed aware of their moment in the spotlight, watched back home by a generation of girls who they wanted to inspire to follow their dreams, whatever they might be.

Right to Dream has pioneered a progressive football academy model, founded in 1999 with its first site in Ghana and now present in Egypt and San Diego as well as Copenhagen, where it owns FC Nordsjælland. The model provides opportunities to young people based on a holistic youth development model that combines education and character development alongside specialist football training. One of my own most moving sporting experiences was seeing the Women's Oxford–Cambridge Boat Race take place on the same course that the men have rowed in this world-famous event, dating back to 1829. Back in the 1990s when I was a student, I was told (by many men) that the women's race would never be equal to the men's. After long years of hard work by many in and around our sport, that change finally happened in 2015. Although our light blue side lost that day, that race was about so much more than who came first. It was about equality, progress and challenging the status quo. It is when sport has meaning beyond the result that we start to glimpse the greater power and potential of sport.

Many brilliant charitable organizations and foundations work through sport to help others and address major social issues at local and international levels. From seeing football as a means of educating children about landmines in Bosnia to seeing sport inspire disadvantaged children to explore their potential when given the opportunity to play, I have found sports (and athletes) are at their best when connected to a wider purpose. More than one Olympic champion have told me that the work they do for charities like the Laureus Foundation has brought greater meaning to their lives than their previous purely competitive existence did.

A sense of purpose, and the social responsibility that comes with that, requires us to develop a wider sense of perspective and Connection to the world around us, linking closely to the third C, Connection. No one can achieve their life's purpose through a quarterly set of results, and no one can sum up what being part of a team means without having connected with others.

Perspective: what is our timescale for success?

A focus on purpose naturally extends our perspective on time. Rather than focusing on a single moment in time that you assume will fulfil your dreams – winning medals, getting promoted or passing exams – you can consider the future and what these trophies may mean over the longer term. What will the world look like when you have been successful? How will others experience the difference you want to make? Then come back to today. What can you do today to set yourself up for the longer term?

Perspective matters. Some of the stories we've seen so far – feeling empty after winning a gold medal or unfulfilled by earning a huge salary and large bonus – show that meaningful success cannot be defined by a single moment in time when a one-off goal or milestone is reached. Indeed, activities innately characterized by a one-off 'win or lose' moment, such as events in the Olympics, seem to lack meaning and fulfilment unless connected to something beyond that moment.

Long Win Thinking stretches our perspective in two directions: firstly, in relating to a longer-term purpose, as discussed above; and, secondly, in thinking about how we find success in each day. If we only focus on a short-term target or deadline, then there are many things we don't *need* to invest in today, such as communication, experimenting and deepening relationships. But if we connect today to our longer-term purpose, then being successful today requires investment in things crucial to achieving our long-term purpose: building collaborative partnerships, trying out new ways of doing things, resting well and investing in reflection time.

Developing a performance mindset

As we saw in Chapter 9, sports psychologists work with athletes to separate concepts of 'performance' and 'results' – the first they can control and work every day to improve; the second sits in the future and is affected by many external factors beyond their control. A constant focus on the former is the best way to achieve the latter. It requires us to let go of thinking about outcomes, which is easier said than done in many sports environments. I believe this shift in perspective was critical to the way I approached competing at my third Olympics.

It really sank in when, at a point when I had few international wins under my belt, I won one particular World Cup race. It was a relief and a joy to experience winning again. We hadn't raced our best race by any means, but the result was good. Often, I had experienced it the other way around. As we walked our boat back to the bay to meet our coach, he didn't look pleased. 'Good result! Tell me about the performance.'

We were celebrating having won; all around us the physiotherapists and support team were cheering us and about to come and give us a celebratory hug. They hesitated as soon as they got close enough to hear that our conversation with our coach was not a simple round of congratulatory comments and back-slapping.

We felt aggrieved and defensive: we had won the race – wasn't that the whole point of what we were doing? But the conversation that followed helped me to understand that it wasn't, and the penny finally dropped about the role of a performance mindset in redefining success and how to pursue it.

We didn't know how to reply to the coach at first and went a few times round the loop of talking about how good it felt to get a winning result, while he grew increasingly irritated. He said: 'The result was good but let's talk about the performance... tell me about it.'

Suddenly, we realized the distinction he was making, and we started to answer his question. We said that the start had been good; we had executed certain key things we had been working on. But our transition from the start into the rhythm hadn't gone as planned. We were still taking too many strokes per minute well after the start to find a sustainable rhythm that we knew we would need to develop by the time of the Olympics. The strong tailwind meant that we managed to scramble along without losing too much boat speed, but in other conditions that strategy could be disastrous. We were chasing a hurried rhythm that made it harder for us to respond to other crews and hadn't executed what we had practised in training to create a more solid rhythm based on longer individual strokes. We weren't able to make any moves in the middle of the race or to manage changes in wind direction very well either. Somehow, we had stumbled through the sprint to the end and stayed ahead. We were unlikely to be able to get away with that again.

Our coach had got a better answer and that meant we could move on to discussing how to improve our performance next time. We were distinguishing between 'performance' and 'result'. Only by analyzing our *performance* could we start to get the information needed to learn how to improve next time. Only by reviewing our *performance* could we work out what had worked well and continue to build on that and decide where to make changes in our next block of training. The *result* told us none of that. In fact, the result was potentially distracting and unhelpful to the process of learning and improving next time.

This separation of performance and result is becoming second nature to most elite athletes. It doesn't mean that results aren't important – far from it – but it recognizes that the way to achieve better results is to focus on optimizing all the performance elements that an athlete can develop. Results can never be guaranteed or controlled. They depend on a range of external factors, ranging from weather conditions to referees and umpires, not to mention competitors. The same principles apply to business contexts, but often the concepts of performance and results overlap and really both refer to results.

I know first-hand that it's a completely different experience to sit on the start line of a race waiting to deliver your best performance than to sit there feeling that you have to win. Those two experiences are worlds apart, and the performances that follow usually are too.

The day that Katherine and I beat the rest of the world at the 2003 World Rowing Championships in Milan, winning had been further from our minds than it had been at any other championships. We went out to race focusing on the performance, not the result. We were free of expectations, focusing simply on how we rowed, unencumbered by thoughts of the impending result. It's a subtle but significant distinction, which brings a hugely positive impact on performance under pressure.

In the final few metres of that race, as we overtook the three leading crews, the boat was flying, skimming over the surface of the water. I was so intensely absorbed in the moment that I was unaware of where we had finished after we crossed the line. Before I looked up to find out, I felt a moment of deep joy, amid the fatigue, that we had been able to reach that place of peak performance where our extreme effort was so synchronized it felt effortless and the boat seemed to accelerate with unstoppable momentum. That was why I got up in the mornings to train in a rowing boat for hours on end.

Once I did look up, I slotted into the conditioned behaviour to look at the screen and respond to the result. Of course, we were overjoyed to win, especially as it was so unexpected. For me, it was a rare highpoint in my career to date. There's no doubt, with my track record, that I was hugely relieved to have a result at last that would give me the credibility in my own mind, as well as in others', that had been lacking for so long. Yet it's still the moment before the line that I treasure most. It's why I loved the sport of rowing, and what enabled me to do it two or three times a day, seven days a week, for years. It's also why I think it's almost impossible to win in a sport you don't fall in love with first. It's perilous to fall in love only with the idea of being world or Olympic champion.

Play, joy, flow

It's that important element of play, of being in the moment and loving what you are doing, regardless of where it will take you, which is so powerful and positive for both a sense of wellbeing and performance. It's the easy win–win that ironically gets overlooked in the obsessive focus on results and desperation to come first. We can learn from an early age that play is not valued by grown-ups, but certain winning results are. I have read so many interviews with cricketers, footballers and Olympians whose experience of competing at the elite level kills the joy of sport, leads to mental health issues or early retirement, or time away from the sport to rekindle that love of simply playing around with a bat, ball or oar.

The one sportsperson who stands out as staying closest to the spirit of pure love for sport is the legendary athlete Daley Thompson. I don't think it's a coincidence that he was also one of the most successful athletes ever, winning the Olympic decathlon title twice, breaking the world record four times and remaining unbeaten for nine years. He had such fun at athletics that he continued to train with friends and former competitors every Saturday morning down at Battersea track after retiring. He gave away all his medals; pieces of metal weren't what brought him joy. When asked why he still went to the track regularly after retirement, he would always ask in return: 'Why would I stop doing something that's so much fun with my friends?'

But it is interesting to look back on how commentators and spectators criticized and even condemned him for his playfulness, for not taking sport seriously enough, for not fitting the image expected of winners and heroes. What they totally failed to appreciate was that it was this ability to maintain a spirit of playfulness in moments of crushing pressure that was his greatest skill and enabled such utter athletic brilliance. I got to know him in the Olympiad leading up to Sydney. When describing the training we were flogging through and our 'sackcloth and ashes' dedication to each session, I remember him saying to me: 'You lot are taking it too seriously. You need to have more fun!' I couldn't relate to it at the time – how could an athlete aiming to win be 'too serious'? In hindsight, it was brilliant advice.

In my year away from the Olympic team, I trained for fun at weekends with Daley and a bunch of friends. I loved the challenge of track sessions that my rower's body had not been honed for; they loved the challenge I set them of sessions on the rowing machine. This was a key part of learning to love sport again that was instrumental in returning for a third Olympics.

Learning scientist Elizabeth Bonawitz emphasizes how essential play is to the human development experience. In research around the benefits of play for children, Bonawitz and colleagues found that 'children chose harder settings when playing for fun rather than trying to win'. They found that what matters is intrinsic rewards: feeling curious, following our creativity, bonding with others. And even when the children exploited the game to win, there was still a part of them that wanted to play for fun. For example, some kids chose to wear silly costumes even when sincerely trying hard to win. There are lots of lessons for education and youth sport from this research, where all too often 'serious sport' removes important fun and play elements too quickly. The state of mind associated with play, with being totally involved in what we are doing, is a crucial part of being 'in the zone', a 'flow' state associated with peak performance, low stress and creativity.[11] Sports psychologists support athletes to move away from a state of 'outcome hijack'[12] towards being much more in the present, accepting and tuning in to our thoughts and feelings, such as through practising mindfulness.

The physiology of being present and getting into the zone involves tapping into a different part of our brain, from where the fight or flight responses are centred. Being in flow is a deeply fulfilling experience: there is no fear of failure, just the complete absorption in the activity itself. It is a timeless rather than time-bound concept and relates to internal values rather than any external markers or results. (It's similar to the unselfconscious immersion which psychologist Abraham Maslow describes as 'peak experiences' and which has become part of the branch of psychology known as positive psychology, a close relative of sports psychology.)

Although being in the zone is often associated with winning sporting performances, it is often overlooked that the state of mind that enables these brilliant performances is one that is completely unfocused on winning, free from fear or anxiety over outcomes.[13]

It's an approach I've since discovered also sits at the heart of comedy improvisation. Businesses trying to improve creative thinking and communication sometimes bring in improv experts to try to help staff reconnect with the playful part of their brain. I remember one comedian working with some managers in small groups asking them to tell a story one word at a time, taking it in turns. It was fascinating seeing the challenges. You can't control where the story is going; you have to rely completely on others and listen and respond in the moment. The groups that created some momentum started having fun, became absorbed in what they were doing and were listening actively to each other. In other groups, some participants tried to exert control on the story and force it in a particular direction, frustrating themselves and others in the process. Some tried to come up with a 'clever strategy' which generally only messed things up and left the group adrift. Summing up, the improv expert shared the fundamental rule of improvisation: 'You have to play to play – not play to win.'

Media perspectives and sporting myths

Of course, the media continue to focus relentlessly on results. Much of what we watch, read and hear hasn't really moved on despite the shifts in focus, training methods, mental preparation of elite athletes and approaches to coaching.

If you start to look for it, you can often see the opposing approaches in sporting interviews. Journalists typically ask athletes after a performance at a major championships, whether it's the World Cup, Commonwealth Games or Olympics, how they feel about finishing first, second, third, fourth, fifth... (Below fifth, they rarely get interviewed!) The athletes' reply typically focuses on their performance rather than purely their placing, in line with the performance mindset described above. They focus on whether they achieved a 'personal best', regardless of the outcome, because they are used to thinking about and analyzing their performance, first and foremost. They want to move on to learn and improve, and to work out what they can take from that race into the next one. Competitions become an opportunity for learning how to go faster next time, as we see in the next chapter on Constant Learning.

After winning a race in the 2018 Commonwealth Games, I remember watching Olympic champion swimmer and world record holder Adam Peaty say in his post-race interview that he wasn't happy with his performance. He knew something wasn't working right. The interviewer seemed confused. How could there be anything wrong if he had won? The athlete seemed confused that the interviewer didn't understand. Peaty was focused on the performance, on what was working and what needed to be improved. For him, the concepts of excellence and winning were inherently distinct. He knew something wasn't quite where it needed to be in his performance but couldn't quite explain, and in another race, a couple of days later, he came second, ending his unbeaten streak of four years.

After that race, the interviewer expected disappointment and asked nervously about how he might feel about ending his long run of victories. This time, Peaty was much more upbeat: he had worked out what it was that wasn't quite right. What he hadn't been able to work out from the first race where he had won, he now understood better, and so felt confident that he and his coach would be able to address the issue. The mismatch again in mood and language between the interviewer and Adam Peaty showed how strongly the performance approach is part of an elite athlete's way of thinking and breathing, and yet how little it is understood outside that world.

Football managers interviewed after matches are typically asked a 'winning'-focused question – 'How do you feel about losing that match?' or 'What do you think about the points you won (or dropped) today?' Football managers used to talk in post-match interviews about league positions and points needed, and be upbeat when winning and downbeat when losing. They were on a constant rollercoaster. Most football managers now give a performance-focused answer. They don't respond much about points won or lost; rather, they focus on the performance on the pitch: 'The defence was good but we didn't create enough chances upfront.' 'The midfield were strong but we need to work on our defence.' In a performance mindset, there are always some elements of the performance which are working well and other areas that require improvement, regardless of the result.

I have been involved with the Oxford–Cambridge Boat Race for some years, having rowed there as a student and then later having joined and chaired the executive committee. If you listen to the

TV commentators each year (and I've been one of them), certain phrases are repeated annually for this classic win or lose race: 'it's a gladiatorial battle on the Thames', 'it's win or lose', 'there are no prizes for coming second', 'the winners are heroes, the losers have nothing'. It's not just in the commentary box that those phrases can be heard. It's a world that seems unavoidably defined by win–lose thinking – but I could see that was limiting performance.

When looking at how we might prepare our Cambridge women's crew to race on the first-ever women's Boat Race on the historic Tideway course in London in 2015 in front of a global audience, I realized we needed to invest in sports psychology support. My experience of how performance thinking had developed at Olympic level was making me question the traditional gladiatorial narrative. I could see how it would prevent our students from performing to their best. The nearly two centuries of culture and mythology about this binary race made losing personally catastrophic to the students in the losing crews. This made no sense. I could see that this was a race that we would have to lose sometimes. While we would always seek to go as fast as we could, the overall event would not last long if one side won all the time. The natural cycle of fortune and talent meant that one side would never win permanently. That meant we needed to make sure we knew what it meant to win well *and* to lose well. Yes, 'losing well'. It can still feel hard to say that out loud.

It was clear to me that we needed to redefine what winning meant: success had to be about delivering the crew's best performance in the race, developing each athlete's potential and maximizing the broader invaluable life skills that are honed in the tough sporting programme run alongside a demanding academic schedule. We were lucky enough to bring in psychological support from Kate Hays, who went on to run the English Institute of Sport's psychology team and then work with the Lionesses, England women's football team. She cut through the old Boat Race myths and helped instil a performance-minded approach.

As a club, we needed to raise our ambitions beyond simply beating Oxford, despite that being the main event of the year; otherwise we would limit ourselves and tie our standards to theirs. We wouldn't be able to support the student rowers to fulfil their potential and improve our programme year on year if we allowed ourselves to ride the win–lose rollercoaster of euphoria and despair each time. Of course, there is sadness on the day if a crew loses, and a shared empathy for that feeling we all know. But what matters far more is reviewing how close they got to their best performance, understanding what worked well and less well to take into the following year's programme (regardless of the result) and, most important of all, celebrating what the students have gained over the season that they'll take with them into the rest of their lives: resilience, self-awareness and friends for life.

Olympic rowing champion Ben Hunt-Davis explains in his book, *Will It Make the Boat Go Faster?*, co-authored with Harriet Beveridge, how crucial it was for his rowing crew to separate performance from results to achieve a step change in the mindset and actions of the crew, which had consistently finished sixth to ninth at World Championships and Olympics for nearly a decade. It gave them a basis on which to change their approach to nearly every aspect of their training and achieve a stunningly different result at the Sydney Olympics in 2000, where they became the first British eight to win gold since 1912.[14]

People love to touch Olympic medals. There's a magic about them that comes from their rarity, the achievement that they represent and the narrative that surrounds them. Olympic champions are celebrated guest speakers at corporate conferences and events. There's a set narrative that almost all champions obey – a story of challenges that ends with a glorious victory. But I think these events, and these athletes, miss a massive trick. Beyond feeling a frisson of excitement and brief motivational surge, I don't think audiences walk away with anything of lasting value. That's simply not how science tells us that we learn. Nor what I've seen in practice. We need to hear a much broader set of stories related to performance, not just a formulaic version of the 'hero's journey'. Only then can we start to think about how their stories have meaning for our own context and learn something useful.

Paradoxically, a performance-focused approach offers a lot to those with a results-only focus, if they could only allow themselves to stop focusing on the results long enough to realize this. But it would be wrong to focus on that as the only benefit. Prioritizing performance over results also shifts the values in an environment and changes the experience of all involved. If 'how' you win matters, then an approach that involves corruption, cheating, doping and bullying has no part in that picture of success. If 'how' you win matters, and performance is prioritized over the next short-term result, then our perspective on time starts to shift too.

Steve Magness collated numerous research studies across business and sport, all demonstrating that 'the inner drive matters more than the outer' when it comes to resilience, satisfaction, engagement, adaptability and motivation to go the extra mile.

Research by Teresa Amabile and Steven Kramer shows the power of managers focusing on progress, rather than results, each day at work if they want to increase joy, engagement and creativity. Amabile and Kramer set out to better understand why dismal management and poor motivation was so prevalent in the workplace. They worked through almost 12,000 diary entries depicting the key events in a working day, revealing what mattered in people's 'inner work lives'. The most positive event influencing people at work was 'making progress in meaningful work', described as 'work that people care about' and then having that progress recognized. 'Nourishing' relationships was also important. Not hitting targets, not stunning annual results, not receiving a bonus. 'Helping [people] succeed at making a difference virtually guarantees good inner work life and strong performance.'[15]

Long-termism

Once we no longer expect value and worth to be justified through short-term outcomes, we can start to play a longer game. Public philosopher Roman Krznaric describes the different parts of our brains that we can choose to develop: the part that he calls our 'acorn brain' (frontal lobe) that is geared for long-term thinking and planning.[16] Working out how to deal with the climate crisis, synthetic biology, global pandemics or AI requires us to think decades ahead.

We've already seen how crucial time is to our picture of success and the behaviours that flow from that. If a government is only in power for four years, it is naturally drawn to depict measures of success in terms of what can be achieved in four years or less. This causes a disconnect in addressing global issues which clearly cannot be 'solved' within four years. In the business world, the relentless short-term rhythm of stock market reporting and quarterly and annual company cycles makes it hard to align work with longer-term purpose and impact, even though evidence shows that this yields better returns and value over time.

Growing numbers of groups and organizations are looking for ways to change this trend towards short-termism across Western society. In 2019, Eric Ries founded the Long-Term Stock Exchange to try and create a new way for companies to raise capital while keeping their focus on long-term rather than short-term results. In *The Lean Startup*, Ries notes that fewer companies had been going public over the previous two decades; those that had, suffered many problems due to pressure from short-term investors. He was determined to create an alternative and reduce a major obstacle for entrepreneurs.[17]

Businesses still report to financial markets based on accounting principles and concepts from the 1970s. In 2017, the Embankment Project for Inclusive Capitalism brought together more than 30 global companies to develop and test a framework to help companies measure and report the long-term value they create. They found that as little as 20% of a company's value was captured on its balance sheet, down from about 83% in 1975. The report notes that the majority of a typical company's real value is reflected in intangible aspects that are difficult to measure, such as innovation, culture, trust and corporate governance.[18]

In 2019, Klaus Schwab, founder and Executive Chairperson of the World Economic Forum, advocated moving away from GDP as the 'key performance indicator' in economic policymaking, embracing independent tracking tools to assess progress under the Paris Agreement on climate change and the Sustainable Development Goals, and ensuring that all businesses report on their ESG impact. Change is happening, but there is still a long way to go. A lot of old ways of thinking still need to be unlearnt and reframed.

In 2018, UK campaigner Ella Saltmarshe and Beatrice Pembroke launched The Long Time Project, sparked by a devastating report from the Intergovernmental Panel on Climate Change. They point to the damage done by prioritizing personal short-term gains over the future collective good and resolve to support the development of 'longer perspectives on our existence' in order to change the way that we behave.[19]

> In the face of global anxiety, we put our heads down and our horizons get closer and closer. The problem is that the tunnel vision of short-term thinking is leading to decisions that might mean we are only left with a short term as a species.

They highlight a distinction between 'long-termism' and 'long-timism'. Long-termism means predicting, forecasting and planning for the future. Long-timism means cultivating an attitude of care for the world beyond our lifetimes. Our workplaces are full of forecasting, and they want to move towards a greater emphasis on care for the future we are forecasting.

Saltmarshe and Pembroke also emphasize the important role that culture can play in creating a longer-term perspective. Concepts such as 'deep time' challenge our short-term mindsets, referring to the philosophical concept of geologic time covering the age of the Earth, determined to be around 4.55 billion years.

Connecting across generations provides greater perspective. Some Indigenous cultures, such as that of the North American Iroquois, emphasize emotional connections to long lineage, inspiring a sense of responsibility to care for future generations. The Oglala Lakota tribe, native to South Dakota, act and take decisions bearing 'in mind that our seven generations are sitting with us already'.[20]

University of California Berkeley has developed a new course in the faculty of engineering called 'Thinking like a good ancestor: Finding meaning in the technology we build', demonstrating a new and broader perspective on a career in engineering. The University of Cambridge set up the Centre for the Study of Existential Risk, to study and mitigate risks that could lead to human extinction or civilizational collapse, and the Institute for Sustainability Leadership. The University of Oxford founded the Future of Humanity Institute to develop multidisciplinary research across mathematics, philosophy and social sciences on 'big-picture questions about humanity and its prospects'.[21]

The Network of Institutions for Future Generations was set up to share knowledge and disseminate best practice of institutions engaged in the promotion of responsible, long-term governance worldwide. Similar institutions are starting to appear at a government level: Wales has a Future Generations Commissioner following the introduction of the Well-being of Future Generations (Wales) Act 2015. This was the first piece of legislation in history to place regenerative and sustainable practice at the heart of a government. The Act connects social, environmental, economic and cultural wellbeing and aims to improve decision-making on the complex interconnected issues of our time. Jane Davidson, the Welsh Minister for Environment, Sustainability and Housing, who introduced the legislation, is one of the Long Winners in Chapter 13. The UK has an All-Party Parliamentary Group for Future Generations, and Finland has a Committee for the Future. Wellbeing now sits at the heart of policy in the Scottish, Icelandic and New Zealand governments. But in many countries, these initiatives are very much in their infancy and remain on the edge of the political debate in most cases.

The Long Now Foundation is a non-profit organization set up in the US in 1966 (or 01966 in their 10,000-year framework, based on the idea that most civilizations last 10,000 years) as a long-term cultural institution. It offers guidelines for slower/better thinking in contrast to today's faster/cheaper mindset, through taking the long view, rewarding patience, allying with competitors and not taking sides.[22] The foundation has several projects, including a clock that will tick for 10,000 years, designed to make us all think about an expanded sense of time and the massive generational impact of our decisions, and encouraging us to become more responsible. A prototype is displayed in the Science Museum in London, and the actual clock is being built inside a mountain in Texas. It is being constructed out of durable materials and is powered by renewable sources. It will be easy to repair using Bronze Age technology (a nod to the theory that human societies of the future could easily be more primitive than our own).

The foundation set up a seminar series to debate areas of long-term concern. These debates are not set up on a win–lose basis but with the purpose of fostering long-term responsibility and deeper understanding of key social issues. There are two debaters. The first takes the podium and makes their argument. Then the next takes their place, but before they can present their counterargument, they must summarize the former's argument to that person's satisfaction. In this way, before the second debater begins to share their own views, they actively demonstrate respect and good faith. Only when the first debater agrees that the second has got it right can the second continue with their own argument. When finished, the first debater must then summarize it to the second's satisfaction. The goal is not to 'win' the debate but to come away with a deeper understanding of the issue after the event than before. It's a far cry from the debating societies of the Oxford Union and other famous societies which have been the learning ground for many politicians.

It's a mindset shift away from the daily to-do list towards 'cathedral thinking'. This is a powerful visual concept stretching back to medieval times when architects, stonemasons and artisans laid plans and began the construction of cathedrals, which took many lifetimes to complete and had an enduring purpose across generations to create safe havens, places of worship and community gathering.

The concept has been applied to space exploration, city planning and any other long-term goals needing decades of foresight and planning for the benefit of future generations. Greta Thunberg calls for cathedral thinking to tackle the climate crisis: 'We must lay the foundation while we may not know exactly how to build the ceiling.'[23] There are super-future thinkers, deep ecologists and black sky thinkers scattered around the world, engaged in different ways in 'cathedral science', with values of collaboration, ambition, faith and adaptability central to their endeavours.

Margaret Heffernan describes the vital importance of 'cathedral projects', which 'challenge to the utmost our capacity to imagine and adapt a future we can't see or predict' while simultaneously demonstrating 'our capacity to deal creatively with what is uncertain, complex, ambiguous, invisible'. Cathedral projects rarely start with a business case or plans to drive economic growth or solve practical problems; instead, they usually have a strong spiritual character. Heffernan's interviews with research leaders at CERN, the European Organization for Nuclear Research, reveal minds that are both disciplined to be scientifically precise and open to improvising, changing, learning and unlearning. The technical director of the Large Hadron Collider explains:

> you can't have prima donnas, you need team players who aren't trying to prove, they're trying to understand. People who are open and share and like searching for surprises. That aren't always worrying about the outcome, aren't always thinking about themselves. People have to share knowledge or the cathedral can never be built.[24]

This brings alive the way in which our interactions and relationships are driven by the perspective that we take.

Personal success

Let's consider how we each create a personal philosophy of success. A substantial body of self-help literature advises on how to 'win at life', and research into happiness is prolific. It is a confusing world to navigate.

Rather than searching for answers, challenging our own assumptions might be most useful. The inclusion of comparison in our definition of personal success is one to question. As we saw in philosopher Alain de Botton's criticism of how society rejects 'an ordinary life', comparison can lead to widespread mental health problems. In *Barking Up the Wrong Tree*, Eric Barker notes that 'trying to be a relative success compared to others is dangerous' and recommends having multiple yardsticks across happiness, achievement, significance and legacy, with quality counting as much as quantity.[25]

Material gains is another obvious area to re-examine. Many people chase salary increases, promotions or lottery wins as the means to happiness, despite the fact that earning above a certain amount has not been found to increase happiness or emotional wellbeing.[26] A 2008 Dutch study into lottery winners found that six months after the fact, winning the lottery did not make households any more or less happy.[27] This built on a classic study in 1978 which compared the experiences of a group of lottery winners, a control group and a group of people who had become paralyzed through accidents. With a focus on material outcomes, you would expect a huge variance in experience between the lottery winners and the accident victims. However, this was not what the research found. Lottery winners weren't significantly happier a year after their win, nor were accident victims as desperately unhappy as you would expect. Moreover, this study found that this perpetual misreading of the situation by observers (that lottery winners are deliriously happy and fulfilled and accident victims tragically distraught) was really damaging to both lottery winners and accident victims.[28] Such assumptions made it much harder for both groups to feel that they belonged and were accepted by their social environment, which was what had the greatest effect on their happiness.

It's another way of looking at the earlier point about the separation of performance from results – that focusing on outcomes is deeply counterproductive. It also highlights how human Connection (regardless of outcomes) is the key factor in our lives, bringing in the third C, explored further in Chapter 12.

The situation of accident victims brings alive the importance of perspective like nothing else. How can people who have lost a leg be happier a year later? Because they have a different frame of reference. They are happy to be alive. They have a changed perspective. Long Win Thinking encourages us to change our perspective on what success means, before accidents or crises might force us to. As Simon Sinek concludes, 'no matter how much money we make, no matter how much power we accumulate, no matter how many promotions we're given, none of us will ever be declared the winner of life'.[29]

Social pressures and norms are huge in this area but many more Long Win voices are starting to challenge these. British writer Emma Gannon unpicks illusions and misconceptions around happiness, productivity, identity, celebrity, money, ambition and 'arrival' in *The Success Myth*. Chief Learning Officer Dr Ruth Gotian echoes the 3Cs in her research for *The Success Factor*, which shows that intrinsic motivation, perseverance, strong foundations and a

Constant Learning mindset are common across astronauts, Olympic champions and Nobel laureates. And Ed Haddon, whose coaching business was the first to be B Corp certified, urges us towards 'writing our own rules' in *The Modern Maverick*. There is no doubt that to clarify what success means to each of us, there are no easy definitions to borrow. We should resist accepting others' views and accept that there can be more than one answer and that it can change through our lives. We should feel free to start defining success on our own terms as we explore what matters most to us over the long term.

National measures of success

A few nations have started to use different metrics to measure national progress. New Zealand became the first nation to officially incorporate measures of wellbeing into its government priorities, adding social dimensions to GDP, including educational, environmental and health indicators. Leaders of Iceland and Scotland also adopted a wellbeing agenda with other social indicators besides traditional GDP data. Time will tell if global health challenges alongside increasing concerns about climate change and other social challenges of equality and inclusion are the catalyst for further revisions of how governments think and behave around the world.

The UN's 17 Sustainable Development Goals, agreed in 2015, are an attempt to create a different shared framework of priorities for the world. These are referred to across businesses, governments and charities, but they haven't taken precedence over GDP metrics.

The UN Sustainable Development Solutions Network produces an annual World Happiness Report. In its research into the reasons for both high and low levels of self-reported happiness across nations, the most important factor is social support. There is no doubt that economic prosperity is also important, along with life expectancy. But the trio of social support, economic growth and health offer a much more balanced perspective of how we might start to view a country's success in a way that relates to real lives.[30]

My work on *The Long Win* has connected me to academics, practitioners and leaders who are part of Harvard's Human Flourishing Program. Their aim is to develop better systematic approaches to understand and promote human flourishing. Cutting across typical divisions between the empirical social sciences and humanities, their work integrates insights from sociology, political science, economics, education, psychology, medicine, public health, philosophy and theology. A Long Win Thinking mindset sits at the heart of their research, debates and emerging recommendations. Attempts to develop 'meaningful metrics' and look beyond GDP are broadening the debate and challenging previous assumptions. Greater visionary leadership is required from political and business leaders to break away further from the status quo.

Reflections on Clarity

Clarifying what matters is an ongoing process, as layers of meaning are continually developed. There is no formula, though a commitment to constant 'why' questions, challenging others to broaden the criteria for success and looking longer-term can help us develop a more meaningful dialogue about what success means to us. We need reflection time to ask these questions, review and challenge our responses, and adapt. This space for growth and adaptation links directly into the second C of Long Win Thinking, Constant Learning, as well as the third C, Connection. It is in our conversations with others that we can really advance our thinking about success and together act in different ways.

How to gain Clarity

1. Ask ongoing clarifying questions about what else matters beyond existing metrics.
2. Develop a sense of purpose and clarify how you want to make a difference to others.
3. Focus your success criteria more on 'how' you show up, not simply 'what' you do.
4. Lengthen the timescale in which you envisage success.
5. Reflect on what has given meaning in your life and what will give meaning in the future.

Chapter 11

Beyond Medals and Grades

The Role of Constant Learning in Long Win Thinking

What would I gain beyond any result?

I knew when I returned to rowing that no one could guarantee me a medal. It wasn't even a given I would be selected for the Olympic team again. What I did know was that with the right mindset, I could learn things I hadn't learnt before. I could stretch myself in a much broader way, challenge my thought processes, assumptions, beliefs and biases, and learn new ways to connect with those around me. I was returning to rowing with a wider perspective, not just my view from nearly a decade of international competition, but a fresh view from a completely different world of work at the Foreign and Commonwealth Office. I'd also had a year away from elite sport to reflect, reassess and reconnect with what mattered to me. Whatever the outcome, trying again in a different way would bring huge learning for me.

When Liverpool Football Club won the much-vaunted Champions League trophy in 2019, endless rhetoric followed in the media about the win's significance, about previous doubts as to whether the team could win and so on. Many of those doubts had been aimed at their manager, Jürgen Klopp, but I can remember watching him being interviewed by the BBC straight after the game, amid all the hysteria, and simply claiming that winning is 'cool', but what he was really interested in was development. Even at this moment of triumph, Klopp acknowledged the winning but focused on the more meaningful part of his role: developing his athletes not just as footballers who win trophies but also as great people. Once again, the media overlooked his answer and returned to their repeated hype about the result. But the new breed of top football managers is starting to have ambitions beyond winning. This is helping them to raise the bar in their performance over a sustained period.

Long Win Thinking embraces learning as a way of living, working and playing. It can fit in any context, create positive momentum and resilience during challenging times, and enable adaptation and innovation within our fast-paced world. It's not just about acquiring knowledge; it's often much more about noticing, listening and tuning in to others around us and the environment we're in. In our noisy, busy lives, mindfulness is becoming an increasingly crucial learning skill to allow us to pay attention to the things that matter most to us and to our path of growth and development.

Constant Learning requires us to be proactive, stay open to new information, seek feedback, listen to other views and challenge our own assumptions. It goes beyond identifying process improvements and increased efficiencies to a deeper, less visible but crucial level of learning about ourselves and others, our experiences and the environment in which we work, study or train. Resilience and performance expert and runner Steve Magness emphasizes that 'being able to see yourself grow is a fundamental human need. As leaders, we need to create environments that allow people to see a brighter future that includes growth and mastery.' Whether you look at the latest research on resilience, high performance or leadership, one theme appears repeatedly: the centrality of learning in order to improve, manage pressure, failure and adversity, and adapt to the changing world around us. No one has all the answers. Those who thrive in our fast-paced, changing world are those who can learn quickest, innovate, make connections across previously separated worlds, review, reflect and adapt. American futurist thinker and businessman Alvin Toffler predicted some years ago that 'The illiterate of the 21st century are not those who cannot read and write but those who cannot learn, unlearn and relearn.'[1]

How do we create a Constant Learning mindset? Just turning up at school, to courses, to work does not mean that we will learn. Leaders should consider how best to create a learning environment for others that stimulates their appetite and provides opportunity to learn informally on a daily basis.

What are the habits that ensure we are learning, regardless of workloads, pressures, results? How do you use feedback, and who do you ask for feedback? Are you still reviewing results or performance, and are you working out what you'll do differently next time or playing the blame game? What assumptions and biases are you bringing to meetings, projects, decisions that may hold you and others back from learning alternative ways? Are we aware of groupthink in our organizations (and homes!) and how might we recognize and shift it? How do we support the growth of cognitive diversity around us?

Psychological safety is an essential prerequisite if we are to be able to fail and learn and take risks – but how consciously are we creating psychologically safe environments around us so that others can speak up and question the status quo? How far does psychological safety form part of our leadership responsibilities and objectives?

Questions really are the home of learning. Don't be afraid to channel your inner three-year-old and keep asking questions, stretching your own thinking and that of others around you. When did you last read, listen to or find out about something that you would previously never normally have taken an interest in? Probably my favourite question is: when did you last try something for the first time?

How we learn and what we learn

Our understanding of how we learn effectively has changed radically through discoveries in neuroscience and psychology. You'd think that our learning and teaching experiences would have changed accordingly, but that's not yet been the case. It's long been known that passive learning – sitting listening to teachers or lecturers – is a poor way to learn. Little knowledge is retained, and even less is translated into action. Yet, you would not have to look far to find schools, universities and academies around the world where pupils and students still spend much of their time learning passively.

This may have worked to a certain extent in the past, in a world where our economy was based on large-scale employers with mass production and largely repetitive work that required employees to carry out instructions rather than think for themselves. But this kind of learning does not befit the home, schools or workplaces of the 21st century.

In surveys led by business schools and business magazines, leaders repeatedly say that the skills they most need in the workplace (and are lacking in) are leadership, creativity, innovation and collaboration.[2] Yet where can children, pupils and employees learn and develop these skills?

When Satya Nadella took over Microsoft in 2014, he saw a key flaw that had developed in the corporate culture: too much fixed mindset thinking and behaviours, and not enough open-mindedness, humility and experimentation. His immediate priority was to lead the organization from a 'know it all' culture to a 'learn it all' culture.[3] Many organizations struggle with this transition. In many schools, teachers believe in a growth mindset yet find themselves in a system based firmly on evaluating fixed outcomes and ranking according to grades. It's a double bind. They want to teach a growth mindset but have to stick to limited parameters which yield the results demanded by the system. At that point, any focus on growth and the individual's own learning and development is undermined and falls away.

A similar pattern can be seen in organizations that want their staff to be open to learning, developing and challenging the status quo, but review and evaluate the same staff by different metrics: short-term sales figures or profit margins and compliance. None of the valuable learning that comes from failure in the workplace gets recorded and valued – quite the contrary. Once again, learning and development is stifled.

Our attitude to failure is key. The idea of 'loss aversion' urges us to avoid failure (see Chapter 2). But cultures that punish failure, particularly if it risks damaging short-term results, inhibit the learning needed for long-term success. A growing body of research focuses on understanding failure better, since it is so crucial to our success. Amy Edmondson's *Right Kind of Wrong* explores what this means in an organizational context. Matthew Syed argues comprehensively in *Blackbox Thinking* that a willingness to engage with failure is crucial to progress and reaching excellence across our lives, whether in business, Formula 1 motorsport or biological evolution.[4]

In the new evolving field of 'failure science', one research study examined the three disparate domains of gaining healthcare grants for research, exiting start-ups and how terrorist organizations maximize casualties in attacks, highlighting the crucial learning that comes from failure, and pointing out in each case that almost every winner starts a loser.[5] Amazon CEO Jeff Bezos confidently told his shareholders: 'If the size of your failures isn't growing, you're not going to be inventing at a size that can actually move the needle.'[6]

The 'entrepreneurial mindset' is commonplace in certain areas of business. Many entrepreneurs have experienced rich learning experiences completely outside conventional education, characterized by risk-taking, experimentation and lack of constraint on working across typical silos of expertise, skills or subject areas. We surely need to close this gap between entrepreneurial thinking and conventional education. Ali Ash, a hugely successful business entrepreneur, who came from a difficult background, describes 'infinite learners' and the challenge of how we traditionally see education as follows:

> A lot of people go through the... education system and they believe that once you've done your diploma, your degree, that's it. I think the world is now about lifelong learning and becoming an infinite learner, learning all the time and becoming self-educated. Self-education is a big piece of how you can continue becoming successful and developing an unfair advantage.[7]

In sport, the performance mindset, discussed earlier, is all about learning constantly. Multiple Olympic cycling champion Chris Hoy was part of a British team famous for its hungry approach to innovation and change. When asked in an interview after one of his multiple world-beating races about his approach, Hoy explained that it's easy to change a losing formula – everyone does that – but it takes bravery to change a winning formula. Adaptive thinking is required to keep developing and sustaining high performance. The same exists in business, perhaps epitomized in Amazon's 'Day 1' philosophy, which requires you 'to experiment patiently, accept failures, plant seeds, protect saplings, and double down when you see customer delight'.[8] The classic examples of Kodak and Nokia reveal what happens to those who don't actively adapt.

Athletes know that they need to find new ways of going faster all the time – simply training harder physically is rarely the answer above a certain limit. It's the same in the workplace. More hours are not going to improve engagement, productivity or results, let alone culture or employee experience. No athlete would ever believe that training all night in the gym would help deliver a better performance. Yet many lawyers, bankers and consultants work regularly through the night in pursuit of better performance. In this mindset, the focus is on short-term gains but at the cost of developing creative and innovative thinking, longer-term learning, adaptation and performance gains.

The learning environment

Large parts of the Western education system perpetuate a focus on 'getting things right' and 'acquiring knowledge', ignoring how we really learn. We learn what the capital of France is but fail to consider why we have countries at all. If success is getting the right answer, then learning comes to be about rehearsing prepared answers and regurgitating information. But if success is about exploring new ways of thinking, then learning comes to be about developing excellent questions, stretching our minds and challenging the way that we think.

David Epstein suggests that learning should involve 'desirable difficulties' – obstacles which make learning more challenging and slower in the short term, but much more effective in the long term. In contrast, making things easier – for instance, through excessive hint-giving – improves immediate performance but undermines longer-term progress. According to Epstein, 'Learning deeply means learning slowly', but not many school systems or workplaces are able to take this on board.[9]

Another important aspect of learning is the 'generative' approach whereby students 'generate' answers, rather than passively receiving and learning answers. Socrates was famous for using this approach with his pupils. Being asked to generate answers is proven to improve subsequent learning, however incorrect the generated answer may be. 'The more confident a learner is of their wrong answer, the better the information sticks when they subsequently learn the right answer. Tolerating big mistakes can create the best learning opportunities.'[10]

Learning without hints and help can feel slow and full of errors, yet is shown to be the best way to create lasting learning that can be applied flexibly and broadly. Repetition is proven to be less effective than struggle, but short-term rehearsal gives only short-term benefits. But that's not how most of us have experienced education. It remains difficult in many educational settings to accept that 'the best learning road is slow, and that doing poorly now is essential for better performance later'.[11]

One of the qualities I observed and learnt most from while watching some of the best diplomatic negotiators at work was their patience. Rush the process, move forward at a pace that others aren't comfortable with, and the whole construct of the negotiation falls apart like a house of cards. Whether it was incredibly skilled police negotiators working on hostage situations in Baghdad during the conflict, or political negotiators working to bring the Balkan states closer to the EU, I saw an approach of Constant Learning and regular reviewing, regardless of outcomes. Every conversation, discussion and exchange of ideas provided new information to explore. There were no answers that could be looked up. But potential new solutions could always be generated if we were open to them. Yet studying and developing patience is rarely on the curriculum at school or in business education.

The PISA (Programme for International Student Assessment) 2015 results showed that '"adaptive instruction" was the second most powerful predictor of high levels of educational outcome, rating above discipline, classroom size and more'. In other words, education based around the needs of students is better than teaching pupils to do the same thing at the same time in the same way. The excellent Finnish system emphasizes diversity in assessment as well as in teaching, ensuring an adaptive approach throughout. Students have their own specific goals and evaluation is always based on the students' strengths. Yet many education systems remain rooted in past methods.

A learning mindset needs to be supported by an environment where Constant Learning behaviours are valued, supported and encouraged. In organizations, the belief that 'knowledge is power' can lead to behaviours that inhibit learning, with ideas not being shared, collaboration being undervalued and acquiring knowledge being prioritized over shifting mindsets, experimenting and innovating.

Many companies claim to be learning organizations, but few actively prioritize developing and supporting learning behaviours above short-term task completion. Even fewer recognize learning in their metrics of success and reward. Those that do typically recognize only traditional 'qualifications'. This usually means that those with conventional qualifications are included, promoted, rewarded and recognized more, all the time bypassing those who practise broader methods of learning and discovery.

The same contradiction exists in schools, which tend to focus more on individuals acquiring fixed knowledge than supporting shared learning, exploration and discovery. In education systems taking on board the need for change, we see more project-based work. Pupils in the Nordic countries spend much of their school day working in project groups, learning how to collaborate, develop, support and challenge each other's thinking and how to experiment together. One of the OECD countries where school students work most often in groups is Denmark. Groupwork makes up the majority of assignments and contributes most to grades, and particular attention is paid to the quality of interaction and contribution. This continues at universities, where assignments often require students to work in groups of two or three. Verbal examinations are much more common than written exams, allowing for ideas and experiences to be discussed and explored alongside knowledge, which tends to be the prime focus in written exams.

Cooperative learning, defined as 'working together to accomplish shared goals',[12] is not a new concept but has yet to be embraced by many education systems. How students interact is often a neglected aspect of instruction. But it is critical to how well students learn and how they feel about school, each other and themselves. Alfie Kohn's research substantiates this approach: 'If there is a single concrete image that represents the transcendence of mutually exclusive goal attainment, it is a picture of three or four children sitting around a table, animatedly exchanging information and ideas.'[13] Given the number of leadership courses I see where companies request sessions on 'communicating with your team' or 'how to have difficult conversations', it seems pretty clear that lifelong benefits would result from learning like this earlier on in life.

In more progressive systems, self-evaluation, initiative and choice play a larger role too. With the help of technology, pupils in history classes in the Netherlands are able to choose which period of history they learn about and which aspect they might focus on within that period. This inclusion of autonomy and choice in the learning experience provides a huge boost to pupils' motivation.

I have always found it puzzling that people in Great Britain have all learnt the same bits of British history: we usually know about events related to the Vikings and the Romans, the Tudors and the Stuarts. Mention an event in British history either side of any of those periods, and no one will know about it. And very little is known about economic, social and cultural history. The rigid curriculum has limited how much history is learnt by a nation. It makes no sense: across a country we could have collectively studied the whole of British history and together could bring multiple perspectives on it. But when we pool our knowledge, we all know the same stuff, making us 'individually perceptive but collectively blind', as Matthew Syed explains in *Rebel Ideas*.[14]

Despite widespread recognition that interaction and experiential learning are important components of learning, they still often exist alongside significant passive learning. A fundamental underappreciation remains of how to achieve shifts in mindset and behaviours and, through that, improved leadership and performance.

Frustratingly, I often see time designed into leadership programmes for reflection and experimentation quickly sacrificed for more content, without proper consideration of the actual outcomes of shoehorning in knowledge. The need to measure (short-term) impact from learning and development programmes has led to a focus on content and key topics that can be 'ticked off'. But knowledge acquisition is largely a waste of time and prevents many executive education programmes from achieving meaningful learning, personal growth and change in the workplace. It has been estimated that only 10% of learning translates into behaviour change[15] and 70% of those who participate in development programmes revert back to previous behaviours a year later.[16]

Beyond whatever is learnt on a programme, there is rarely sufficient follow-up and support to help with putting the learning into practice. Changes aren't made overnight; habits take time to change. Yet coaching or line manager support to aid the translation of learning into the workplace is rarely prioritized. Nor is there sufficient space within the day job to experiment and try things out with feedback, as part of an ongoing learning environment. I have heard many executives express guilt and apologize to colleagues for taking time out to learn, making it almost impossible for them to take more time out to reflect or share their learnings on return to their roles. This undermines any potential gains and makes the return to previous behaviour inevitable.

Tailored learning remains underutilized in many workplaces, schools and sports clubs. Elite sports teams are realizing the opportunity for performance gains from creating athlete profiles and individualizing training to develop players' strengths. At work, leadership programmes still tend to be standardized, so every leader goes through the same course, regardless of their background and experience. This often reflects a culture that focuses on the system rather than the individuals within it, reinforcing conformity rather than diversity and creativity.

I found it ironic when I encountered 'special needs education' in UK schools that there was an individualized approach in complete contrast to standard education. With less of a focus on curriculum and set knowledge, teachers are free to focus on pupils' needs and aptitudes, often doing great work and maximizing the children's progress. There is less of a focus on results and grades, and children have individualized learning plans. It seems baffling that my child with special needs is supported to reach their potential, while my child without special needs has to learn what they are told to learn, regardless of any other factors. (Of course, by opting out of the curriculum and exam system, children with additional needs will never get the 'winning tickets' required to be 'accepted' later on, as their slightly less conventional skills and abilities are left unmeasured and undervalued.)

Our aims for learning play an important role in how we learn. Two studies found a significant difference in the learning experience, behaviours and performance of individuals focused on winning and competing compared with those focused on personal development. Those prioritizing learning over outperforming others were more cooperative and collaborative than those focused on winning. They also felt lower fluctuations in self-esteem and greater connectedness with others.[17] Whether we take a 'performance' or 'results' approach to learning significantly shifts outcomes.

Constant Learning behaviours

Once there is an openness to learning and a psychologically safe environment to do so, then the stage is set for a number of learning behaviours to develop. These include coaching and mentoring, review and reflection.

The growth of a 'coaching' approach in schools, sport and organizations reflects an increasing awareness of how we learn, though it is often still not fully understood and therefore poorly implemented. John Whitmore, leading thinker and developer of coaching methods, describes coaching as 'unlocking people's potential to maximize their own performance. It is helping them to learn rather than teaching them.'[18]

Executive coaching and team coaching are typically offered only to senior leaders, usually for a short period, and come in a poor second place to larger (more expensive) set piece development programmes. Organizations commonly state they support a coaching culture yet underinvest in the process of learning to coach and fail to develop managers and leaders, not realizing the potential cultural and performance gains. Technology is increasing access to coaching tools and guidance through apps, though it's still the safe, reflective space between a coach and coachee that facilitates the deepest learning.

There are misconceptions too. Research led by Julia Milner and Trenton Milner found that managers thought they were coaching when in fact they were directing or micromanaging, regularly using phrases like: 'Why don't you do this?' or 'First you do this.'[19] Instead, coaching involves listening, questioning, giving feedback, showing empathy, recognizing and pointing out strengths and letting the coachee arrive at their own solution (the latter was found to be one of the hardest things for traditional directive managers to enable but one of the most important).

Coaching is seen as one of the key ingredients for leaders within 'teal' organizations, a term coined by Frederic Laloux, who writes about the evolution of management. Laloux describes different phases of organization, moving through hierarchical organizations to target-focused, profit-driven approaches, then more empowered, employee-focused cultures and, finally, the teal stage, which sees much greater self-management and deeper sense of purpose. Leaders in teal organizations see their role as coaches and facilitators. If a team can't make a decision, then rather than sending it to a leader higher up the chain to make a decision, that leader sees their role as coaching the team to have a better conversation and learn the skills that enable them to make a decision. It's Long Win Thinking in action.

Progressive coaches in sport are role-modelling more supportive, question-based approaches that allow the athlete to learn for themselves, rather than being directed and told what to do. This enhances performance, motivation and decision-making under pressure. But you don't have to look far to find coaches (or parents) yelling at players about what they should be doing from the sidelines!

I experienced both approaches and can honestly say that the experience of each was strikingly different, and the effect on my performance similarly significant. It's hard to process a string of instructions effectively. You want to carry them out, you think you're carrying them out and then you're frequently yelled at for not doing them, without the space to explore where things are going amiss. It's not an enabling or motivating experience.

But when you are asked for your views and challenged to think things through for yourself, to realize where the gaps are and to start to fill them in yourself, with the support of a coach, it's a completely different experience that hugely expands your capability, adaptability and confidence, and creates learning that lasts. More importantly, it develops crucial decision-making skills and thought processes for when you need them most – in a race, under pressure.

Mentoring is also on the rise as its effectiveness is increasingly understood. Similar to coaching, there is a move away from the old-fashioned view that mentoring is about wiser, older people telling younger people how to do things, and it's becoming one of our most effective tools for building more inclusive environments and safe spaces for expansive learning.

Feedback is another familiar concept that is often poorly implemented. I am constantly struck by how feedback can vary in different organizations – how damaging it can be in some contexts yet how positive in others.

In the high-performance sporting world I was part of, feedback was a critical part of our everyday interactions. In the Olympic rowing team, feedback was about how to make the boat go faster. It wasn't personal; it was simply about what else could be done to help improve boat speed. It's definitely easier to give feedback if you can connect it to a common purpose and shared vision of success. Without this, feedback can seem personal and more threatening. Feedback also relies on trusted relationships in order to have open conversations about how to improve. We quickly see how the 3Cs interconnect and mutually support each other.

In the rowing environment, everyone accepted that there were more ways to gain speed, as there was always a gap between where we were and where we were aiming to get to, and no single person had all the answers. There wasn't the division between 'negative' and 'positive' feedback that I later heard in the workplace. All feedback was listened to through the lens of how it could help the boat go faster. However feedback was conveyed – and it could certainly be robustly delivered at times – we were looking for what we could learn from it.

Feedback came from everyone in that environment: fellow athletes, coaches and the various experts who supported us – the sports psychologist, nutritionist, physiologist, biomechanist and medical team. We also went out and sought feedback. I spoke to retired athletes for advice and sought out athletes from other sports who had come into sport relatively late in their lives, as I had, so that I could learn from them.

When I first entered the working world of the Civil Service, I was stunned by how different the experience of feedback was. Firstly, it was rare. Secondly, nobody really liked it or wanted it. Thirdly, it felt incredibly awkward. Fourthly, and most damagingly, it could feel personal and judgmental. Fifthly, it was tainted by its association with a dysfunctional and demoralizing appraisal process. Feedback was linked to a performance review process that few trusted and which focused on past failures rather than future possibilities.

There were attempts to revamp this while I was there, but as in many organizations, there was an underestimation of the investment in managerial capabilities required to help managers to have effective conversations and understand the 'purpose' of reviews. As with poor coaching, poor reviewing diminishes learning gains and performance improvements.

I have often reflected on why it can feel so hard to establish a constructive feedback culture in the workplace compared to a sporting environment. Clunky appraisals are one part of it, but it goes beyond that. Like any skill, feedback requires regular practice, and it was a given that everything we needed to do well to improve performance needed practising, and that included how we gave and received feedback. We practised, reviewed and adapted how we gave feedback just as we practised, reviewed and adapted how we put our oars in the water.

Feedback is a rich source of learning right under our noses – there are so many people in our organizations with useful information and relevant experience. Yet how often do we proactively seek out their input? Organizational neuroscientists looked at how our brains react when receiving feedback and saw that the 'threat' part of the brain frequently lit up. But they saw a different response when individuals sought feedback, deciding what they need, when and from whom. This autonomy allows our brains to avoid the 'threatened' defensive response which lessens our receptiveness and ability to learn. One study suggested that 'feedback' has such poor connotations from bad experiences in the past that we should instead think about asking others for 'advice'. I don't mind what it's called, as long as we are tapping into the potential for learning that is constantly around us.

The benefit of feedback often comes from how you reflect on it, review it and make sense of it in order to turn it into a new way of thinking and behaving. I have been struck over the last decade with how the theme of reflection has become more sought after in all the leadership programmes I have been involved in. At the start of a programme, when I ask participants 'What do you most want to get out of this leadership programme?', the answer now is consistently 'time for reflection'. It speaks volumes about the noisy, 'busy' workplaces that leaders find themselves in. It also tells us that while leaders are aware of the importance of reflection and the need to do more of it, many find it incredibly hard to incorporate this into their roles, and the workplace is not helping.

NASA famously spend two years debriefing their missions, meticulously drawing out the lessons over time, harnessing initial feedback as well as the insights that come with greater hindsight and experience. There are numerous stories of leaders with less time than any of us, Bill Gates and Barack Obama spring to mind, who carve out regular time to think, read and reflect in order to keep developing the way they think. Reflection and review were part of the DNA of the best sports environments I've experienced. We didn't just review how fast we went on the water; we reviewed all of the performance elements, such as how well we communicated and collaborated, how our mindsets were affecting our performance and, of course, how well we were reviewing and maximizing our potential to learn.

We would review races regardless of result and always look for what was working well as well as what needed to be improved. This applied to daily training as much as to racing and was carried out the same, win or lose. If you don't review your successes, you are passing up great opportunities to learn about what helped you to be successful. If you only review when you lose, it can feel more like a blame game or witch-hunt, and it can be hard to get good at it because those occasions are more laden with emotions and negative feelings. Reviewing needs to be simply part of how you operate. It can provide huge ongoing momentum and prevent the destabilizing huge highs and lows that come if you allow results to dictate your emotions, your experience and how much you learn.

After British rowers Katherine Grainger and Anna Watkins won a gold in the London 2012 Olympics, Anna revealed that following the medal ceremony, anti-doping processes and immediate press requests, they got into a taxi to take them to the BBC studios in London for a longer interview. In the car, Anna, a lover of spreadsheets and with a PhD in Mathematics, pulled out their crew spreadsheet, which they always carried with them and had used to review their performance regularly over the last four years. Some might have thought that the Olympics had ended when they crossed the line, but their performance mindsets and learning approach hadn't. It was in their DNA to keep reviewing and learning.

A mindset of Constant Learning starts to reshape success away from a single result or moment when you may or may not cross the line first and towards a much broader world of ongoing growth that is useful for both that single moment and the longer term. This ongoing learning perspective also means that crossing the finishing line is placed in a continuum of practice, rather than there being a 'cliff edge' moment, and this enables athletes to enjoy those pressure moments much more and deliver their best performances. Another win–win!

The same applies equally to the workplace. If learning is occasional, limited to short external development opportunities and results focused, then improvement and potential remains massively underdeveloped on a daily basis.

Another Constant Learning behaviour that plays to the motivating power of progress and Connection to purpose is the 'marginal gains' approach. This allows everyone in a team or organization to identify and recognize small gains as well as big game-changing opportunities (with the former often providing opportunities for the latter). This mentality was one of the keys to the revolution of the British Olympic team that took Great Britain from number 36 in the medal table with one gold medal in Atlanta 1996 to 29 gold medals in London 2012 and number 2 in the medal table in Rio 2016. It is often associated with Sir Dave Brailsford, the British cycling performance director who pursued this approach to the extreme and attributed the cycling team's spectacular results in the Beijing, London and Rio Games to it, but it was used across Olympic sport. Examples ranged from athletes taking pillows with them to competitions – taking control of a small aspect of their environment, which would have benefits for sleep, recovery and wellbeing – to athletes establishing proactive habits around hygiene – in order to minimize risks of infection in training and competition – and athletes in cycling and bobsleigh wearing aerodynamic helmets that had been refined through the use of Formula 1 wind tunnels. The marginal gains philosophy enabled everyone to contribute to the overall purpose; each contribution mattered. Everyone took responsibility to experiment and share their learning with others proactively, and that included bringing in ideas from outside sport too. Significant positive momentum was created by this learning approach as it spread across British Olympic sports and connected them in all sorts of previously unexplored ways.

It mirrors a process adopted by Japanese businesses after the Second World War, summed up by the Japanese word *kaizen*, meaning 'improvement'. It was part of the much-documented 'Toyota Way', which set up an approach of continuous improvement across the whole business with huge success. The idea isn't new, but applying it to less obvious aspects of what we do – our mindsets, behaviours and relationships – is less explored and offers further performance gains across our lives.

It's important to say that a Constant Learning approach requires us to enjoy the experience of growth and development that comes from learning, not use it to judge ourselves or imply that we are not good enough. At times, I have seen this approach distorted in the sports and business world to mean that individuals are seen as inadequate, resulting in a lack of self-acceptance and self-worth because of constant striving without a sense that gains are being made through learning. That is not a true learning approach. In Long Win Thinking, we are learning in order to grow in a constantly changing world, exploring untapped potential and possibilities, failure included.

Learning is both 'a lifelong challenge and opportunity from which we can derive meaning and discover purpose'.[20] Learning isn't an isolated activity; it requires us to be part of a community we learn with, linking us to the third and final part of Long Win Thinking, Connection.

How to practise Constant Learning

1. Notice what makes the difference between when you are on automatic pilot or fixed in your views and when you are open to learning within each day.

2. Work out how to create a safe Constant Learning environment for those around you, personally and professionally.

3. Invest in developing learning behaviours, including coaching, mentoring, feedback, reflection, review.

4. Include (formal and informal) learning and growth for individuals and teams within your vision and measures of success.

5. Reflect on the best questions to ensure you learn about yourself, and others, including those related to mindset, behaviours and relationships. Consider how you might need to adapt what you have learnt in the past and what you need to learn, unlearn or relearn to become the best version of yourself.

Chapter 12

People First

The Role of Connection in Long Win Thinking

It can't just be about me.

When I returned to row in my third Olympics, I knew that I couldn't do it alone. I also knew that whatever the outcome, whatever medal might or might not be part of that, what I'd carry with me for life would be the experience I shared with others and the relationships made along the way. I wanted a different experience from this Olympic adventure. That required a shift in my thinking. It was really a completely natural ambition to have, and a relief to realize it as such. But it was not easy, given that I'd been conditioned for so many years to focus on results above everything and to prioritize the physical training environment above feelings, emotions, experiences and people.

Echoing the Greek statesman Pericles, who advised that 'what you leave behind is not what is engraved in stone monuments, but what is woven into the lives of others',[1] Professor Clayton Christensen used to advise Harvard's graduating class every year: 'Don't worry about the level of individual prominence you have achieved; worry about the individuals you have helped become better people.'[2] Relationships are central to helping us be at our best, both as individuals and as societies. They are the 'essence of human flourishing' as 'we seek, more than anything else, to establish deeper and more complete connections'.[3]

On retiring after a stellar career as one of Britain's leading hockey players, with a collection of multiple world and Olympic medals, Alex Danson cited 'human connection' as what she valued most from her impressive 18-year career: 'It's not the winning, it's how you win, the people you win with, the group of people you are connected to... I think that human connection is the ultimate marker of success.'[4]

Research on resilience and wellbeing always acknowledges the importance of 'social capital' that comes through those who support us, family and friends within a safe, inclusive environment. It's not by battening down the hatches and toughing things out on our own that we display resilience; it's by reaching out, asking for help and learning from others. Relationships, with the teams we work with or family members at home, define our daily lives and relate directly to our sense of wellbeing and whether we feel cared for and able to care for ourselves. Research into experiences during the COVID-19 pandemic, with isolation causing so much suffering, confirms how crucial connections are to our wellbeing and that 'resilience is a team sport'.

Experiences of Connection of course start from the earliest point in our lives. Psychologist Terry Orlick, having carried out extensive work with children, concludes that 'experiences in human cooperation are the most essential ingredient for the development of psychological health'.[5] The same continues to apply throughout our lives, but how much are we prioritizing and consciously developing the quality of connections in our lives? We might reflect on who we feel most closely connected to in our families and communities, and why. What does good Connection, cooperation and collaboration look like on a daily basis, and what is required of our mindset and behaviours to enable that? We might consider how connected we and others around us are to a purpose greater than ourselves and our pursuit of that purpose? Rather than simply ticking the day's to-do list, we might ask ourselves about what we have done to create an environment for ourselves and others to thrive in? What experience do we want others who live and work with us to have? Finally, who else could we connect with to bring further dimensions to our lives?

Connection

Connection is the glue that interconnects the 3Cs. If we don't have Connection as a team, then it's hard to create Clarity about the why and the what. If we don't connect with friends, colleagues and customers then we won't have Constant Learning about new things, anticipate emerging needs and be prepared for the unknown, uncertain future and, perhaps most importantly of all, grow and flourish together. If we don't develop Connection across our lives, we lose the potential to achieve our purpose, which by its nature requires cooperation and collaboration.[6]

If we are clear that success involves learning behaviours, such as coaching, feedback and challenging the status quo, then we need collaborative relationships to enable and support those behaviours. Only through those behaviours can we gain the different perspectives and alternative thinking we need to stimulate our own thinking.

We should consider what stands in the way of connecting, cooperating, collaborating and communicating effectively when it seems such a natural path. Despite it being easier than ever before to connect (at least technologically) with others across the world, we are experiencing increasing rates of isolation and loneliness, a loss of community and sociability, and increased anxiety and hostility across Western societies.[7] The ease of technological connections has not been matched by an increase in the quality and depth of Connection. We must also acknowledge the impact of a dehumanizing approach to workplaces, schools and other aspects of society, where processes, procedures and systems have been prioritized over people for decades.

Establishing genuine connectedness and working relationships that deepen over time requires going beyond a merely transactional, superficial level. Author and management professor Brené Brown defines 'connection' as finding 'the energy that exists between people when they feel seen, heard, and valued; when they can give and receive without judgement; and when they derive sustenance and strength from the relationship'.[8]

The basis of our diplomatic work was to find ways to deepen relationships and build alliances with partners with whom there were all sorts of seemingly unpassable hurdles. There might be cultural, linguistic, historical and political barriers, and the main tool we had at our disposal was building authentic, collaborative relationships to help us find a way through.

Learning how to connect and negotiate involved a mixture of formal training and on-the-job training, studying those around us, observing skilled negotiators in action, reflecting on each negotiating experience and thinking about how to play to and adapt our own strengths and weaknesses to influence others better. There were no hard and fast rules, and learning was ongoing, whatever career stage we were in. What worked in one negotiation setting might be ineffective in another. We learnt to become more flexible in our approach, to be present and to think about the opportunities in the moment of each negotiation, not to prejudge or make assumptions about how things might go. It always came down to how well we built connections with others.

I remember Condoleezza Rice visiting the Foreign and Commonwealth Office on her farewell visit as US Secretary of State: she gave an inspirational talk, the core of which was about the relationships that had been critical to the successes and failures of her time in government. No matter the challenges, no matter the complexity of the issues, no matter the brilliance of her policy teams, if she didn't manage to find a human Connection with her opposite numbers around the world, little progress was made.

I also remember talking to a wise, experienced ambassador before I went on my first posting to Sarajevo. He had extensive experience of working in the Balkans and I expected to get his highly informed geopolitical view of that part of the world. In fact, he spoke very little about history or politics. Instead, he advised me on the importance of connecting authentically with everyone I would get the chance to work with. I would learn from them all and gain deeper perspectives about Bosnia than I could ever get from a book. He advised that we never know who has influence behind the scenes, so avoid underestimating or leaping to judgements about that. He gave me three pieces of advice when looking to build a relationship with anyone who I initially think I have nothing in common with:

- *Look beyond the job title* – find out who they really are, regardless of whether they are the president, ambassador or taxi driver. Find out what gets them out of bed in the morning, what they really care about deep down, what will really matter to them when they're fatigued from negotiations lasting hours or days on end.

- *Listen more than you speak* – in order to achieve the above, you'll need to listen. People are nearly always willing to share; the question is whether you're willing to listen. Listen to what's said (and what's not said), how it's said and the meaning behind it. Listening is the key to influencing and persuasion, though many people still think speaking and communicating is.

- *Find what you have in common* – you'll quickly become aware of what you don't have in common (language, history, politics, culture), but forget that and focus on what you do have in common. There will always be something; you just have to find it and then collaboration can begin.

His words continued to echo in my mind – not just during my diplomatic work but throughout my work and life experiences since. If you don't build that common ground as a team, then your performance will be limited and less sustainable. In negotiations, experts from former hostage negotiator Chris Voss to business psychologist Adam Grant emphasize the importance of building common ground and reinforcing that. Connectedness sits at the heart of Owen Eastwood's transformational work with Gareth Southgate and the England football team, the South African cricket team, the Royal Ballet School, the NATO Command Group and European Ryder Cup team. Owen says there is a simplicity to his work that focuses on two main elements: connecting everyone to something greater than themselves and connecting everyone to each other.

Connection requires us to learn about less easily visible, measurable areas of culture, experience and wellbeing, and then develop our mindset, behaviours and relationships accordingly.

Culture, experience and wellbeing

It is not a new idea that culture matters and directly affects 'the bottom line'. There is no shortage of examples where culture has played a central role in major economic and social disasters, from Enron to Chernobyl to healthcare crises across the world. Culture concerns a deeper world of thoughts and feelings, often not talked about in workplaces, where we are more accustomed to discussing spreadsheets and KPIs. It will be by now no surprise that harnessing deeper thoughts and feelings as a route to building connections is crucial to Long Win Thinking and our journey to longer-term and more meaningful success in our lives.

Developing and changing culture requires acknowledging what's happening at that deeper level beyond the surface level of what gets articulated. It's not what the CEO says in a town hall meeting or the mission statement on the wall that tells us about the culture of an organization and how things are done; it's how people feel, what they believe and experience – which then drives their thinking and behaviour and the results that ensue.

Companies quickly look for metrics to understand a topic. 'Culture checks' and 'engagement surveys' are favourite tools but in practice can provide only superficial snapshots about what is happening at single points in time. Understanding culture requires information to be gathered on a regular and ongoing basis, based on informal and formal feedback. It requires asking not just about tasks and results but about how those tasks are experienced, what team members enjoy about their work, what they find challenging, what causes stress and what causes satisfaction. Outsourcing 'culture' to a survey or seeing it as the remit of the HR department (or worse, marketing) neglects the reality that everyone is responsible for the culture of an organization. Time and again, it is only when there's a culture crisis that boards are finding out what it's actually like to work in their organization. This was seen vividly when, out of the blue, the board of the CBI (Confederation of British Industry) faced a culture crisis in 2023 following allegations of sexual harassment and a toxic culture, and when the board of British Gymnastics were completely unaware of the levels of abuse in their sport at a time when they had five stars from the NSPCC (National Society for the Prevention of Cruelty to Children) for their integrity unit and were celebrating improving performance and membership statistics. Neither of these organizations were interested in or aware of the real culture in their organizations.

Edgar Schein, Professor of Organizational Development, sets out the different layers of culture and the concept of 'deep culture' (which is what really matters) in his seminal works on organizational culture and leadership.[9] Schein showed the different levels that exist within a workplace, from the 'espoused values' – the mission statement, a company's values that are posted on its website, a leader's speech to the company – to what is actually experienced by the people that work there and the beliefs that then grow out of those experiences. Looking for and understanding where there is a gap between what is articulated by senior leaders and what is experienced by everyone else is the prime mission of understanding culture and should be the area that senior leaders and boards are interested in, regardless of whether it can fit into a neat spreadsheet or not.

When, at the request of the chief coach, I was researching the culture of the British Olympic women's rowing team with organizational culture expert Dr Alison Maitland, we carried out interviews, focus groups and qualitative analysis, using the power of metaphor to unlock deep lived experience. It is sometimes hard to know what the unwritten rules are, but when we asked interviewees what were the 'ten commandments' for their team or workplace, they responded instinctively and opened up at the level of their deep lived experience.

This helped us to unlock greater understanding about the subculture across the group, which was an important part of how the rowers supported each other at times of great pressure and stress. Some of this involved conversations that went on in the changing rooms, where vulnerability and vital support could be shared, which didn't feel like acceptable behaviour outside those walls in the more macho, competitive environment of the gym.

Our research also highlighted aspects of the environment that felt hostile or unwelcoming to women, such as the pictures of winning male athletes dominating the walls as you arrived and the priority given to male athletes in the gym. There were several areas where the chief coach could make immediate changes, as well as other areas, such as the values and behaviours of the team, which could start to be openly discussed for the first time and co-created consciously for the future.

We saw in Chapter 6 how sporting narratives across multiple sporting bodies and national Olympic organizations are starting to shift as leaders learn more about how to develop high-performance cultures that both enable performance and support athletes. In the wake of increasing stories of GB athletes struggling with transition after retiring or with experiencing mental health issues during and after competition, UK Sport created an Integrity department after the Rio Olympics in 2016. Every British Olympic and Paralympic sport is now subject to regular 'culture health checks', signalling that culture, not just winning medals, is now an important indicator of progress and success. But the long-entrenched culture of counting medals runs deep, and these checks are still often too focused on what's happening on the surface (statements, policies, what leaders say but not what they do). 'Walk the floor' exercises are used to try and open up environments, but again, these can be contrived, not always reflecting everyday reality. The language used by the leadership at UK Sport has moved from a focus purely on medals to a narrative of 'medals and more'. Yet it still puts medals first, leaving the 'and more' unclear.

The English Institute of Sport started a campaign in 2019 called #More2Me to encourage balance in athletes' lives and promote the benefits of planning for life after sport. The challenge is for these initiatives to be a full part of the daily high-performance training environment, not an optional add-on, and for coaches to believe that they are as crucial to athletes' performance as lifting weights or technique drills. This requires different conversations between athletes, coaches, performance directors and managers, and a more connected relationship with the world outside sport, based on a genuine interest in exploring sport's greater potential social value.

Poor retention rates at both grassroots and elite level have also increased the focus of governing bodies and other organizations on experience. Having looked at a number of 'marginal gains' to sustain competitive advantage for the British Olympic team, such as investing in talent identification programmes and new technology, athlete retention is the latest area of focus. Too many athletes are choosing to retire after one Olympics when they could have a career lasting much longer. If governing bodies can improve the experience of high-performance athletes, then there could be more than a marginal gain to be found.

Gareth Southgate has been a role model when it comes to thinking differently and prioritizing culture within performance sport. On taking over the position of England football manager (frequently described as harder than being UK prime minister), Southgate adopted an approach of constantly learning. This included talking to coaches and performance directors of the 'poor cousin' sports of the Olympics which football, with its independent wealth, fanbase and brand, had previously looked down on. But Southgate could see that there had been so much innovation around performance in the Olympic world and was keen to draw on it.

The language of 'experience' leapt out in all the media interviews Gareth Southgate gave as the manager of a rejuvenated England Football Team. In strong contrast to his predecessors, when asked by sports journalists and media interviewers what his aims were for the 2018 FIFA World Cup, Southgate repeatedly gave answers about the 'experience' he wanted the team and support team to have. Seemingly confused, and operating on a completely different wavelength, the journalists simply repeated their question: 'What does success look like, Gareth? Is it reaching the group stages, or the quarter-finals, or semi-finals?' Again, Gareth repeated his aims: he wanted the players and the support team to have 'the best experience' at the World Cup. He knew that if his players and support team had the best experience, they would thrive and perform at the top of their game. If they were able to be at their best and deliver their best performance, then that would put them in the best position to get the best results possible, always mindful of the uncertainties and uncontrollable factors (crossbars and referees to name just two) that would also affect the results.

It was striking how clearly Southgate saw his leadership role as creating an environment that supported his players and the support team (he always mentioned both in the same breath) to have a positive experience. The rest – that is, the results – would take care of itself. It was also striking how hard it was for sports journalists and others used to old ways of thinking to understand this new language. What Southgate and his team went on to do, by delivering England's best performance at a World Cup for over 25 years and sustaining this level of results over a number of years, was demonstrate how this thinking works in practice.

Another striking and refreshing change in the leadership behaviour shown by an England football manager was Southgate's spontaneous display of compassion for the unfortunate Colombian penalty taker after a tense match that took England into the quarter-finals of the 2018 World Cup. At the moment when the rest of the team, media and fans were whooping and hollering about England's success in the match, he was empathizing and connecting with a member of the opposing team. And Southgate's agreeing to, and even insisting on, Fabian Delph's return home *during* the World Cup for the birth of his child also brought a refreshing dose of perspective to this sporting event. (This provides a welcome contrast to many less enlightened experiences, such as the Olympic athlete who told me they were not allowed to join their wife by phone for the Caesarean section delivery of their baby because it clashed with a scheduled gym training session on an overseas camp they had to go on.)

When the FA selected Dutch football coach Sarina Wiegman to take over the England women's team, it was clear that they were developing a cultural blueprint for the approach they wanted to see from their coaches. Wiegman continued an emphasis on strong support and compassion in her work with a team that also performed at the highest levels, winning the 2022 Euros and being runner-up at the 2023 World Cup. When 19-year old Lauren James was red-carded for a moment of madness, standing on a player's back after a tackle, Wiegman avoided the mistakes of the past when players making similar mistakes have been ostracized by coaches and media alike, emphasizing her youth, inexperience and potential, and noting her own intention to put an arm round Lauren and help her learn from the experience.

The importance of 'experience' translates into most other contexts. Retention is a critical factor in business in the race for 'talent', innovation and reputation, and plays a major part in developing diverse, inclusive workplaces. In the world of education, universities have been forced to rethink and reorganize significantly because of the influence that student experience now has on how universities get ranked and recommended by a generation of fee-paying students. By taking an interest in the *experience* of others, we gain insight into what is happening at a deeper level culturally. These insights then give us the opportunity to start shaping culture proactively.

Another aspect of culture that underpins how we thrive in our workplaces, schools and sports clubs is whether there is a genuine interest and willingness to invest in each other's wellbeing.[10]

One of the most genuinely supportive teams that I have ever worked in was the one I was part of when working as a diplomat and living on a military base in Iraq during conflict there. Even though we had permanently heavy workloads (work never stops in a war), we always checked in with each other several times daily. We were organized into small groups of four to five, with no hierarchy, and had a simple protocol for the almost daily occurrence of incoming fire: loud sirens would sound and after immediately lying down on the floor and putting on body armour (or moving quickly to a safe*ish* place to do that), we would connect with each other by radio, and we would connect again once the all clear happened, to check that everyone was OK before carrying on with work. We'd always meet up in the evenings too. Of course, we had no families or homes to go to in the evenings, so it was incredibly reassuring that no one took wellbeing for granted in such a challenging environment. Our proactive care for each other went across roles and hierarchy. Sadly, once I returned to a 'normal' desk job in Whitehall, this wasn't the case any more, regardless of the crisis of the day or other personal issues that might have been going on. Choices we make (or don't make) to connect with and support others proactively can make a big difference.

Arguably the COVID-19 pandemic, starting in 2020, might have helped to accelerate the importance and space given to understanding the important role of wellbeing in our definitions of personal and professional success. With the strangeness of working from home and increased social distance, everyone seemed to feel they had permission to start meetings checking in with how other colleagues were feeling. (It was amazing how many companies described this – starting a meeting asking how others were – as a fundamentally new approach to wellbeing.) What had stopped that from being normal previously? Why did it need a pandemic for blue chip companies to provide online mindfulness and counselling sessions? But pretty quickly after the height of the pandemic, companies started worrying about productivity of employees working from home and, in some cases, demanded a return to the office, driven by a mindset of control and mistrust, forgetting all notions of genuine wellbeing.

As sport attempts to redefine what a high-performance culture looks like, to avoid the abuse, mental health struggles and demoralizing environments we have glimpsed in earlier chapters, there is an increasing focus on wellbeing. Working out what that means alongside a demanding training regime that optimizes performance progress at the boundaries of human capability offers a huge opportunity for sport to lead the way in the area of organizational culture change.

One international non-profit organization that is trying to provide guidance and practical support for promoting wellbeing as a fundamental part of sport is The True Athlete Project (TAP). It aims to '[re-imagine] sport as a training ground for compassion, mindfulness, and good mental health'.[11] I have become more closely connected with their work, as it aligns so closely with Long Win Thinking. TAP runs a global mentoring programme and provides mindfulness-based support as part of athlete development and coaching practice, stimulating discussions about values, identity and the role of compassion in sport, as well as helping athletes consider issues of social responsibility and the meaning of their journey in high-performance sport. This approach offers a way of reimagining what sport could be, of creating ambition that includes and goes beyond medals, and of redefining success with a wider social impact alongside individual performance excellence. It offers an exciting glimpse of what sporting success could look like.

A core area of wellbeing for all of us, regardless of career or interests, is our connectedness with nature. The biophilia hypothesis affirms our innate need to affiliate with nature, whether plants or animals. An increasingly popular branch of psychology, called ecopsychology, explores the relationship between humans and the natural environment, building on the evidence that connectedness to nature is a huge part of human flourishing.[12] It's a challenge for those stuck in workplace environments without natural light and surrounded by technology, but critical to enabling employees to thrive. However dire some of the rowing experiences were in the early years of my international career, I always felt able to look around on the river and appreciate the stunning natural environment that surrounded me. (It's still one of the places I feel happiest.)

Feeling connected with nature may seem about as far as you can get from the macho tough talk of who the winners might be in the office hierarchy. But high levels of burnout, depression and low engagement should make us think again about the environments we are asking people to perform in.

It is staggering how little interest there has been in understanding or supporting the health of employees, usually the single biggest factor in any organization's long-term performance. In the UK, Business for Health is starting to change this. This business-led coalition aims to bring 'health' into ESG (HESG) in order to enhance health and economic resilience. They introduced the Work Health Index and want to help businesses understand why it's in their interest to play a proactive part in enhancing their employees' health and reducing health and wellbeing inequalities in society.

Improving culture, experience and wellbeing requires a different leadership approach that values and prioritizes these fundamental building blocks of performance. None of these areas can be plotted out and project-managed in 12 weeks with clear monthly targets along the way. This still frustrates organizations who work to a quarterly rhythm with action plans based around set time frames. But this isn't about fixing a machine: it's about releasing human potential, taking account of the way we learn, develop and grow. It's where the older mechanistic, industrial language of work is clashing with how we learn and think as humans, and where a more flexible, human and developmental approach is needed to generate thriving workplaces and flourishing organizations. Professor Gianpiero Petriglieri calls for 'a management that pursues existential growth as passionately as it pursues instrumental growth... where we can be fully human, with all our contradictions, in pluralistic institutions'.[13]

Developing collaborative relationships

Most people sign up to the theory and principles of collaboration and wellbeing – who wouldn't? The critical part is bringing those principles into how we think, behave and interact on a daily basis. How quickly do those collaborative aspirations get ignored or forgotten when operational priorities are drawn up? And how might our assumptions, biases and habits prevent us from being open to collaboration?

Business school programmes use simple activities (like the old classic of building a tower out of spaghetti, marshmallow and string) to help leaders explore the relationships, conversations and interactions within a group that is required to collaborate. Habits of speaking over others, not listening to ideas, failing to see things through a different perspective, making assumptions about our own capability and the 'right' way to act, combined with a competitive comparison with others, usually all appear prominently. It's only afterwards when we debrief and reflect on what happened that we can begin the process of realizing how we might not be as open to collaboration as we thought we were. At that point, it is wholly in our power to make different choices and develop this area proactively if we believe that collaboration will make a difference. We are often so unpractised at collaboration, an area that we have seen is poorly addressed during our early life education as well as workplace training.

Proactive collaboration requires us to tap into the part of our brains that is stimulated by being part of a socially rewarding process, rather than the part of our brains activated by competition and stimulated by a short-term (and short-lived) extrinsic reward. This is the path to thinking beyond bonuses and medals towards longer-lasting, meaningful success.

To think collaboratively, we may need to challenge the assumptions that we need to fix problems by ourselves, that our success is defined by others' failure and that asking others for help is 'cheating'. As Paul Skinner explains:

> Our greatest failures to create Collaborative Advantage may likely occur when we overlook the process of exploring how others might help us better address a problem or challenge in the first place and instead concentrate exclusively on trying to respond to a situation ourselves... Most of the value that could be created through building Collaborative Advantage remains left on the table.[14]

It is in that lost value that we see how a narrow focus on winning holds us back. John Vincent, co-founder and CEO of the restaurant chain Leon, testifies in *Winning Not Fighting*: 'wherever I have worked... I have seen cooperation deliver more results than annihilation'.[15]

Collaboration is an active learning process, learning from and with others, exploring possibilities and working with influence and possibility. There is an emerging contrast between the 'old ways' of creating value and competitive advantage – through efficiency and controlling knowledge, resources and power – and the 'new way' of creating value – through collaboration, innovation and embracing uncertainty.

The opportunities of our highly interconnected world, the increasingly complex social and economic landscape, and a deeper understanding of human decision-making are leading to new collaborative business models in areas never seen before, typified by the 'sharing economy'.

The sharing economy works on a fundamentally collaborative basis. Unlike Disney or Warner Bros., which built their success on the assets they owned, YouTube depends on its users to create its core value. And Wikipedia and Airbnb challenge the traditional models of *Encyclopaedia Britannica* and large hotel chains. Collaborative business models such as those used by Airbnb and easyCar (a peer-to-peer car rental service) typically rely on trust and have feedback mechanisms at their core. The success of these organizations is another form of proof that it's not against human nature to collaborate.

As a GB rower, I knew lots of people across the rowing community, I knew which schools rowed, knew people from lots of university rowing clubs, knew lots of past GB rowers. But I didn't know any cyclists, canoeists or swimmers. Yet we had so much in common as fellow endurance athletes, water sports specialists and Olympians. Dame Sue Campbell told me a story about how, early on in her leading role in UK Sport, she used up all her political capital to bring all the performance directors of the Olympic sports together for a day to try and set a new path of collaboration. There was initially some scepticism, reluctance to waste precious time if it wasn't going to directly benefit them and their sport, and questioning from some of the more successful sports about what they could really learn from the others. She asked them all to share what they thought their sport did brilliantly, where their sport was truly world leading. She paired up directors across sports – cycling with synchronized swimming, sailing with archery – and waited. Within minutes, the performance directors were engrossed in intense conversations, and notebooks came out to take notes and share methods. Sue Campbell knew that she had struck gold by getting the endurance sports scientists to share their expertise, the water sports leaders to talk to each other, and many others to discover mutual interests, ideas and solutions. After all, they were all trying to create environments for excellence, motivate and maximize the performance of their athletes and achieve at a level never seen before by a British Olympic team.

As much as Connection and collaboration increased the sharing of best practice and new ideas, it also brought a powerful psychological effect. All the sports became interconnected and started to see themselves as part of Team GB. Their siloed ways of working were challenged and broadened. When one sport was doing well, not only did other sports get quicker access to the successful strategy, they also felt buoyed by that sport's success, knowing that if one sport could try new things and go faster, then so could they. The experience of being part of something exciting, groundbreaking and meaningful is as important as the knowledge that is shared. That's how silos are gradually broken down.

Collaboration combines different aspects of our mindset, behaviour and relationships. The first step is to dispel the myth that it's more natural for us to compete than collaborate. As we saw in Chapter 2, there is no biological or psychological reason why we can't collaborate on a much greater scale if we choose to. Margaret Heffernan sums up passionately how decades of Western culture have focused purely on competition to make us 'bigger, tougher, meaner, more successful competitors':

> As though the entire culture has been caught up in a testosterone-fuelled feedback loop, we've been persuaded that if we aren't top dog, we must be underdogs; if we aren't winners, we're losers. What's striking in its absence is the equivalent effort to hone our collaborative gifts. We know they're in there – we just don't make much effort to refine them.[16]

A learning approach, a willingness to adapt, learn from and collaborate with our rivals, rather than focusing on beating them, offers us an alternative route. Going back to the origin of 'competition' – *competere* (to strive together) – we can start thinking of our 'competitors' as essential to our performance, thereby reducing stress and fear. Sports psychologists and coaches distinguish between 'challenge' and 'threat' states in competition: if you are losing to someone you hate or fear, you feel threatened and your body is flooded by cortisol, the stress hormone, increasing tension and reducing the ability to think clearly and effectively, thereby diminishing performance. If you are losing to someone you respect and want to be at your best to compete with (striving together), then you feel positively challenged, able to think clearly and raise your game.

Simon Sinek talks about 'worthy rivals' as the way he reframes competition through considering his own personal battle with business academic Adam Grant. He says of Grant: 'He was my main competitor and I wanted to win.' But Sinek realizes that 'instead of investing my energy on improving myself... it was easier to focus on beating him'. He says:

> That's how competition works, right? It's a drive to win. The problem was, all the metrics of who was ahead and who was behind were arbitrary and I set the standards for comparison. Plus there was no finish line, so I was attempting to compete in an unwinnable race.[17]

He now recognizes Grant as his worthy rival, not competitor, who helps him become better at what he does.

Numerous sporting examples illustrate this too. Chris Evert and Martina Navratilova have publicly described their appreciation for each other, each helping the other to reach new heights on the tennis court. In later years, they both supported each other through parallel experiences of cancer. Over years of grand slam finals between Federer and Nadal, the two demonstrated a huge respect and friendship for each other, enabling each other to transcend the game to reach new heights in their performance. After Federer announced his retirement and played his final competitive match at the Laver Cup in September 2022 against Nadal, both players sat together with tears streaming down their faces, their hands interlocked.

New research about reciprocity and giving in the workplace challenges the persistent myths that generosity only gets exploited, that those who willingly offer help, time and energy to others are lacking in ambition or desire to succeed, and that 'good guys finish last'. Adam Grant's study of 'giving', 'matching' and 'taking' behaviours in the workplace shows that:

> Successful givers are every bit as ambitious as takers and matchers. They simply have a different way of pursuing their goals... there's something distinctive that happens when givers succeed: it spreads and cascades. When takers win, there's usually someone else who loses... Givers succeed in a way that creates a ripple effect, enhancing the success of people around them.[18]

Different attitudes to how we connect with those around us in the workplace offer a real opportunity to change our work environments and move away from a zero-sum game culture that limits what's possible. The way we connect shapes the experiences we have as part of teams, groups, departments and classes. The quality of our conversations becomes a critical cultural tool. In the diplomatic world, our daily work centred on interactions. Our only means of changing, developing and improving a situation was through relationships, and this led us to constantly review, reflect and invest in how we connected with others. This is not always the case in other settings. I have spoken to athletes where the domination of one coach, whose ultimate power it was to select who goes to the Olympics or not, created an unsafe environment where it was hard to challenge or take risks in speaking up. In the work environment, the threat of annual reviews and appraisals can stifle vital conversations.

Research around effective communication, influencing and high-performance teams reveals some common themes:[19]

- the need for open and frequent communication (with communication being about listening as much as about speaking);
- the importance of safety to take risks, make mistakes, share alternative views and challenge the status quo (psychological safety);
- the need to build confidence to show vulnerability in communication, ask for help (seeing this as a sign of strength rather than weakness) and have constant curiosity about colleagues and about the issues being worked on.

Most people would sign up to the idea of improving these areas – but in practice, how many of us consciously work to develop these areas on a daily basis? Who has this scheduled in to their work objectives? Who has these areas as priority agenda points in meetings about an organization's performance? Who specifies them within their learning and development programmes? Who measures, values and works to improve these areas? Yet our interactions are critical building blocks in the process of building trust and sustainable workplace cultures where people can thrive.

Collaboration requires interpersonal trust. Trust is a part of all of our lives. We're aware of it from a young age, consciously and subconsciously, as we experience our first relationships within our families and early friendships. We start to learn about what trust means, how it's built and how it's broken. It remains fundamental to us throughout our lives.

In every world I have been in, trust has been critical for success: whether as an Olympic athlete in an elite rowing crew looking to be the best in the world or as a diplomat working in negotiating teams trying to resolve complex, difficult international disputes, from negotiating an EU directive to supporting Bosnian politicians to agree reforms to move the country forward after the bitter conflict of the 1990s. Now, in my work with organizations, trust is required to challenge norms and enable conversations on a deeper level than many are used to, in order to create more effective teams.

Research around trust shows its enormous benefits in the workplace. Yet how many organizations value and prioritize trust? How many give trust the same standing as the other metrics and KPIs that get rigorously reviewed?

Compared with people in low-trust companies, people in high-trust companies report less stress, more energy at work, higher productivity, fewer sick days, more engagement, more satisfaction with their lives, less burnout. The results of increased engagement, less stress and more energy are that employees are more motivated to tackle difficult problems, more open to learn and, therefore, more able to improve and develop, and retention also improves as a result.

If the basic message from a range of research is that people at higher-trust companies suffer less chronic stress and are happier with their lives, fuelling stronger performance at work, you would expect companies to be investing in and improving trust. But everywhere we turn, trust is on the decline. Trust in our culture at large, in our institutions, in our politicians and in our companies is significantly lower than a generation ago. In one study, only 49% of employees trusted senior management and only 28% believed CEOs were a credible source of information. The costs included poorer communications, interactions and decisions, just as a start.[20]

Trust requires workplace environments where staff really belong and can connect with each other. Not where they turn up at the door, leave a large part of who they are at the threshold, perform a set of tasks and leave, picking up the rest of their identity on the way out. It's another crucial human area of development ignored in traditional metrics of success. But we cannot afford to ignore it any longer if we are serious about improving performance and exploring our collective potential, whether in the workplace or on the sports pitch.

Themes of trust, collaboration and quality conversations always form the foundation of workshops and discussions I've been involved in to improve inclusion in the workplace. In one company, senior leaders came to an inclusive leadership workshop straight from a board discussion where they were looking at quarterly results. When asked to explain the company's strategic aims to build a more inclusive environment, there was an initial blankness. It took a moment for these senior executives to access a different way of thinking than they had used in the previous meeting when looking intensively at the quarterly figures and poring over spreadsheets. It required different language, broader perspective and Connection with the human character of the company that produced those quarterly results. We started discussing the quality of conversations, what psychological safety looked like and the lived experience of colleagues outside the room. Enormous energy came from embarking together on that new conversation. But these conversations can't be rushed or squeezed into meetings with heavy agendas.

Business success in the 21st century depends on a company's agility to unlock the ideas that exist within it and listen to a richer diversity of voices and opinions than are currently being heard. Success is becoming more related to creativity, innovation and embracing uncertainty than simply financial management, efficiency and cost-cutting.

Inclusive, collaborative, trusting behaviour requires us to find new ways to connect with people we might not previously have connected with and to be curious about difference and tap into the greater potential that it offers. Connection with a broader set of people develops a stronger sense of community that we can draw on personally and professionally. The purpose-led movement, discussed in Chapter 10, emphasizes the need for companies – if they want to be successful and develop an engaged workforce and loyal customers over the long term – to contribute positively to the communities and environments in which they operate. Beyond local communities, the pressing issues of our time require us to feel connected to the wider world and the communities around us, and to understand how our actions can have potential consequences for millions of others now and in the future.

I have referenced the ongoing global challenges of the 21st century throughout this book. It is not the purpose of the book to look in depth at each complex subject, but to consider the mindsets, behaviours and relationships through which we approach them. It is clear that the greatest problems humanity faces – from climate change to international security, from global health to migration flows, and beyond – require a collective response, an understanding of multiple perspectives and collaborative solutions. One can even go so far as to say that the future of humanity depends on our capability to connect more deeply, ambitiously and diversely. This book has shown that this capability exists but we need consciously to invest in it further. Yuval Noah Harari describes 'the unique ability of homo sapiens to create narratives that drive large-scale cooperation as the key driver of our unique evolutionary success so far'.[21] It's time for that unique ability to come to the fore as we consider what the Long Win for the human race could look like.

How to deepen Connection

1. Reflect on the quality of your connections, conversations and interactions, and how you could further invest in and improve these.
2. Consider the experience that you want to have and that you want others around you to have, and how you might consciously shape this and set ambitions around this.
3. Reach out and connect on a deeper level with colleagues, traditional 'enemies' or 'rivals', those who are different from you and those who you don't know yet but who could add an extra dimension to your life over the longer term.
4. Develop connecting behaviours and keep reviewing and adapting these through quality conversations, collaboration rather than competition, trust, inclusion, shared purpose and deepening sense of community.
5. Reflect on the different ways in which you currently prioritize people in your life and how you might change or develop this further.

Strive not to be a success, but rather to be of value

Albert Einstein

Chapter 13

The Long Winners

Short Stories of Leaders Putting the Long Win into Practice

I always feel fascinated by examples of Long Win Thinking coming to life. The Long Win has never been a formulaic, prescriptive approach that looks the same for everyone. The 3Cs aren't a tick-box formula; they offer a way of reshaping our thinking to lead to different behaviours, interactions and outcomes. Having been consistently asked for more 'how to' tips and guidance, here I bring together some short stories of Long Win leaders with whom I've worked or connected.

The leaders' stories are intended to offer additional insights and spark further thought about what the Long Win could look like in your own personal and professional context. There are vignettes from three business leaders, two entrepreneurs reimagining and redesigning career development, three leaders reframing sport from the ground up and two leaders working to change society through alternative approaches. I share a snapshot of each leader with some practical insights and then draw out particular aspects of Long Win Thinking. We learn best through stories, reflecting on what resonates most and then considering how we might adapt these elements into our own contexts.

Gary Hendler, Chairman and CEO of Eisai EMEA

Committed to connecting pioneering pharmaceutical work to its life-changing social impact

The 3Cs of the Long Win connect closely with Eisai's 'human healthcare philosophy' and Gary's commitment to strengthen workplace culture to underpin their groundbreaking pharmaceutical work.

Eisai's leaders have many complex processes to integrate and manage. Gary realizes these mechanistic processes need to link clearly to the bigger picture: the life-changing impact of their work across society. Their work is difficult and requires resilience, creativity and innovation – it can't be reduced to chasing targets and endless task lists.

The Eisai culture is guided by six motivational behaviours: teamwork; emotional leadership; extreme ownership; discretionary effort; positive energy; and resilience. These follow from a carefully thought-through approach to the mindset and attitudes needed to help colleagues thrive in pursuit of Eisai's healthcare mission.

Gary and I recorded a series of interviews during the COVID-19 pandemic to share the ideas from *The Long Win* directly with colleagues and help connect them to the bigger picture. Eisai now run an internal podcast featuring colleagues from all parts of the company, interviewed by Gary. This maintains connectedness in their world of hybrid working and shows genuine interest in colleagues for who they are and what they do both in and outside the office.

Eisai also runs a volunteer programme where colleagues (from anywhere in the company) go to a care home to visit and spend time with people experiencing health conditions in therapeutic areas their work supports. There's a long waiting list for it and incredible personal, emotional feedback has come from colleagues describing how powerful it feels to connect directly to the people their work is intended to support.

I worked with Eisai leaders to use the 3Cs to connect the company's purpose to their everyday (finite) objectives, projects and tasks: gaining Clarity about what matters beyond short-term deadlines, investing in Constant Learning as part of the daily ways of working and prioritizing human Connection in their work. They drew posters to think creatively and visually about the 3Cs and align their own work areas better to Eisai's purpose.

The Long Win in action

Clarity and purpose: These form a thread through Gary's vocabulary when he speaks and underpin Eisai's work to help patients. Leaders go the extra mile to deliberately weave the company's purpose into everyday life and, through that, improve performance and wellbeing, prioritization and decision-making, innovation and motivation.

Constant Learning: This needs to be part of the psyche that fuels groundbreaking pharmaceutical work. Learning, failing and stretching themselves are central to Eisai's definition of success.

Connection: This is critical internally and externally to ensure that everyone understands the part they have to play. The new treatments they are developing cannot move forward without a vast array of partners each playing their part. The stronger that feeling of Connection, the greater the motivation, resilience and creativity available for their progressive endeavour.

Mindset: Eisai staff have to work at pace and under pressure yet need constant innovation and collaboration to make progress. It's essential that technical and logistical aspects of their work never crowd out the human and societal aspects. That requires mindsets, behaviours and relationships that remain open, creative and collaborative.

Jane Davidson, former Welsh Government minister and architect of the Well-being of Future Generations (Wales) Act 2015

Bringing long-term thinking and a multigenerational sense of responsibility into the heart of governing

After a stint as Welsh Minister for Education, Jane Davidson became Minister for Environment, Sustainability and Housing, where she pioneered the Well-being of Future Generations (Wales) Act to ensure regenerative and sustainable development became the prime organizing principle for government in Wales. This law embeds long-term thinking across Wales transforming government, education, environment, transport and beyond in a way few other countries have ever attempted.

The law is unprecedented, requiring Jane and colleagues to work out both the theory and the practice without a blueprint. From the start, Jane knew this law had to be more about changing mindsets than setting out detailed policy. The behaviour change required for ministers, civil servants, community organizations, business leaders and Welsh citizens could never be mandated – a collaborative, inclusive approach was vital.

The Act was always envisaged as embodying and facilitating the voices of the Welsh nation. It was informed by dialogue and conversations throughout society, invigorated by 'The Wales we want' conversations across, among others, schools, colleges, youth forums, young farmers' clubs, Welsh language groups and community groups prior to its coming into law.

The idea of ensuring that everything that government does takes into consideration the impact and needs of future generations requires a mindset shift to see government from a long-term perspective. That leads to different choices and actions with life-changing consequences. It's nothing short of revolutionary. Changes affected by the law include a reshaped school curriculum based on areas – not subjects – with a higher level of outdoor teaching for foundation years. Approaches to housing, building roads and community development have been transformed too.

Jane Davidson and the Welsh Government adopt a supportive learning approach in the legislation. Deliberately not punitive in the traditional legal sense, it aims to help and encourage leaders in public life to learn and adapt in order to find constantly new and better ways to achieve their aims for the wellbeing of future generations. The role of the independent Future Generations Commissioner for Wales is an essential part of identifying and supporting good practice and holding organizations accountable, based on the seven connected wellbeing goals for Wales:

- A prosperous Wales
- A resilient Wales
- A healthier Wales
- A more equal Wales
- A Wales of more cohesive communities
- A Wales of vibrant culture and thriving Welsh language
- A globally responsible Wales

In contrast to repeated failures to tackle inequality, attainment gaps in education, transport issues, housing issues and accelerating global environmental crises, the impact of this law shows how a values-based approach to government based on long-term thinking and underpinned by sustainability principles can transform society.

The Long Win in action

Clarity: Jane demonstrates the importance of visioning to create challenging, long-term goals, using the language of possibility and expanding our perspective to understand what we're capable of, not just what's probable if we carry on as we have until now. All too often, our systems of government focus on reacting to and policing small-scale problems rather than articulating the vision upstream of what's required, to create a different world without the issue in question becoming a problem.

Leadership: Sustainability and purpose can't be superficial. They require practical integration into every part of society and life. Long Win Thinking supports leaders to understand how this can provide the central, defining thread to their work, a process which then also transforms how they develop as leaders.

Connection: The public services networks essential to understand, engage and deliver the Act form a non-hierarchical 'web of connections among equals, held together not by force, obligation, material incentive, or social contract, but by shared values and the understanding that some tasks can be accomplished together that could never be accomplished separately'.

Sam Parfitt, CEO and Founder of The True Athlete Project

Advancing a holistic approach to human development and social impact through sport

Sam set up The True Athlete Project (TAP) as a non-profit organization committed to cultivate a more compassionate world through sport. TAP's ambitious vision is brought to life through patient, practical work that shows athletes, coaches and sporting leaders how to break free from the status quo where sport fails to live up to its potential, as discussed in Chapter 6.

TAP works with community sports centres, individual athletes, schools, elite teams, national governing bodies and international federations. Their approach encourages leaders to bring the same care to crafting a PE curriculum as a plan for high-performance training, and understands that as much can be learnt from a youth worker supporting youngsters in a local community club as from an Olympic hero.

The TAP spirit – humble, open, inclusive, kind – is critical to their approach of embody, deliver, influence. It's embodied in how they lead meetings, plan programmes and deliver workshops. TAP offers any programme participant free lifetime membership to their monthly 'sangha' (community of practice) and offers scholarships on a trust basis. Sam and colleagues always start meetings with a mix of mindfulness practices.

In one initiative with a Scottish gymnastics club in an area of high socioeconomic deprivation, Sam brought together 20 club volunteers, with ages ranging from 13 to 73, for weekly evening workshops. The programme was designed to support volunteers as 'social change makers', providing a space to come together, talk openly and learn new techniques, including mindfulness, compassionate communication and deep listening. They learnt how to prioritize wellbeing and then design together ways of applying what they'd learnt to support young people in their community. Outcomes ranged hugely in nature and participants said: 'My sleep improved'; 'I am better able to notice if a gymnast needs extra support'; 'I'm less anxious about exams'; 'I managed to defuse tension between my parents'; 'I'm more focused when I'm coaching'; 'I can regain myself when things are difficult'; 'I'm using more open questions and it's helping me understand and be closer with others.'

Their positive impact and outcomes butt up regularly against entrenched approaches. As Sam told me:

> people want black and white – 'X programme will achieve Y impact and in five years we will reach Z people', all trackable in a simple spreadsheet. It's so important that we don't get sucked into this ritual business speak, and that we continue to trust

in what happens and emerges from participants, rather than forcing certain outcomes. It's worked so far. Young people tell us how different it feels to interact with TAP when previously they've been used to such dehumanizing environments.

TAP designed the pioneering Powered by Purpose (PbP) programme to support UK Olympic and Paralympic athletes interested in developing a platform for positive social change. Causes range from sport's role in supporting environmental sustainability to increasing inclusion in sport and beyond. Traditionally, sport has focused on raising media profiles and athletes' commercial value, yet this often contributed to a diminished experience of sport. PbP is rooted in a longer-term belief that athletes can be powerful social change makers and enhance their performance and wellbeing through connecting with a purpose beyond themselves.

Eilidh McIntyre, Olympic sailing champion and PbP participant, says:

> As an athlete, it can feel the only way to win is to be totally single minded and selfish towards the cause but it's becoming increasingly obvious that sport is missing the opportunity to unite and empower people behind the important issues of the day... If I can inspire one child to love sport and protect the ocean; if I can teach one child that their tears might become their greatest strength, that's success too.

The Long Win in action

Connection: TAP's approach blends mindfulness training, play, movement practices, mentoring, and reflective spaces to support the growth of communities in which every individual feels free to explore who they are and who they want to become alongside others. Like the Long Win, their work is not prescriptive but strongly relational, long-term, where each individual has space to follow their own journey.

3Cs: TAP's three pillars of performance, wellbeing and social impact naturally map onto the 3Cs. Their programmes enable participants to Clarify identities beyond sport, and purpose beyond medals, facilitate the development of values-based environments underpinned by mastery and Constant Learning, and prioritize Connection through both relationships and wider social impact.

John Morgan, Co-founder and CEO of Morgan Sindall Group

Committed to a values-based workplace that feels connected to a shared purpose of enhancing communities

Co-founder and CEO of Morgan Sindall Group, John believes deeply in the company's values, which he has been developing since co-founding the original company Morgan Lovell in 1977. These values form a critical thread across the group of companies:

- Consistent achievement is key to our future.
- The customer comes first.
- Talented people are key to our success.
- We must challenge the status quo.
- We have a decentralized philosophy.

The last point about a decentralized philosophy distinguishes the companies from their competitors, empowering decision-making close to the frontline and giving more autonomy to their leaders. With the lack of centralized communication and functions, the values provide a natural link across the Morgan Sindall Group.

John takes leadership development seriously and attends every single one of the leadership programmes, without fail – the programmes are never confirmed until the dates are in his diary. How many CEOs prioritize that? In the time spent on each programme, he focuses entirely on the company's values. John leads interactive sessions to connect the leaders more closely to the values. He may ask leaders to mime them or act them out, to debate which they think is most important or least important. He never discusses the latest financial figures or future growth targets. If asked about this, John emphasizes that the company focus is on being 'better' not 'bigger', though this has in practice led to strong growth.

The company has clear priorities on the sort of community projects they do best and is willing to turn down those that don't fit their strengths. Taking on projects where the company can add most value to the local community helps the overall ambition to be better not bigger, feeds into decision-making about future projects and supports a relentless focus on quality and positive social impact – all of which adds up to long-term stability, performance and sustainability for the company, even in difficult times.

The Long Win in action

Clarity: John wants to build Clarity across the group's leaders about how the values underpin the long-term success of their company. It's a priority for leaders to role-model the values and use them to connect colleagues and external stakeholders. It's moments where values are upheld or overlooked – a joke made at someone's expense that's tolerated rather than challenged, a decision about a customer's project – that feed into a customer's gut feel and Connection to the company or an employee's sense of belonging.

Long-Term Thinking: John highlights the importance of taking a long-term view and staying focused on that despite other pressures. He shared that 'We find a lot of people in our organization like things like awards (which I don't) as they like to see a measure of perceived success. We try to get our teams to enjoy the journey as there is no final destination and no finite measure of what winning means.'

Purpose: a strong focus on communities rather than profit enables better decision-making about future projects and higher quality within the projects that the company takes on, and through that a higher long-term success rate is achieved.

Constant Learning: Leadership is about 'how' we work as much as 'what' we do. Leaders need space to learn and reflect on how to become role models for the culture required to sustain long-term performance. Learning experiences are more effective when interactive, experiential and collaborative.

Helen Tupper and Sarah Ellis, Co-founders of Amazing If and *Squiggly Careers* podcast hosts

On a mission to make careers better for everyone

Helen and Sarah, friends since university, both spent nearly 20 years working in different big businesses. Over a coffee one day, they reflected on how their successful careers had deviated from the expected ladder-like path. They could see they were so much better off because they'd developed in different directions, explored possibilities and been open to unexpected opportunities.

So Helen and Sarah set out on a mission to democratize career development and bust myths that careers are and should be linear, coining the term the 'squiggly career'. Their company provides easy ways for people to take ownership of their own careers.

Amazing If provides practical materials addressing a whole area of our working lives that was previously only considered by a select few. Their books offer practical exercises and tools around career development. Some organizations give these to new joiners or long-term staff members as a way of giving them support and freedom to carve out their own career paths.

In 2022, Amazing If launched the global 'squiggle and stay' experiment, involving 16 organizations who wanted to test ways to reimagine 'talent retention'. Experiments range from replacing ladder-like language in job specifications to 'squiggly safaris' (where employees are given a safari allowance to spend time in different teams). Everyone involved in this pioneering project committed to sharing their learning externally, embodying a spirit of open collaboration rather than closed competition.

Sarah points out that

> frequently, many of us felt we had little control over our own work lives. Giving the reins of our careers back to us and facilitating open conversations in the workplace about our careers, how we lead, how we work in teams, how we can thrive at work and what we want from work, is playing a part in transforming the way we think about our working lives.

Their work comes at a crucial point of significant social, technological and demographic change. Modern careers no longer resemble those of older generations; career development clearly needs to move in step.

The Long Win in action

Long-Term thinking and reframing success: Long Win Thinking connects naturally with the 'squiggly career' philosophy, which sets out to help people find the right career path for them. Both approaches help us understand what brings meaning to our work lives, and how to think about the values and purpose in our work, rather than simply seeing our careers in terms of the next promotion.

Clarity of Purpose: The mission to increase accessibility to career development skills runs like a thread throughout Amazing If's work. As the company grows, Sarah and Helen constantly focus on where they can add most value to others, where they can be most unique in what they offer and where they can have greatest impact. They refer to Amazing If's values constantly in their conversations and use them as a filter for decisions and priorities:

Action: We are motivated by doing and the practical 'how to' of learning.

Energy: We generate energy and commitment to career development.

Useful: Everything we create is relevant, relatable, and can be put into practice.

Work in progress: We are always learning and improving.

Constant Learning: Despite the rapid growth of their company, both put aside time to read the latest business books and distil the key ideas into useful, practical nuggets for their audiences to gain from and to inform the growth of their own business. Learning and helping others to learn underpins their mission.

Connection: Both are wonderful connectors. They consciously develop and draw on their powerful, diverse networks, just as they support others to develop Connection skills, networks and relationships at work. Competing over careers is probably one of the most common yet most counterproductive activities in our work lives, where it's hard to see any positive impact on performance over the long term and a lot of potential for reducing fulfilment and achievement. Their collaborative approach profoundly reimagines career development.

Debbie Sayers, founder of Salisbury Rovers FC
Transforming youth sport through a human rights-based approach

Debbie Sayers started a youth football club in Salisbury in 2016 after her son's experiences of football left her alarmed. She founded Salisbury Rovers FC to be truly based around children, prioritizing their voices and respecting their rights, with 'play at the beating heart of their club'.

Having grown up on a council estate where unsupervised play was the norm, and being a lifelong football fan, Debbie felt that the current system failed to see the game as children experienced it. A human rights lawyer by profession, Debbie noted the lack of awareness in youth sport of the UN Convention on the Rights of the Child, which enshrines children's rights in international law, including the right to be heard, the right to develop and the right to play.

Instead, the prevailing and largely unchallenged status quo in youth sport revolves around adult objectives such as early selection, 'talent scouting' and 'elite' programmes recruiting children at young ages. Even well-meaning attempts to 'make sport fun for kids' remain based on adult aims and perceptions. Youth football basically mirrors the adult paradigm of structure and leagues, or in Debbie's words, 'kids in kits in teams in leagues'.

In contrast, Salisbury Rovers has a clear philosophy based on rights and pedagogical principles. Their coaching approach is based on the theory of self-determination. Football planning and delivery reflects a deeply embedded process of dialogue with children about what they want from their game. Children are constantly encouraged to express their views and participate in decision-making. Session plans are built on their views and can be thrown out of the window (and frequently are) when they have different ideas. Coaches don't direct children's play in matches; instead they ask questions, engage, discuss and listen.

The club doesn't always play in traditional competitions, as these can cause behaviours which impede a child's development. For instance, coaches start shouting, the best players are drafted in at the expense of the rest, mistakes are seen as bad and learning is soon squeezed out. This is not a rejection but a redefinition of competition. The club believes in competitive play for all children, but not giving certain 'more talented' players more time in games and leaving others on the side. Competition is owned by the young person, not the coach, and it involves effort, learning, leading and having fun – not just beating the local club opponents. They do play matches but don't always stay within the confines of traditional rules and formats, enabling greater creativity and learning of both football and thinking skills.

Echoing the research of US educationalist Alfie Kohn, cited in Chapter 5, Debbie understands that 'Children learn most when they solve problems themselves. Not if we constantly offer them what we think is the "right" solution.' There are no screamed instructions from the touchline; nor is there an overarching focus on the scoreline. Instead, success means 'the kids lead the play', a process that is also developing confident, thoughtful future citizens.

The Long Win in action

Clarity: Having a values-based culture, a rights-based framework and an evidence-based pedagogy gives Salisbury Rovers Clarity on what they stand for: placing the child at the centre of youth sport. 'If you don't step back and let young people lead, you'll never know what they can do.'

Constant Learning: Free play and children's autonomy are the starting point for football at Salisbury Rovers. This results in a completely different experience of the game with lots of flexibility, questioning and problem-solving led by the children themselves – a much more transformative learning and developmental environment than is traditionally offered in youth sport.

Connection and social impact: This is a grassroots sports club that aims to connect across the local community, proactively unblocking barriers to accessing football. The rights-based approach sets up different types of conversation, giving young people a much greater voice and say in what happens and a different development experience as they grow up.

Long-Term Thinking: Taking a rights-based approach means Salisbury Rovers FC sees all its young people as future citizens, not short-term talent machines. It sets up the club with the foundations to sustain this broader perspective on what matters most for sport and for society.

Chris Dossett, former Director of Sport, Health and Fitness at Solihull School and Chair of PADSIS (Professional Association of Directors of Sport in Independent Schools)

Bringing Long Win Thinking into schools

Chris is an experienced school leader who recognizes that sport in schools typically creates an experience that is too narrow – based on specific skills and winning fixtures – and misses out on the potential for a broader, more positive long-term impact on pupils.

Chris incorporated the ideas of *The Long Win* into his school's sports programme with the long-term aim of influencing the wider school community (pupils, academic departments, senior leadership, staff and parents). His department broadened 'Physical Education' into 'Sport, Health and Fitness', and created a long-term purpose for the department:

> For Sport, Health and Fitness to be fun and enjoyable for every single one of our pupils. To develop a lifelong love of Sport, Health and Fitness so that our pupils are still physically active at 25, 45 and even 95!

The programme focused on values, learning and embracing failure, and rewarded values-based behaviour. There was a clear shift away from a traditional tick-box emphasis on technical skills and narrow national curriculum goals. Lessons were less directive and delivered in a coaching style to help pupils develop their own coaching and feedback expertise – vital skills for their future lives.

At a previous school during the pandemic, when there were no fixtures or sport lessons outside, Chris connected with fellow teachers to create a mental skills programme in collaboration with Aaron Walsh (a mental skills coach who has worked with teams including Scottish Rugby and women's hockey and football teams in New Zealand). I fed into it too and enjoyed the energy and excitement around it during a difficult time. Topics included identity, pressure, process versus outcome, fear and authenticity, and the programme was eagerly received by pupils. The teachers suddenly realized that in their previously busy fixture-driven life, they had not created enough time for the mental, emotional and spiritual side of sport, and vowed this should remain a core part of school sport.

The Long Win in action

Clarity and Purpose: Chris saw the need and benefits of defining school sport in a much broader way, creating a longer-term purpose with the potential for deeper, longer-term impact on pupils' lives beyond their time at school. It's a Long Win perspective that underpins both the vision and purpose of school sport and how that translates into daily lessons.

Long-Term Thinking: Short-term metrics mean that schools tend to look at weekly match results rather than considering their responsibility to set up children to be active 10, 20, 30 years after they leave school. While a harder metric to measure, Chris and I discussed how it would be more meaningful if school sports departments could start exploring with their alumni how active they are later in life, and the role that school experiences play in that. That kind of learning would help school sport to explore better how to fulfill the subject's greater potential for individual pupils and the positive consequences that could have for society, particularly considering long-term health. (It would also help governments to understand more clearly what gets in the way of children staying active as they become teenagers and then adults.)

Constant Learning: The focus on a coaching approach, rather than 'teaching' and directing basic technical skills, changes how pupils experience a lesson and how much they learn, and role-models skills for them to learn and use way beyond their experiences of sport. This approach sees school sport as a more transformative educational and developmental experience than is often currently the case.

Alejandro Cadena, Co-founder and CEO of Caravela

A purpose-driven, quality coffee company on a mission to reshape the coffee industry and their own company culture

Caravela's mission to 'make coffee better' works on two interconnected levels – constantly improving the quality of their coffee and pursuing their wider social aims to improve the coffee industry. In relation to the latter, they aim to increase awareness and action to address inequalities across the supply chain, including addressing the traditionally poor treatment of farmers.

When I met Alejandro, Caravela was already a registered B Corp but he knew that in order to reach the next level, the company's culture and ways of working needed to shift. He wanted the next tier of leaders, those running country operations, to step up and become more engaged in the company's future strategy. This proved difficult: although the leaders were full of energy and ideas when they came together, when they returned to their country operations, they fell straight back into focusing on short-term metrics and sales targets. Alejandro knew they had to diversify metrics away from simply the number of 'bags sold' and reshape their ways of working and culture.

The challenge was how to encourage leaders to think simultaneously about what was necessary to deliver strong sales today and the longer-term twin ambitions of improving the quality of their coffee and strengthening the coffee industry. Increasing climate and global financial instability has only made this challenge more urgent.

When he became the company's interim Head of Guatemala and El Salvador in addition to his CEO role, Alejandro saw an opportunity to experiment with a new, collaborative way of leading: acting more as a coach than an instructor and encouraging greater self-management.

He started by gathering the Guatemala and El Salvador teams together to clarify their 'why' and talk through the strategic framework, including the company's core purpose, values, principles and strategic goals, aiming to develop greater alignment and sense of belonging to Caravela's purpose. Together they created objectives related to the long-term purpose. As Alejandro explained:

> For instance, our objective wasn't merely to export a set volume of coffee, but also to source that coffee from individual producers with whom we could nurture enduring relationships. In other words, we placed [the same] importance on 'how' we sourced the coffee as we did on achieving our targets.

The team members were entrusted with their agreed responsibilities and given the tools and information necessary to make decisions themselves. Alejandro, for his part, had to refrain from micromanagement – as he put it, 'demonstrating trust, treating them as responsible adults'.

This process took nearly a year, during which time Alejandro increasingly distanced himself from day-to-day operations. In his words: 'Trust was cultivated by empowering team members to make their own decisions while keeping the collective objectives in focus, over and above personal ambitions.' The team eventually went on to deliver remarkable results, further reinforcing their self-belief, capabilities and trust in a different way of working.

The Long Win in action

Purpose and Connection: Combining the essence of their business (quality coffee) with their wider social purpose (improving the coffee industry) in one phrase keeps the company purpose integrated into everyday work. Making it easy for everyone, whatever their position, to connect to a company's purpose in their everyday working lives is critical to bringing it to life and creating a strong thread of Connection and belonging across different roles in different countries.

Long Win Culture: To turn a company purpose from a mission statement into a way of working requires deep cultural change, challenging and disrupting existing ways of working throughout the organization. As well as our discussions, Alejandro drew on the theory and practical examples in Frederick Laloux's work *Reinventing Organizations* and consulted business experts to learn more about bringing self-management into Caravela's ways of working.

Constant Learning: By showing up as a coach rather than simply the boss, Alejandro facilitated a different type of engagement, with greater collaboration and autonomy. It makes sense to enable more self-management across a lean, dynamic organization where the operations can look quite different from Taiwan to Guatemala, from Australia to Peru. Colleagues were galvanized to learn actively from the past and take this into consideration when thinking about future possibilities. Powerful freedom and agency is unlocked by a strong sense of purpose, autonomy and Constant Learning (the fundamentals of intrinsic motivation set out by Daniel Pink in Chapter 5), which create the best performance fuel for any company looking to explore its potential.

Jon Alexander, co-founder of the New Citizenship Project and author of *Citizens*

Supporting us to think and act like citizens, not consumers, and see the greater possibilities that brings

Jon, with Irenie Ekkeshis, started the New Citizenship Project (NCP) to change the way society addresses challenges and opportunities. They facilitate greater collaboration and engagement in a way that has died out during the last decades of the social contract, where we have become 'consumers' of what government or business offers us rather than agents and participants shaping society.

In his book, *Citizens: Why the Key to Fixing Everything Is All of Us*, Jon shares examples from around the world of how different leaders and groups have come together to solve a range of problems, from Taiwan crowdsourcing what was arguably the world's most successful COVID-19 response to the National Trust treating members and visitors as collaborators in the work of protecting and championing the importance of beauty in the world, not just as consumers of days out.

Jon and the NCP start from the fundamental question: what if we treated people as participants in causes rather than consumers of products? Their approach invites groups and organizations to reimagine what's possible (rather than simply how to tweak existing, usually vastly suboptimal, systems and processes) and explore how greater collaboration with others can enable better outcomes.

They use approaches based on collaboration, consultation, giving voices to all citizens – not just those in authority – and amplifying the voice of those traditionally excluded from decision-making in policy and government locally and nationally.

A recent example of their work is the process design of the People's Plan for Nature, combining input from thousands of people across the UK – from government bodies to businesses, charities, farmers and communities – in an initiative to protect and fundamentally change how we value nature. It provides a vision for the future and sets out the actions we must all take. The first stage was to bring together people from all walks of life for a National Conversation; the second was a citizens' assembly to deliberate the key issues, and find and strengthen the common ground; then, with the resulting Plan, the third is not only to challenge businesses and governments but also to support community organizations to take meaningful action to protect nature.

The aim is never just to come up with a new plan, but to bring about a creative, collaborative approach where we think differently about our role in national life and gain a voice and opportunity to get involved alongside others with different perspectives. In other words, they draw on a practical process for developing Long Win Thinking on some of the biggest issues of our day.

The Long Win in action

Clarity and Long-Term Thinking: Thinking long-term is essential if we are to address issues such as environmental protection or social inequality. Short-term fixes, policy changes and projects imposed on communities from the centre have failed. A different mindset is needed to consider things beyond electoral timescales, annual metrics and other rigid frameworks that stifle long-term thinking, and to allow multiple perspectives to come together.

Language: Jon, Irenie and the team at the NCP use language as a key tool for thinking differently. They challenge the dominant language of consumerism to help groups reframe their purpose and how they engage others in that. Even changing prepositions to use 'with' more than 'to', 'for' or 'against' can signal a different relationship of interdependence rather than dependence and control. This echoes discussions on language in *The Long Win*, and there are tools at the end of the book to help you develop different conversations.

3Cs/3Ps: In conversation with Jon, we realized the 3Ps framework – Purpose, Prototype, Platform – that the NCP use to facilitate their work with organizations maps closely onto the 3Cs of *The Long Win*. We've seen how Purpose sits at the heart of our theme of Clarity; Prototype mirrors Constant Learning and testing, experimenting and further refining of what's possible when working in a different way; and the focus on Platform is about Connection to build communities with a greater voice, input and involvement in how they want their lives to be.

Possibility: Jon, Irenie and the team at NCP take as a starting point the question 'What would you do in this time if you truly believed in yourself and in those around you?' It's a question based on exploring possibilities, not probabilities, in broadening our thinking and actions, not constraining them, and on taking positive action collaboratively, not reacting passively and individually. This question echoes the vision at the heart of *The Long Win* to provide a way of thinking and practical framework to help us better explore what's possible, together.

Reflections on our Long Winners

We've glimpsed how a range of leaders are redefining success and applying Long Win Thinking to support their colleagues to thrive and sustain performance with a positive impact on society. Although the leaders differ hugely in the work they do and in their own leadership styles, there are some common threads that run through these snapshots. These leaders all show a willingness to challenge the status quo where it isn't working; they are committed to a purpose greater than themselves, accompanied by a sense of humility and constant openness to learning; and there is a strong relational focus in their work priorities. These leaders lead some of the most empowered, creative and 'human' work environments that I've seen.

The world is beyond the winning.
Lao Tzu (*The Complete Works of Lao Tzu*)

Concluding Thoughts

New Language, Different Questions, Fresh Stories

Language

We looked in the first chapter at where the word 'winning' comes from and then traced how a dominant definition of winning has emerged and become distorted over time to drive an increasingly narrow way of thinking, behaving and interacting. In contrast, Long Win Thinking redefines winning through a broader emphasis on what matters over the longer term, a focus on learning and growth rather than short-term outcomes, and a recognition of the extent of collaboration and connectedness that is essential to fulfilling our ambitions.

In this redefining process, language is a crucial tool that underpins how we think, behave and interact. How we put ideas into words determines how those thoughts come alive. Language offers a window into the mind and as such forms a thread through this book as we have uncovered more about what winning has come to mean in our lives and more about our beliefs, biases and assumptions on this topic.

I have become increasingly aware of this in both personal and professional settings. We intend to say one thing, but the language we use reveals that we don't fully believe it. For example, team leaders at work say that they want their team to speak up more and share their ideas. But what I then observe in the meetings which follow is that the leader's language (verbal and non-verbal) says the opposite. Either they turn away when new ideas are shared or quickly close them down, act impatiently or even interrupt. At times, they can be completely unaware they are doing this.

This highlights one of the difficulties of challenging cultural concepts: we need to look for signs of our subconscious thinking if we are to change our behaviours. Most leaders set out with good intentions in their ambitions to win, wanting to engage, value others and improve inclusion without realizing that their definitions of success may actually demotivate, devalue and exclude others.

Changing what we say requires us to develop a new radar and consciousness about our language. This shouldn't be frightening or something to be nervous of: it's a natural process. Language is dynamic; it changes and grows all the time, so our use of language should grow and develop similarly. This requires a commitment to care not just about what we intend to say, but the impact of what we actually say. Reflecting on our impact on others requires us to get feedback from a range of sources, to stop and listen to what is happening around us, notice the language used and start to understand what it's telling us. That's a great way to connect to our environments and start shaping them together.

As we notice, review and challenge language and what it means around us, we may start to see things differently and adjust our vision of success and the words we use to describe it. In conversation with Brené Brown, sports and ecopsychologist Dr Pippa Grange uses the words 'shallow' and 'deep' to distinguish between 'winning born of comparison and scarcity and self-doubt' and 'winning where you actually can feel the richness of your journey, you are attached to the joy and the struggle, you are attached to the mess... It is done more from a soul level.' Whether it's adding adjectives or asking questions, painting a different picture or telling a different story, the language we choose plays a key role in developing Long Win Thinking.

Questions

We need to be vigilant to challenge the status quo effectively, and questions provide a useful tool and guide. With a coaching style, we can challenge some of the winning-related language that we used to take for granted and begin to explore what a redefined, Long Win vision might look like. When we hear the staple phrase 'it's all about winning', we have an opportunity to find out more: Is it? Why? What are you trying to win? Who are you trying to beat? What else matters?

When the awards come round, think about what you are rewarding and who the winners are. Who have the heroes been in the past, and who do you want to be recognized in the future? Consider the criteria for who gets valued and undervalued, and whether you are rewarding short-term outcomes or looking for a deeper contribution. As leaders, think about the traditional heroic trappings of feeling like we need to know all the answers, being unbendingly tough and full of direction. Then step out of those and think about what we can do to create an environment where connections grow, collaboration is the norm and colleagues can thrive. Asking ourselves 'What do I need to let go of that has served me in the past but won't help in the future?' can spark useful reflections.

It's time to challenge empty phrases like 'no pain, no gain', 'you're only as good as your last result' and 'you'll prove your worth if you win'. Find some better ones or replace them with questions. Why does the past have to predict the future? What else is possible? What have you learnt from your recent experience? And if you hear anyone dismissing others as losers, or categorizing the top talent from the rest, then step in and get curious. What is driving this thinking? Is it fear of difference or fear of change? What role is ego playing? What could be gained by seeing the world through a fresh, Long Win perspective?

The language we choose and the questions we ask determine whether we keep our perspective broad and open to future possibilities or constrain ourselves and reinforce a too narrow world. By moving beyond simple, binary 'win–lose' language, we can start to see the world differently, allow ourselves to adapt and grow, and open up new possibilities.

It's useful to consider what sort of questions drive our thinking and actions each day and whether we might want to ask some different questions as we go about our daily lives. Here are some suggestions to kickstart some daily Long Win Thinking. They all concern choices that are within our control, even though other aspects of our daily life and environment may not be.

Daily questions to ask as part of the Long Win mindset (an alternative to simply reviewing a daily to-do list)

1. What's the longer-term difference you want to see and what can you do today to contribute to that? What are the short-term tasks and measures that you are working on and how will those help you work towards your longer-term purpose?
2. How will you judge whether today has been a success? What frame of mind do you want to be in? What questions will you ask of yourself and others around you? What perspective will you bring to whatever happens today, good or bad?
3. What will you learn today? And what will you gain, even if you don't get the short-term outcomes you're hoping for today?
4. Who loses out if you do well today? Do they need to? Who are your competitors, and what could you do to start to collaborate with them and create greater shared value?
5. How will you connect with those you encounter during the day? What's the impact on others (and yourself) that you want to make? How do you want to show up today?

Stories

It is striking to see how some of the 'new' sports in the Olympic fold are bringing with them refreshing language and stories, different from the old winning-obsessed mantras. Interviews with athletes competing in winter sports events like big air skiing, moguls and aerials show a huge sense of connectedness and community across the athletes, seen cheering each other on and sharing a culture of playfulness and discovery. There's huge honour and pride in going for something adventurous rather than doing what's required to win a medal. There has to be, as their sports are about risk-taking, trying to push the boundaries of what's possible, rather than playing safe to come out with a medal. The bigger mission and reward for the community of competitors is being part of pushing the sport on.

The Invictus Games founded in 2014 added a different dimension to what sporting competition could be about. Set up like a traditional multi-sport event, these Games are not just about who wins. The Invictus Games showcase adaptive sports, such as wheelchair basketball, sitting volleyball and indoor rowing for wounded, injured or sick armed services personnel and veterans. The name Invictus is the Latin word for 'unconquered' or 'undefeated'. The aim is to use the power of sport to inspire recovery, support rehabilitation and generate a wider understanding and respect for members of the armed forces who are wounded, injured and sick.[1] Prince Harry, the Duke of Sussex and Patron of the Invictus Games, spoke of

> guys sprinting for the finish line and then turning round to clap the last man in. [The Invictus Games] have been about team mates choosing to cross the line together; not wanting to come second, but not wanting the other guys [to] either. These Games have shown the very best of the human spirit.[2]

After feedback and reflection, US gymnastics coach Valorie Kondos Field, 'Miss Val', changed her whole philosophy of coaching from being a 'dogmatic dictator' focused on winning to developing 'champions in life for our world, win or lose', developing trust through patience, respectful honesty and accountability.[3] She also went on to achieve even greater competition results with that strategy. One of the finest examples of what she was able to achieve through changing her approach was with Katelyn Ohashi, a brilliant US junior gymnast who arrived at college saying she 'hated everything associated with being great'; as Kondos Field puts it: 'Katelyn didn't want to be a winner because winning had cost her her joy.'[4] Miss Val realized that her job was to help Katelyn find joy in sport again, through investing in her as a whole person, taking an interest in her life beyond gymnastics and showing that she cared about her regardless of her results. It worked, and the passion slowly returned. Video footage of Ohashi's stunning performance went viral around the world in January 2019, watched by more than 150 million viewers. She scored a perfect 10 in a brilliantly executed floor routine at the 2019 Collegiate Challenge. It's the sheer joy that she exuded in performing that makes it such compelling viewing.

Spectators and commentators alike seemed surprised and yet moved by the attitude of cyclist Geraint Thomas towards his teammate and competitor Egan Bernal in the 2019 Tour de France. His selflessness and strong team ethic in supporting the younger

Colombian rider to take the title that Thomas had hoped to retain stood out, creating a new narrative about performance and success in this most gruelling of international races. Writer and venture capitalist Mike Moritz notes that 'the real winner of the race was the man who came in second', and praises above all his 'ability to relish the achievement of others'.[5]

Jason Dorland, a Canadian Olympic rower whose experience as an athlete and coach was bred in a fear-driven 'win at all costs' world, told me how he reached rock bottom before realizing that there was an alternative approach. Jason has seen the power of sport to destroy or inspire. He uses his 'losing' story as a powerful force to show others a different way to approach sport, work and life. He sees the potential for a different vision of how sport could contribute to our lives:

> Sport can choose to maintain the status quo that says competition is a battlefield where combatants use any means to destroy one another in the pursuit of winning. Or, it can choose something more meaningful. Therein lies the truest opportunity for sport.[6]

One of the most inspirational athletes I have ever met has not won any Olympic medals. He is the only Nike-sponsored ironman triathlete, not because he is the top of the world rankings but because of the power of his story. John McAvoy served time in jail for armed robbery and was one of the UK's most wanted criminals until sport transformed his life. One of the officers who ran the prison gym realized that John had athletic talent after watching him on the rowing machine one day. Years later, after prison, he has become a professional triathlete. Alongside training, he works on many fronts to support youngsters in deprived communities and youth offender institutions. As an athlete, McAvoy prioritizes social responsibility as high as competing. When he speaks, he has a story like no other, and whether it's told to schoolchildren, university graduates, young offenders or business leaders, his story of what matters in life, of what winning means to him, reminds all of us of the choices we have and the opportunities beyond simply placing first.[7]

Many athletes are starting to explore the deeper meaning in their sporting journey – sometimes setting out to do so, sometimes discovering it by chance or in the face of adversity. The nature of pushing your boundaries as an elite athlete can develop a mindset ready to look for what's possible beyond the immediate. It need not just be about sacrifice, pain and fighting. The vocabulary of elite sport is starting to include concepts of friendship, love, human connections, emotional safety, meaning, support, values and integrity. The same exists and applies to our worlds outside sport. The challenge is to notice and develop these concepts further.

The short stories of Long Winners in Chapter 13 showed us leaders following a different approach to success across society. As we have seen throughout the book, Long Win Thinking urges us to embrace, listen to and tell different stories. It encourages us to ask more questions about the stories we think we know as part of resetting our view of what winning means for ourselves and the world around us. It is through stories that we change and shape our lives.

In *David & Goliath*, Malcolm Gladwell reinterprets the story most of us will know. He challenges the simplistic picture we have heard, accepted and admired without question: the small boy winning against the odds in the face of the all-powerful mighty warrior. But Gladwell takes a fresh look at the scene where David encounters Goliath. He points out how the giant was weighed down by his armour – which he wore in line with the ritual of single combat – how it prevented him from moving fast or even seeing clearly. He observes that David had no intention to fight like that. He plans to fight Goliath using a slingshot, playing to his strengths and using the method he had learnt to fight wild animals with. Without armour, David has speed and manoeuvrability.

Usually we don't consider such an interpretation of the story or even consider that there might be such an alternative view. Our blanket judgement on the unlikelihood of David winning shows how quickly we make assumptions about who the winners are and what power looks like. Gladwell points out how King Saul – who doubts David but agrees that he should face Goliath anyway – only sees power in terms of physical might and doesn't appreciate that power comes in other forms, for example 'substituting speed and surprise for strength'. He goes on to use this analogy to explain that 'we continue to make that error today, in ways that have consequences for everything from how we educate our children to how we fight crime and disorder'.[8]

Turning this well-known story on its head enables Gladwell to illustrate the need to challenge dominant narratives based on narrow assumptions:

much of what we consider valuable in our world arises out of these kinds of lopsided conflicts, because the act of facing overwhelming odds produces greatness and beauty... we consistently get these kinds of conflicts wrong. We misread them. We misinterpret them. Giants are not what we think they are. The same qualities that give them strength are often the sources of great weakness.[9]

In the same way, we can see that we have misunderstood what winning looks like. That winning isn't what we think it is. That the same qualities that help people win in the short term can lead them to lose over the longer term. That failing can change people positively in ways we overlook. And that success could look altogether quite different, opening up possibilities and creating opportunities to explore together much greater ambitions that were previously hard to imagine.

Sharing, listening to and searching out different stories and perspectives is the daily fuel for Long Win Thinking. One story within a story stands out to me. At one corporate dinner, I can remember listening to an Olympic champion rower telling his story of how he had been in losing crews for years but by taking a completely different approach and interrogating the way they did things, he and his crew transformed their performance and went on to become Olympic champions. It was an inspirational story and was told brilliantly. At the table where I was sitting, the business leader next to me turned to me after the dinner as everyone was clapping euphorically and gazing with admiration at the beautiful Olympic gold medal; he said:

That's a fantastic story and hugely inspirational. But... [lowering his voice as if about to speak some heresy] I can't help wondering about everyone else in that race. What about them? That race wouldn't have been as brilliant without everyone in it. And they may have trained at least as hard, maybe harder, and questioned what they did just as much too. But they don't get to stand up there, we don't get to see them or learn from them or acknowledge them, because they didn't win. But I think they probably have stories that help add value too.

That comment stayed with me because it confirmed one of the driving forces for this book: that it's time to consider some different stories that could be a vital part of our success now and in the future.

Storytelling is one of the richest ways we can reshape how we think and how others around us think. The stories we choose and seek out can widen our perspectives and bring different meanings to what we do. I have used stories throughout this book – some are my own, others are from those I have trained or worked with over my career, still others are from those I have interviewed or read about. I hope to have sparked the memory of more of your own stories, helped you to see them through a different lens and encouraged you to consider the wider meaning of those stories. Those are the first steps in shaping and defining what the Long Win looks like for you.

Concluding reflections

This is a book underpinned by questions. Throughout I have explored, probed and reflected on the question 'What does winning really mean?', viewing it from as wide a set of perspectives as possible. I have not tried to find the right answer or a simple formula. I hope that the stories, questions and ideas in this book have stirred up examples, thoughts and reflections from your own experiences of winning. Once you start to look out for something, you tend to see it more. Notice which stories from your own life are emerging in your mind, which memories of winning (or not winning) are strongest, which aspects of your work, school or home environment you might be starting to see through different eyes.

We have uncovered and discussed the full reality of winning and all its paradoxes. We have seen how something that may seem so universally simple, positive and good can, in fact, have multiple other faces. We have explored how what is held up to be winning in life – personally, socially, organizationally or globally – does not always prove as positive or meaningful over the longer term. And we have established that we have other choices.

We have dared to challenge and look in the face of what it really means when we say 'winning isn't everything; it's the only thing'. We have found that if that is true, then 'the only thing' is temporary, without lasting meaning, and a shackle around us that may hold us back from exploring what's possible long-term.

By freeing us up from the constraints and dangers of a short-term, narrow definition of winning, I aim to help us explore our potential with greater ambition. In many discussions about this book, I have contemplated, imagined and wondered what a Long Win education system, high-performance sporting environment, business environment and political system would look like. Some have asked me to describe these in more detail, but it is not the job of this book to prescribe. I have provided ideas, challenges and provocations, along with multiple stories of how business leaders, athletes, coaches and teachers are already exploring Long Win alternatives.

Our Long Win journeys start with challenging the status quo in our minds wherever it is based on a narrow, short-term definition of winning. From there, we can start to clarify our purpose in a way that gives us meaning over our lives and connects with the communities and societies we live in; continue to learn and develop throughout life, exploring new ideas and challenging old ones; and build connections that help us collaborate in different ways to be the best that we can be, together.

This book and the multiple lives behind it are part of a search for a better way to succeed that we have, at times, cut ourselves off from. There is more to success than you think. There's a bigger game to play with more riches to be won than simply winners' medals. It's time to redefine what winning in the 21st century could mean for all of us.

Epilogue

When we arrived in Athens for what was to be my third and final Olympic Games, we had a clear plan: win the heat, qualify direct to the final and then focus on delivering our best performance there. As so often in life, things didn't go to plan. We lost the first race by quite a large margin to a rival crew from Belarus. After the race, we felt shell-shocked. I could feel panic rising inside me as we returned to the dock. With just days to go until the final, for which we now had only one opportunity left to qualify, we were not in a great position.

It had not been a smooth year since winning the World Championships. The back injury that my crewmate, Katherine, had sustained during those championships had disrupted our winter and we had been left playing catch-up from there. The knowledge that a new life and career was waiting for me after Athens was a vital lifeline that helped me to dig in and keep finding ways round the obstacles in our path. I knew I had learnt and grown so much through risking a return to the sport and exploring a new approach. But I also knew I had literally only a few minutes of racing left to see that bear fruit within my sporting career. The nearer to the Games we got, the more my poor past record was playing on my mind. And after our disappointing first race in Athens, I noticed people within our team literally move away from us, talk to us less, approach us less in the team hotel.

A few hours after that race, we sat down with our coach and had one of those eyeball-to-eyeball conversations. We had five days left to qualify through the repechage and, if we got through it, then race in the final. We needed to be ready to write our own story, try some new things, take some risks, make some changes and trust in each other. We had to cut out what others were saying – that we had lost it or that we'd never come back from such a poor start to our Olympic campaign or that Katherine's injury challenges and my poor past performances would predict what would happen next. It was yet another giant challenge, following on from a decade-long experience of working out how to scale one challenging peak after another.

An incredibly intense few days followed as we wrestled our demons to rebuild ourselves to win the next round and then prepare for the Olympic final. We challenged ourselves to make changes and refine our technique with just hours left for us to hone it. A stream of thoughts and feelings surged through us night and day as we lived with the uncertainty of how things would play out through those last few days.

Five days after that first race, we sat on the start line of the Olympic final. For me, the first and only Olympic final of my sporting career. It was a lung-busting, adrenaline-fuelled seven minutes, eight and a half seconds of my life, into which I poured my heart and soul, laid out bare on that 2,000-metre stretch of water in Athens.

When I crossed the line on Lake Schinias on 21 August 2004, I experienced the broadest set of emotions possible and a tide of questions that have challenged my thinking ever since. Those questions have stayed with me – sometimes in the back of my mind as I have embarked on what I thought would be new worlds less defined by winning; sometimes at the front of my mind as I have found the issue recurring around me. It's been a thread through my professional life as I worked with individuals, teams and organizations looking to be successful yet trapped in many habits, processes and assumptions which hold them back. It's also been a thread through my personal life as I have tried to work out what matters for me, for my family, for my children.

I started off wrestling with doubts about whether I was a 'loser' or not, wondering whether I was looking for a justification to make myself feel better about not finishing first and worrying whether the 'winners' would laugh at my reflections on this issue. I now know that deep down the winners feel the same way, and that the questions don't go away whatever the result.

I know that what I experienced on Lake Schinias can never be wholly summed up by a shiny round piece of metal, whatever its colour. That medal is important to me but it's really just one part of a much richer story, from before and since then, that goes well beyond that moment of crossing the line.

I realize now that on that hot, sunny August day in Athens, I took a step forward on the path to gaining a new way of thinking and a deeper sense of what matters. I dispelled some myths that had long held sway over my mind and stood at the beginning of a fascinating adventure to explore the possibilities of what winning could mean for us all.

Long Win Thinking Tips and Tools

The following tools illustrate some of the language, characteristics and thinking patterns that support the Long Win approach. These examples aim to help us bring Long Win Thinking to life and to work out how we might consciously start to develop it further around us.

I: Characteristics of Long Win Thinking in practice

Short win thinking	Long Win thinking
	Clarity
Narrow, short-term focus, not being willing or being afraid to explore or look beyond immediate frameworks	Broader perspective that helps us connect constantly to the bigger picture
Narrow metrics and measures (sales figures; profits; KPIs and other targets; election results; exam grades; rankings) matter the most	Pluralist definition of success and 'meaningful metrics' (experiences; stories of lived values; collaboration; progress towards our purpose, health and wellbeing, and social impact)
Values are jettisoned for short-term gain or when the pressure is on	Values are connected to everyone's work, and leaders uphold them in good times and bad
Articulated culture (what is announced, what goes on the walls and in the policies) is what counts	Deeper culture and the experience of everyone in an organization matters most

Short-term results and short-term decision-making are constantly prioritized	Willingness to sacrifice results in the short term to learn from a mistake, adapt or change in order to thrive in the long term
Success is about results, whatever the cost	Success is defined by culture, the way things are done (the experience of employees, athletes, pupils and so on are foremost; excellence is celebrated; the focus is on long-term impact
	Constant Learning
Only interested in and keen to emulate those who finish first in sport or business	Open to listen to and learn from a wide set of stories, including those with different outcomes than coming first
Immediate skills are recognized and highly valued	Longer-term development (critical thinking, innovation, creativity, collaboration) is valued and invested in
Winners are those who come first	Winners are those with valuable perspectives to learn from, with new ideas, questions and experiences to contribute
Focus is on short-term actions	Focus is on being willing to explore all ideas, curious, open to learn, not leaping to judge (people or ideas)
Prioritizes strategies for quick wins	Prioritizes efforts important to longer-term outcomes and wider outcomes
Focus is on tasks, task execution, to-do lists; celebrate 'hero-fixers'	Focus is on how we show up, whether we are willing to slow down to connect with others, to practise mindfulness to grow awareness of ourself and others, to show compassion for ourself and others

Prioritizes narrow expertise, specialisms and categories	Prioritizes multidisciplinary thinking and broad, creative skills that can't be easily categorized
Connection	
People are defined by their achievements, as athletes, engineers, lawyers...	People are embraced for who they are rather than for their achievements
Management style relies on control, compliance and domination	Management style relies on trust, collaboration and inclusion
Onus is on striving for certainty wherever possible	Uncertainty and ambiguity are tolerated and embraced
In negotiations and work conversations, it's a zero-sum game – someone has to win and someone has to lose	In negotiations and work conversations, a 'win–win' approach is taken, looking for both sides to gain benefits; everyone works together to create an overall greater outcome for both sides to share
Competitiveness is a key desired behaviour, recognized and rewarded extrinsically	Collaboration is a key desired behaviour, with opportunities to broaden connections and relationships valued
Successful meetings are defined by decisions and action points	Successful meetings are defined by connecting to the shared purpose, giving time to alternative ideas and unheard voices, building relationships, developing a common understanding and ensuring wide buy-in

II: Language of Long Win Thinking

Short win language	Long Win language
Temporary, transient, short-term	Lasting value, long-term
Targets, KPIs, deadlines, simple outcome metrics (e.g. sales, final results)	Shared vision, variety of quantitative and qualitative metrics and processes (not just outcome goals)
Inanimate, mechanistic, non-human, extrinsic focus	Human experience, meaning, emotions, intrinsic focus
Emphasis on uniformity, conformity	Diversity, creativity, originality are praised
Compliance, control, goals imposed	Participation, involvement, autonomy, having a voice
Task driven	People first, purpose driven
Success based on individual benefit	Success based on social impact and community development
Stories of status or ego	Stories of human growth, collective progress, shared learning
Binary thinking, right/wrong polarity, fixed mindsets	Pluralist thinking, multiple possibilities and perspectives are embraced
Taking the probable path	Exploring all possible paths

Note: It's not a question of either-or here... you can benefit from both perspectives. However, it is Long Win Thinking which sustains performance and unlocks collective potential over the long term.

III: Practices to bring the 3Cs of the Long Win into the workplace

Clarity

- *Relate each daily conversation, meeting and activity to the broader purpose.* It can be done with a sentence at the start of a meeting, if you are chairing, or it can be how you open and frame a conversation.

- *Use the five 'whys'* to help link people at all levels of an organization to the broader purpose: Why is this meeting important? To share information. Why do we need to do that? To make the best-informed decision on the next step. Why is that decision important? To start the next project. Why is that project important? To reach our clients. Why do we want to reach our clients? To improve the quality of their lives. You can even go beyond five sometimes: Why does that matter? To improve social cohesion.)

- *Agree 'how' you want to work* as a team, as a department, as an organization. 'How' matters – it's your culture, the way you go about the work you want to do, setting common standards and norms for behaviours and interactions. These provide a framework and structure to review when things may not be working well within a team, and provide a route to supporting people to thrive. Some call these 'ground rules', or 'charters'. It doesn't matter what they're called; it's about having an explicit inclusive discussion about 'how' we want to go about things – for example, getting feedback, making decisions, managing conflict – and then regularly reviewing and updating that. It's usually when this is left to chance that difficulties, misunderstandings, dysfunctionality – or at times, serious reputational damage or unethical behaviour – happen.

Constant Learning

- *Review regularly,* not just when things go badly. Be sure to do it when things go well. Learning should be the norm. Regardless of outcomes, review what's worked well, what could be improved and what things you could do differently next time. Stick with that tripartite structure to create a habit that maximizes the learning across your organization and builds resilience in teams through a Constant Learning mindset. Don't just review outcomes, review the process, the experience and the way your teams went about things (the 'performance process'), which can be where most performance improvement opportunities lie.

- *Give yourself time to reflect and learn* in small moments during the day. You might want to keep a diary to jot down things you notice. Take a moment to notice at the end of the day which moments, positive or negative, have stayed with you, and explore why these have made an impact on you. Don't leap to judge when reflecting; seek to understand first. From there, different ways forward emerge.

- *Build a coaching culture.* Invest in coaching skills at all levels of the organization, as these are crucial to building a learning culture that gives everyone a voice. Remember that often people think they're coaching when they're not! We need training and frequent refreshers to develop strong coaching skills, and then support to ensure we're really using them.

Connection

Experiment with practical ways to ensure that people and relationships come first:

- *Look at your diary through a relational lens.* Usually our electronic calendars have meetings, agendas and timings on them, detailing the 'what' and the 'when'. Let's bring people into our schedule. Add more relationship-building information into your calendar, agenda, to-do lists and organization tools. Ask yourself: Who's in the meeting? What do I want to learn from them? How I can use this meeting to deepen my relationship with them?

- *Set relationship-building goals,* not just task-related goals. Ensure people-related goals are highest on your to-do list. When goal-setting, include goals about the experience you want to have doing the job that you do, and the experience you want others in your team and organization to have working with you.

- Take a look at your team or organizational organogram and *start exploring, understanding and developing what's happening in the white space between people*. That's where relationships, teamwork, collaboration, communication, learning and innovation take place – the 'glue' in our teams and organizations which we want to develop intentionally. Try drawing different shaped lines or using different colours to represent communication, collaboration and energy. Use the thickness of lines to represent the strength and depth of the relationship, and use arrows to show if communication is two-way or one-way. This humanizes our organization charts and allows us to start seeing and investing in areas that can hugely impact performance and wellbeing, and spotting gaps where increased Connection can usefully be fostered.

- Finally, *stories* offer a brilliant way to clarify what matters, help us explain our purpose and how our work connects to it, and learn about the culture of our workplaces. What are the stories that you currently hear about how you lead, about what it's like to be in your team or in your organization? Are they 'short win' or Long Win stories? Think about the stories you'd like to be part of creating and what'd be required of you to shape that. Stories often offer us the most meaningful metric of success.

Acknowledgements

This second edition has continued to grow out of aspects of every part of my life, personal and professional. I am grateful to more people than I can name, with whom the ideas, experiences and thoughts in this book continue to be developed, discussed and debated.

I owe much to all those who have won and lost alongside me – especially crewmates from two Olympic coxless pair campaigns, Dot Blackie and Katherine Grainger – as well as many more behind the scenes who brought me far more than any round piece of metal ever could.

Numerous conversations have been pivotal to the development of this book. Being able to discuss this topic with Margaret Heffernan and Matthew Syed was a privilege; their personal generosity and encouragement are hugely appreciated. Thanks also go to Sam Parfitt; Laurence Halsted; Ben Ryan; Helen Tupper and Sarah Ellis from Amazing If; Debbie Sayers; Alejandro Cadena and the Caravela team; Jane Davidson; John Morgan; Chris Dossett; Gary Hendler and the Eisai team; Simon Mundie; Jon Alexander; Ben Hunt-Davis and the Will It? Team; Steve Ingham; Chris Shambrook; Jason Dorland; Annie Vernon; Goldie Sayers; Valorie Kondos Field; Josie Perry; Al Smith; Andrew Hill; Eva Carneiro; Roger Bayly; Matt Brittin; and Alison Maitland. Thanks to Professor Ian Robertson for the use of his words as an epigraph. Heartfelt thanks to all who have read and shared feedback, comments, questions and personal stories since *The Long Win* was first published.

The opportunity to teach on Executive Education programmes at the Judge Business School remains formative in shaping my thinking and gaining fresh business perspectives. Particular thanks to colleagues Mark de Rond, Philip Stiles, Mark Smith, Patrizia Vecchi, Smaranda Gosa-Mensing, the late and much-missed Sucheta Nadkarni and the rest of the team who make it a joy to work on those programmes.

I am immensely indebted to Alison Jones and the Practical Inspiration Publishing team for helping me enter and continue to explore the mind-stretching, inspiring world of authorship.

Last but not least, I am deeply grateful to my family. I have a habit of taking on challenges that stretch me to the extreme. First writing and now revising this book has certainly been one of those. I am thankful they have accepted my intense preoccupation with this project.

Any errors and omissions are, of course, my own, and I hope you can look past them to the ideas, questions and suggestions that I wanted to share in this book as part of my own Long Win journey and in support of yours.

About the Author

Cath Bishop is an Olympian and former diplomat who now works as a consultant and coach in leadership, team development and cultural change. She grew up in Leigh-on-Sea, Essex, and studied at Pembroke College, University of Cambridge, where she learnt to row, competing twice in the Boat Race against Oxford. She represented Great Britain at three Olympic Games and six World Championships. She won a silver medal in the coxless pairs with Dot Blackie at the 1998 World Championships and a gold medal at the same event with Katherine Grainger in 2003, before winning silver at the 2004 Athens Olympics. (But as this book attests, it was about so much more than the medals!)

Cath has an MA in Modern and Medieval Languages from Pembroke College, Cambridge, an MPhil in International Politics from the University of Wales, Aberystwyth, and a PhD in German from the University of Reading. She is an honorary fellow of Pembroke College, Cambridge, and the University of Aberystwyth, and a Steward of Henley Royal Regatta.

Cath was a diplomat in the Foreign & Commonwealth Office between 2001 and 2013, specializing in policy, negotiations and conflict issues, with postings to Bosnia and Iraq. Since leaving the Foreign & Commonwealth Office, Cath has worked in team and leadership development as a consultant, facilitator and coach. She teaches on executive education programmes at Judge Business School, University of Cambridge, and is a sought-after speaker at events around the world. She writes regular articles on culture in sport for *The Guardian* and lives in London with her husband and two children.

More details about Cath and how to contact her can be found at www.cathbishop.com and more materials and insights related to the book can be found at www.thelongwin.com

Endnotes

¹ This is the earliest recorded source of the modern-day saying 'all that glitters is not gold', from Alain de Lille, a French monk who translated a popular local saying into Latin in the 12th century. It echoes in *Aesop's Fables* and can be found in many works of literature since, such as works by Chaucer ('Hit is not al gold, that glareth', *The House of Fame, a*nd 'The Canon's Yeoman's Tale' in *The Canterbury Tales*), the poetry of Chaucer's successor John Lydgate (*The Fall of Princes*), Shakespeare ('All that glisters is not gold', *The Merchant of Venice*), Thomas Gray (*Ode on the Death of a Favourite Cat, Drowned in a Tub of Goldfishes*), Miguel de Cervantes ('no es oro todo lo que reluce', *Don Quixote*) and JRR Tolkien ('All that is gold does not glitter', from a poem originally written for *The Fellowship of the Ring*), as well as many songs, poems and other works. More recently, there were strong Hollywood echoes in *Indiana Jones and the Last Crusade* when the villain, Donovan, is attracted to the gold, bejewelled vessel which he believes must be the Holy Grail, when in fact he's been tricked by his accomplice, Elsa, and the real Grail is a much simpler cup.

Introduction

¹ Buzz Aldrin, *Magnificent Desolation: The Long Journey Home from the Moon*, Harmony, 2009.

² Andy Bull, 'Jonny Wilkinson: "It took a few years for the pressure to really build. And then it exploded"', *The Guardian*, 9 September 2019.

³ Valorie Kondos Field, *Why Winning Doesn't Always Equal Success*, TED Talk, 2019.

Chapter 1

¹ Donald Trump, electoral campaign speech, May 2016.

² Danielle Gaucher, Justin Friesen and Aaron C. Kay, 'Evidence that gendered wording in job advertisements exists and sustains gender inequality', *Journal of Personality and Social Psychology*, 101 (1), 109–128, 2011.

³ Alfie Kohn, *No Contest: The Case Against Competition: Why We Lose in Our Race to Win*, Houghton Mifflin, 1986, p. 30.

⁴ David Hauser and Norbert Schwarz, 'The war on prevention II: Battle metaphors undermine cancer treatment and prevention and do not increase vigilance', *Health Communication*, 35 (13), 1698–1704, 2019.

⁵ Jerry Z. Muller, *The Tyranny of Metrics*, Princeton University Press, 2018, p. 79.

⁶ Joseph Stiglitz, 'It's time to retire metrics like GDP. They don't measure everything that matters', *The Guardian*, 24 November 2019.

[7] Jay Winsten, 'Science and the media: The boundaries of truth', *Health Affairs*, 4 (1), 5–23, 1985.

[8] For example, Eva-Maria Jacobsson, Lee B. Becker, Tudor Vlad, C. Ann Hollifield and Adam Jacobsson, 'The impact of market competition on journalistic performance', paper presented to the Journalism Research and Education section of the *International Association for Media and Communication Research* conference, Stockholm, July 2008.

Chapter 2

[1] The Prisoner's dilemma is one of the best-known models of game theory. It shows why two rational individuals might not cooperate, even if it is in their best interests to do so. It dates back to psychological research in 1950 by Merrill Flood and Melvin Dresher, and was formalized by Albert W. Tucker, who presented it as follows: Two members of a criminal gang are arrested and imprisoned. They are put in solitary confinement so are unable to communicate with each other. The prosecutors offer each prisoner a bargain – each is given the opportunity either to betray the other by testifying that the other committed the crime or to cooperate with the other by remaining silent. If they betray each other, both serve two years in prison. If both remain silent, both will serve only one year in prison. But if one betrays the other, the first is set free and the other serves three years in prison (and vice versa).

The two prisoners are more rewarded if they both cooperate than if they both defect, but one individual stands to gain even more if they defect while the opponent cooperates. What is rational for the individual is not rational when applied to them both. In the long run, each does best when both cooperate.

[2] I first encountered this exercise at the Leadership Trust, an organization that prioritizes experiential learning and reflection time within their courses. I have seen it used at many business schools too.

[3] Kohn, *No Contest*, p. 12.

[4] Frans De Waal, *Moral Behaviour in Animals*, TED Talk, 2012.

[5] Kohn, *No Contest* p. 21.

[6] Ibid.

[7] Charles Darwin, *On the Origin of Species*, Chapter III, John Murray, 1859, p. 6.

[8] Albert Bandura, *Social Learning Theory*, Pearson, 1976.

[9] *Ibid.*

[10] Amy Cuddy, *Your Body Language May Shape Who You Are*, TED Talk, 2012. Interestingly, the reaction to Cuddy's success with the power pose research was extremely hostile and many still dispute her findings. She has had to fight back and refute the criticism.

[11] Emma Vickers, 'Problem gambling among athletes: Why are they susceptible?', *Believe Perform*, https://believeperform.com/problem-gambling-among-athletes-why-are-they-susceptible/

[12] Matthew Syed, *Bounce: The Myth of Talent and the Power of Practice*, HarperCollins, 2010, p. 195.

[13] Bull, 'Jonny Wilkinson'.

[14] Bob Goldman and Ronald Klatz, *Death in the Locker Room: Drugs & Sports* (2nd ed.), Elite Sports Medicine Publications, 1992, p. 24.

[15] James Connor, Jules Woolf and Jason Mazanov, 'Would they dope? Revisiting the Goldman dilemma', *British Journal of Sports Medicine*, 47 (11), 697–700, January 2013.

[16] Frank Ryan, *Sports and Psychology*, Prentice Hall, 1981, p. 205.

Chapter 3

[1] Caroline Criado Perez, *Invisible Women: Exposing Data Bias in a World Designed for Men*, Chatto & Windus, 2019, p. xi.

[2] Anand Giridharadas, *Winners Take All: The Elite Charade of Changing the World*, Knopf, 2018.

[3] Translated to mean 'I am because we are', Ubuntu thinking has become more widely known outside Africa thanks to the theology of Desmond Tutu and Nelson Mandela.

[4] A mixed martial art which combined boxing and wrestling.

[5] 'The Olympic motto', www.olympic.org/the-olympic-motto

Chapter 4

[1] *Monopoly* was originally invented in the early 20th century by Elizabeth Magie to warn players of the dangers of 'land grabbing' and capitalist monopolist thinking.

[2] Margaret Heffernan, 'Hierarchies lie at the root of corporate decay', *Financial Times*, 7 December 2017.

[3] Rich Karlgaard, *Late Bloomers: The Power of Patience in a World Obsessed with Early Achievement*, Currency, 2019.

Chapter 5

[1] Ibid.

[2] Margaret Heffernan, *A Bigger Prize*, Simon & Schuster, 2014, p. 53.

[3] Benjamin Zander and Rosamund Stone Zander, *The Art of Possibility*, Penguin, 2000, p. 31.

[4] Zander and Zander, *The Art of Possibility*, p. 46. Will Crutchfield had earlier lamented that piano competitions resulted in interpretations that were far too similar to each other – that in trying to win, performers avoided taking technical risks and in so doing diminished the potential of their performance: 'The ills of piano competitions', *New York Times*, 16 May 1985.

[5] Muller, *The Tyranny of Metrics*, p. 92.

[6] David Boyle, *Tickbox*, Little Brown, 2020, p. 232.

[7] Zander and Zander, *The Art of Possibility*, p. 25.

[8] Arnold's research is cited in Eric Barker, *Barking Up the Wrong Tree: The Surprising Science Behind Why Everything You Know about Success Is (Mostly) Wrong*, HarperOne, 2017, pp. 9–10.

[9] Kohn, *No Contest*, p. 100.

[10] James P. Carse, *Finite and Infinite Games*, Free Press, 1986, p. 73.

[11] Hanna Sistek, 'South Korean students wracked with stress: South Korea has one of the best education systems in the world, but student suicide rates remain high', *Aljazeera*, 8 December 2013, www.aljazeera.com/indepth/features/2013/12/south-korean-students-wracked-with-stress-201312884628494144.html

[12] Carol Dweck, *Mindset: The New Psychology of Success*, Random House, 2006.

[13] Stephen M. Kosslyn, 'Are you developing skills that won't be automated?' *Harvard Business Review*, September 2019.

[14] School House, 'Anthony Seldon on the future of education', *Country and Town House*, www.schoolhousemagazine.co.uk/education/anthony-seldon/

[15] Cited in Margaret Heffernan, 'How to kill creativity, the Microsoft way', *Inc.*, 6 February 2014, www.inc.com/margaret-heffernan/how-to-kill-creativity.html

[16] Daniel H. Pink, *Drive: The Surprising Truth About What Motivates Us*, Canongate, 2009.

[17] Ibid.

[18] Quoted in Annie Vernon, *Mind Games: Determination, Doubt and Lucky Socks: An Insider's Guide to the Psychology of Elite Athletes*, Bloomsbury, 2019, p. 209.

Chapter 6

[1] Matthew Syed, 'Thomas Bjorn: I felt empty winning tournaments on my own, but this Ryder Cup victory was great', *The Times*, 3 October 2018.

[2] Tyson Fury, *Behind the Mask: My Autobiography*, Century, 2019, p. 142.

[3] Michael Hutchinson, *Faster: The Obsession, Science and Luck Behind the World's Fastest Cyclists*, Bloomsbury, 2014

[4] Quoted in 'British rower Tom Ransley retires after Games delay', *BBC Sport*, 3 April 2020, www.bbc.co.uk/sport/rowing/52140705

[5] Andre Agassi, *Open: An Autobiography*, HarperCollins 2009, location 3241 [e-book].

[6] Vernon, *Mind Games*, p. 214.

[7] Adriaan Kalwij, *The Effects of Competition Outcomes on Health: Evidence from the Lifespans of US Olympic Medalists*, CESR-Schaeffer Working Paper No. 2017-006, 20 September 2017.

[8] Quoted in Tom Whipple, 'Disappointment sends silver medallists to an early grave', *The Times*, 13 October 2018.

[9] Jerry Seinfeld, *I'm Telling You for the Last Time* (part 4 of 5), filmed live in Broadhurst Theatre, New York, *YouTube*, 1998, www.youtube.com/watch?time_continue=5&v=PbIEjy_ww90&feature=emb_title

[10] Jason G. Goldman, 'Why bronze medalists are happier than silver winners', *Scientific American*, 9 August 2012.

[11] For a thorough discussion of the various research relating to 'silver medal syndrome', see Dr Laurie Santos' podcast *The Happiness Lab*, episode 3, 'A silver lining', 1 October 2019.

[12] Jason Dorland, *Chariots and Horses: Life Lessons from an Olympic Rower,* Heritage House, 2011, p. 119.

[13] Cited in Geraint Hughes, 'Team GB's men's rowers emotional over Tokyo Olympic Games 2020 training', *Sky Sports News*, 8 January 2020.

[14] Hutchinson, *Faster*, p. 152

[15] Quoted in Lily Nothling, 'Cate Campbell opens up on being "Australia's poster girl for failure" after open letter to trolls', *Australian Broadcasting Corporation*, 31 August 2018, www.abc.net.au/news/2018-08-31/olympian-cate-campbell-pens-letter-to-trolls-qld/10186576; Cate Campbell, 'A letter to... the keyboard warriors', 29 August 2018, www.exclusiveinsight.com/cate-campbell-a-letter-to-the-keyboard-warriors/

[16] 'State of Sport 2018: Half of retired sportspeople have concerns over mental and emotional wellbeing', *BBC Sport*, 5 February 2018, www.bbc.co.uk/sport/42871491

[17] 'EY Personal Performance Programme', *EY*, www.ey.com/en_uk/workforce/personal-performance-programme

[18] Baroness Tanni Grey-Thompson, *Duty of Care in Sport: Independent Report to Government*, April 2017, www.gov.uk/government/publications/duty-of-care-in-sport-review, p. 4. At the time of writing, many recommendations from this report have not been implemented.

[19] Francesca Cavallerio, 'Sportsmen must develop identities outside sport', *The Statesman*, 21 June 2020.

[20] There is increasing research informing our understanding of athlete transition, such as A. Dacyshyn, 'When the balance is gone: The sport and retirement experiences of elite female gymnasts', in Jay Coakley and Peter Donnelly (eds), *Inside Sports*, Routledge, 1999, pp. 212–222.

[21] Kitrina Douglas, 'Storying myself: Negotiating a relational identity in professional sport', *Qualitative Research in Sport and Exercise*, 1 (2), 176–190, 2009.

[22] Douglas Harper, *Online Etymology Dictionary*, www.etymonline.com

[23] Hutchinson, *Faster*, p. 10.

[24] Sean Ingle, 'British bobsleigh team told: Keep quiet about bullying or miss Olympics', *The Observer*, 17 June 2017; Sean Ingle, 'Inside British bobsleigh's "toxic" culture: The latest Olympic sport in the dock', *The Guardian*, 9 October 2017. The 2017 Independent Review into British cycling found shortcomings in governance,

leadership and culture. See *Report of the Independent Review Panel into the Climate and Culture of the World Class Programme in British Cycling*, www.uksport.gov.uk/news/2017/06/14/british-cycling

[25] 'Values', *Canadian Olympic Committee*, https://olympic.ca/canadian-olympic-committee/values/

[26] Research has shown that over-conformity to the norms and values embodied in the traditional 'sport ethic' – the narrative of sacrifice, seeking distinction, taking risks, challenging limits – leaves athletes particularly vulnerable to corruption. Robert Hughes and Jay Coakley, 'Positive deviance among athletes: The implications of overconformity to the sport ethic', *Sociology of Sport Journal*, 8 (4), 307–325.

[27] Simon Barnes, *Epic: In Search of the Soul of Sport and Why it Matters*, Simon & Schuster, 2019.

[28] Richard Moore, *The Dirtiest Race in History: Ben Johnson, Carl Lewis and the 1988 Olympic 100m Final*, Wisden, 2013, p. 299.

[29] Atherton, Mike, 'It's sport, not business. Australia's sandpaper-gate report is vital for administrators everywhere. Mike Atherton says findings show damage of "win at all costs" ethos', *The Times*, 30 October 2018

[30] Sport England, *Go Where Women Are: Insight on Engaging Women and Girls in Sport and Exercise*, p. 13, https://sportengland-production-files.s3.eu-west-2.amazonaws.com/s3fs-public/insight_go-where-women-are.pdf?VersionId=eYAoAledAKaOOlngZqC6_DFYjF7_rfAI

[31] Amanda J. Visek, Heather M. Mannix, Avinash Chandran, Sean D. Cleary, Karen McDonnell and Loretta DiPietro, 'Perceived importance of the fun integration theory's factors and determinants: A comparison amongst players, parents and coaches', *International Journal of Sports Science and Coaching*, 13 (6), 849–862, 2018; Amanda J. Visek, Sara M. Achrati, Heather Mannix, Karen McDonnell, Brandonn S. Harris, and Loretta DiPietro, 'The fun integration theory: Towards sustaining children and adolescents sport participation', *Journal of Physical Activity and Health*, 12 (3), 424–433, 2015.

Chapter 7

[1] Jeffrey Pfeffer and Robert Sutton, 'The knowing-doing gap', *Stanford Business*, 1 November 1999, www.gsb.stanford.edu/insights/knowing-doing-gap

[2] Jeffrey Pfeffer and Robert Sutton, *The Knowing-Doing Gap: How Smart Companies Turn Knowledge into Action*, Harvard Business School Press, 2000, p. 211.

[3] Andrew Hill, 'The difficulty in managing things that cannot easily be measured', *Financial Times*, 26 November 2018.

[4] Quoted in Andrew Hill, 'The executive success factors that lead directly to jail', *Financial Times*, 10 February 2020.

[5] Muller, *The Tyranny of Metrics*, p. 20.

[6] David Pilling, *The Growth Delusion*, Bloomsbury, 2018, p. 3.

[7] Stiglitz, 'It's time to retire metrics like GDP'.

[8] Heffernan, *A Bigger Prize*, p. 113.

[9] Megan Reitz and John Higgins, *Speak Up: Say What Needs to be Said and Hear What Needs to be Heard,* Pearson, 2019, p. xxx.

[10] Anthony Salz, *Salz Review: An Independent Review of Barclays' Business Practices,* Barclays, April 2013, p. 82.

[11] Quoted in Heffernan, *A Bigger Prize*, p. 287.

[12] Bruce Daisley, *The Joy of Work*, Penguin Random House, 2019, pp. 3, 21.

[13] Thomas J. DeLong and Vineeta Vijayaraghavan, 'Let's hear it for B players', *Harvard Business Review*, June 2003.

Chapter 8

[1] 'Ministerial statements—mosque terror attacks—Christchurch', *New Zealand Parliament*, 19 March 2019, www.parliament.nz/en/pb/hansard-debates/rhr/combined/HansDeb_20190319_20190319_08

[2] Edward Luttwak, *The Pentagon and the Art of War*, Simon & Schuster, 1985.

[3] Andrew Mackay and Steve Tatham, *Behavioural Conflict: Why Understanding People and Their Motivations Will Prove Decisive in Future Conflict,* Military Studies Press, 2011.

[4] General Stanley McChrystal, *Team of Teams: New Rules of Engagement for a Complex World,* Penguin, 2015, p. 249.

[5] '"You did not act in time": Greta Thunberg's full speech to MPs', *The Guardian*, 23 April 2019.

Chapter 9

[1] Simon Sinek, *The Infinite Game*, Penguin, 2019, p. 128.

[2] David Brooks, *The Social Animal: A Story of How Success Happens,* Random House, 2011, p. x.

Chapter 10

[1] Dan Cable, *Alive: The Neuroscience of Helping Your People Love What They Do,* Harvard Business Review Press, 2019, p. 123.

[2] Gianpiero Petriglieri, 'Are our management theories outdated?', *Harvard Business Review*, June 2020.

[3] Alex Hill, Liz Mellon and Jules Goddard, 'How winning organizations last 100 years', *Harvard Business Review*, September 2018. The article points out that the average lifespan of a US S&P 500 company fell by 80% in the 80 years up to 2018 (from 67 to 15 years), and 76% of UK FTSE 100 companies disappeared in the 30 years up to 2018.

[4] Jim Collins, *Good to Great: Why Some Companies Make the Leap… And Others Don't,* Collins, 2001, p. 194.

[5] For example, 'Apple's Worldwide Developers Conference 2020 kicks off in June with an all-new online format', press release, *Apple,* 13 March 2020, www.apple.com/uk/newsroom/2020/03/apples-wwdc-2020-kicks-off-in-june-with-an-all-new-online-format/

[6] 'Our approach to Search', *Google,* www.google.com/search/howsearchworks/mission/

[7] EY, 'The Business Case for Purpose', *Harvard Business Review,* 2016, pp. 1, 4, https://assets.ey.com/content/dam/ey-sites/ey-com/en_gl/topics/digital/ey-the-business-case-for-purpose.pdf

[8] George Serafeim, 'Facebook, BlackRock, and the case for purpose-driven companies', *Harvard Business Review,* January 2018; George Serafeim, 'The type of socially responsible investments that make firms more profitable', *Harvard Business Review,* April 2015.

[9] Robert Phillips, 'Accountability: A business answer to a world in crisis', *Jericho,* 19 November 2019, www.jerichochambers.com

[10] James Kerr, *Legacy: What the All Blacks Can Teach Us about the Business of Life,* Constable, 2013, p. 13.

[11] Mihalyi Czihsentmihalyi, *Flow: The Psychology of Optimal Experience,* CreateSpace Independent Publishing, 1990.

[12] GB rowing sports psychologist Chris Shambrook coined the phrase 'outcome hijack' to help us notice when our thinking slips back to thoughts of whether we will win or not, and the importance of results and defining ourselves through them. Then we can refocus on our performance, and all the things that we can do to make our boats go as fast as possible.

[13] Although only designated formally as a branch of psychology in 1998, positive psychology builds on religious and historic concepts that go back millennia, particularly the notion of 'eudaimonia', referred to as 'the good life' or 'flourishing', which sits at the heart of Aristotelian ethics, mentioned in Chapter 3. It has developed strongly in Western Europe and the US, and focuses on wellbeing through positive emotions, social ties rather than any material outcomes. Associated with optimism and a focus on purpose and a 'meaningful life', positive psychology encourages us to consider our inner values and sense of what really matters in life. It involves a change in our orientation to time, believing that we should be drawn by future possibilities more than we are driven by problems in the past.

[14] Ben Hunt-Davis and Harriet Beveridge, *Will It Make the Boat Go Faster? Olympic-Winning Strategies for Everyday Success,* Matador, 2012; see also the Will It Make the Boat Go Faster? website, www.willitmaketheboatgofaster.com

[15] Teresa Amabile and Steven Kramer, *The Progress Principle: Using Small Wins to Ignite Joy, Engagement, and Creativity at Work,* Harvard Business Review Press, 2011, pp. 7, 10.

[16] BBC Radio 4, 'The cathedral thinkers', *BBC Sounds,* 24 March 2020.

[17] Eric Ries, *The Lean Startup: How Today's Entrepreneurs Use Continuous Innovation to Create Radically Successful Businesses,* Crown, 2011.

[18] Embankment Project for Inclusive Capitalism, https://coalitionforinclusive capitalism.com/epic/

[19] Beatrice Pembroke and Ella Saltmarshe, 'The long time', *Medium,* 29 October 2018, https://medium.com/@thelongtimeinquiry/the-long-time-3383b43d42ab

[20] 'Do we need to re-think our ideas of time?', *BBC Ideas,* www.bbc.co.uk/ideas/ videos/do-we-need-to-re-think-our-ideas-of-time/p0818lnv

[21] Future of Humanity Institute, www.fhi.ox.ac.uk/

[22] The Long Now Foundation, www.longnow.org

[23] Greta Thunberg, Speech to UK Parliament, 23 April 2019.

[24] Quoted in ibid., p. 214.

[25] Barker, *Barking Up the Wrong Tree,* pp. 239.

[26] Daniel Kahneman and Angus Deaton, 'High income improves evaluation of life but not emotional well-being', *Proceedings of the National Academy of Sciences,* 107 (38), 16489–16493, 2010.

[27] Peter J. Kuhn, Peter Kooreman, Adriaan Soetevent and Arie Kapteyn, *The Own and Social Effects of an Unexpected Income Shock: Evidence from the Dutch Postcode Lottery,* Department of Economics, University of California Santa Barbara, 2008.

[28] Philip Brickman, Dan Coates and Ronnie Janoff-Bulman, 'Lottery winners and accident victims: Is happiness relative?', *Journal of Personality and Social Psychology,* 36 (8), 917–927, 1978.

[29] Sinek, *The Infinite Game,* pp. 221.

[30] Deloitte worked with the Social Progress Imperative, a US non-profit organization, to develop its Social Progress Index, launched in 2015. The index focuses on social and environmental indicators, supporting the view that to measure a country's development, measuring economic growth is no longer enough.

Chapter 11

[1] Alvin Toffler, *Powershift: Knowledge, Wealth and Power at the Edge of the 21st Century,* Bantam, 1990.

[2] There have been many surveys asking what skills CEOs are looking for, such as: Sangeeta Bharadwa Badal, 'Skills learned in school differ from those demanded at work', *Gallup,* 26 January 2016; World Economic Forum, *The Future of Jobs,* 2016, http://reports.weforum.org/future-of-jobs-2016/. See also Joseph Pistrui, 'The future of human work is imagination, creativity and strategy', *Harvard Business Review,* January 2018.

[3] Satya Nadella, *Hit Refresh: The Quest to Rediscover Microsoft's Soul and Imagine a Better Future for Everyone,* Harper, 2017.

[4] Matthew Syed, *Blackbox Thinking: The Surprising Truth About Success*, John Murray, 2015.

[5] Yian Yin, Yang Wang and Dashun Wang, 'Quantifying the dynamics of failure across science, startups and security', *Nature*, 575, 190–194, 2019.

[6] Jeff Bezos, '2018 letter to shareholders', *Amazon*, 11 April 2019, https://blog.aboutamazon.com/company-news/2018-letter-to-shareholders?utm_source=social&utm_medium=tw&utm_term=amznews&utm_content=2018letter

[7] Ali Ash talking about his book, *The Unfair Advantage*, co-written with Hasan Kubba, on Alison Jones' *The Extraordinary Business Book Club* podcast, episode 202.

[8] 'What is Jeff Bezos' "Day 1" philosophy?', *Forbes*, 21 April 2017, www.forbes.com/sites/quora/2017/04/21/what-is-jeff-bezos-day-1-philosophy/#49a720c91052

[9] David Epstein, *Range: Why Specialists Triumph in a Specialized World*, Riverhead, 2019, p. 97.

[10] Ibid, p. 86.

[11] Ibid, p. 90.

[12] 'An overview of cooperative learning', *Cooperative Learning Institute*, www.co-operation.org/what-is-cooperative-learning

[13] Alfie Kohn, 'Learning together: A defense and analysis of cooperative learning', *Alfie Kohn*, www.alfiekohn.org/cl/

[14] Matthew Syed, *Rebel Ideas: The Power of Diverse Thinking*, John Murray, 2019, p.37

[15] David L. Georgenson, 'The problem of transfer calls for partnership', *Training and Development Journal*, 36 (10), 75–78, 1982.

[16] Alan M. Saks, 'So what is a good transfer of training estimate? A reply to Fitzpatrick', *The Industrial-Organizational Psychologist*, 39, 29–30, 2002.

[17] David Hibbard and Duane Buhrmester, 'Competitiveness, gender, and adjustment among adolescents', *Sex Roles*, 63 (5–6), 412–424, 2010; Richard M. Ryckman, Cary R. Libby, Bart van den Borne, Joel A. Gold and Marc A. Lindner, 'Values of hypercompetitive and personal development competitive individuals', *Journal of Personality Assessment*, 69 (2), 271–283, 1997.

[18] John Whitmore, *Coaching for Performance: The Principles and Practice of Coaching and Leadership*, Nicholas Brealey, 1992.

[19] Julia Milner and Trenton Milner, 'Most managers don't know how to coach people. But they can learn', *Harvard Business Review*, August 2018.

[20] Kenneth Mikkelsen and Richard Martin, *The Neo-Generalist*, LID, 2016, p. 114.

Chapter 12

[1] Quoted in Jeffrey Thompson Parker, *Flicker to Flame: Living with Purpose, Meaning, and Happiness*, self-published, 2006, p. 118.

[2] Clayton Christensen, *How Will You Measure Your Life?* Harvard University Press, 2017, pp. 29–30.

[3] Brooks, *The Social Animal*, pp. xx, xviii.

[4] Quoted in Jeremy Wilson, 'Alex Danson has "zero regrets" after bringing glittering career to an end following cruel head injury', *The Telegraph*, 20 February 2020.

[5] Terry Orlick, *Winning Through Cooperation: Competitive Insanity, Cooperative Alternatives*, Acropolis, 1978, p. 121.

[6] I use 'cooperation' and 'collaboration' in this chapter, as through the book, without drawing tight distinctions. In general, definitions of collaboration involve greater shared interest, ownership and purpose than cooperation, but in different fields, from education to politics, from business to sport, the extent to which these are distinct varies. Suffice to say, both require genuine Connection.

[7] There are many reports from organizations such as the National Institute of Mental Health in the UK which have tracked these trends over recent years in some detail, looking at different sections of the population and different aspects of mental health issues. Paul Wachtel's *The Poverty of Affluence: A Psychological Portrait of the American Way of Life*, Free Press, 1983, traces the source of what he calls 'isolating individualism' in the US back to the insatiable desire for growth. The Global Initiative on Loneliness and Connection, set up in 2021, supports national initiatives as the socio-psychological-economic effects of loneliness are being understood further (see www.gilc.global). In 2018 the UK government launched A Connected Society, a strategy for tackling loneliness, drawing on a range of sources and organizations, including The Jo Cox Foundation, which focuses on research and recommendations to tackle loneliness and isolation.

[8] Brené Brown, *The Gifts of Imperfection*, Hazelden, 2010, p. 19.

[9] Edgar Schein, *Organizational Culture and Leadership*, Wiley, 1985.

[10] A positive culture is essential to wellbeing. The depth of our friendships and bonds actually has an impact physiologically on our immunity, blood pressure and outlook on life. Emma Seppälä and Kim Cameron, 'Proof that positive work cultures are more productive', *Harvard Business Review*, December 2015.

[11] The True Athlete Project, *Change the World, One True Athlete at a Time*, p. 2, www.activityalliance.org.uk/assets/000/002/688/The_True_Athlete_Project_Brochure_(Spreads)_original.pdf?1551459748

[12] Andrew J. Howell, Raelyne L. Dopko, Holli-Anne Passmore and Karen Buro, 'Nature connectedness: Associations with well-being and mindfulness', *Personality and Individual Differences*, 51 (2), 166–171, 2011.

[13] Petriglieri, 'Are our management theories outdated?'

[14] Paul Skinner, *Collaborative Advantage: How Collaboration Beats Competition as a Strategy for Success*, Robinson, 2018, p. 143.

[15] John Vincent and Sifu Julian Hitch, *Winning Not Fighting: Why You Need to Rethink Success and How You Achieve it with the Ancient Art of Wing Tsun*, Penguin, 2019, p. 60.

[16] Heffernan, *A Bigger Prize*, p. 33.

[17] Sinek, *The Infinite Game*, pp. 159–160.

[18] Adam Grant, *Give and Take: A Revolutionary Approach to Success*, Weidenfeld & Nicolson, 2013, pp. 11–12.

[19] There are a number of works in this area. See: Amy C. Edmondson's *Teaming*, Jossey-Bass, 2012, and *The Fearless Organization*, Wiley, 2008; Sandy Pentland's work at MIT's Human Dynamics Lab; Alex Pentland, 'The new science of building great teams', *Harvard Business Review*, 2012; and Brené Brown, *The Power of Vulnerability*, TED Talk.

[20] Paul J. Zak, 'The neuroscience of trust', *Harvard Business Review*, January–February 2017.

[21] Yuval Noah Harari, *Sapiens: A Brief History of Humankind*, Harvill Secker, 2011.

Concluding Thoughts

[1] Invictus Games Foundation, www.invictusgamesfoundation.org

[2] 'A speech by Prince Harry at the closing ceremony of the Invictus Games, London, 2014', *The Royal Household*, 14 September 2014, www.royal.uk/speech-hrh-prince-harry-closing-ceremony-invictus-games-london

[3] Valorie Kondos Field, *Why Winning Doesn't Always Equal Success*.

[4] Ibid.

[5] Michael Moritz, 'Geraint Thomas is the true champion of the Tour de France: Teamwork beat personal ambition as "G" helped Egan Bernal ride to victory', *Financial Times*, 2 August 2019.

[6] Jason Dorland, *Pulling Together: A Coach's Journey to Uncover the Mindset of True Potential*, Heritage House, 2017, p. 241.

[7] John McAvoy, *Redemption: From Iron Bars to Ironman*, Pitch, 2016.

[8] Malcolm Gladwell, *David & Goliath: Underdogs, Misfits and the Art of Battling Giants*, Little, Brown & Company, 2013, pp. 12–13.

[9] Ibid, p. 6.

Index

Index

Index

A quick word from Practical Inspiration Publishing...

We hope you found this book both practical and inspiring – that's what we aim for with every book we publish.

We publish titles on topics ranging from leadership, entrepreneurship, HR and marketing to self-development and wellbeing.

Find details of all our books at: www.practicalinspiration.com

 Did you know...

We can offer discounts on bulk sales of all our titles – ideal if you want to use them for training purposes, corporate giveaways or simply because you feel these ideas deserve to be shared with your network.

We can even produce bespoke versions of our books, for example with your organization's logo and/or a tailored foreword.

To discuss further, contact us on info@practicalinspiration.com.

 Got an idea for a business book?

We may be able to help. Find out more about publishing in partnership with us at: bit.ly/PIpublishing.

Follow us on social media...

@PIPTalking

@pip_talking

@practicalinspiration

@piptalking

Practical Inspiration Publishing

Printed in the USA
CPSIA information can be obtained
at www.ICGtesting.com
JSHW011926130524
63053JS00016B/448